FUNDAMENTALS OF
ENGLISH
GRAMMAR
Second Edition

TEACHER'S GUIDE
Volume A

Betty Schrampfer Azar
Barbara F. Matthies

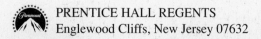
PRENTICE HALL REGENTS
Englewood Cliffs, New Jersey 07632

Publisher: *Tina B. Carver*
Managing editor, production: *Dominick Mosco*
Editorial/production supervisor: *Janet Johnston*
Editiorial assistant: *Shelley Hartle*
Buyer and Scheduler: *Ray Keating*
Cover supervisor: *Marianne Frasco*
Cover designer: *Joel Mitnick Design*
Interior designer: *Ros Herion Freese*

Printed in the United States of America

10 9 8 7 6 5 4 3 2 1

ISBN 0-13-347113-6

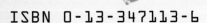

Prentice-Hall International (UK) Limited, *London*
Prentice-Hall of Australia Pty. Limited, *Sydney*
Prentice-Hall Canada Inc., *Toronto*
Prentice-Hall Hispanoamericana, S.A., *Mexico*
Prentice-Hall of India Private Limited, *New Delhi*
Prentice-Hall of Japan, Inc., *Tokyo*
Simon & Schuster Asia Pte. Ltd., *Singapore*
Editora Prentice-Hall do Brasil, Ltda., *Rio de Janeiro*

Contents

NOTES AND ANSWERS

Preface

This *Teachers' Guide* is intended as a practical aid to teachers. You can turn to it for notes on the content of a unit and how to approach the exercises, for suggestions for classroom activities, and for answers to the exercises in the main text and to the Guided Study practices in the workbooks.

General teaching information can be found in the introduction. It includes:
- the rationale and general aims of *Fundamentals of English Grammar*
- classroom techniques for presenting charts and using exercises
- suggestions on the use of the workbook in connection with the main text
- comments on differences between American and British English
- a key to the pronunciation symbols used in this *Guide*

The rest of the *Guide* contains notes on charts and exercises.

The notes about the charts may include:
- suggestions for presenting the information to students
- points to emphasize
- common problems to anticipate
- assumptions underlying the contents
- additional background notes on grammar and usage

The notes that accompany the exercises may include:
- the focus of the exercise
- suggested techniques as outlined in the introduction
- possible specialized techniques for particular exercises
- points to emphasize
- assumptions
- answers
- expansion activities
- item notes on cultural content, vocabulary, and idiomatic usage (Some of these item notes are specifically intended to aid teachers who are non-native speakers of English.)

The author would enjoy hearing comments and suggestions from other teachers who have ideas they would like to share.

Betty S. Azar
4149 S. Saratoga Road
Langley, WA 98260
USA

Introduction

General Aims of *Fundamentals of English Grammar*

Fundamentals of English Grammar is a mid-level ESL/EFL developmental skills text. In the experience of many classroom teachers, adult language learners like to spend at least some time on grammar with a teacher to help them. The process of looking at and practicing grammar becomes a springboard for expanding the learners' abilities in speaking, writing, listening, and reading.

Most students find benefit and comfort in studying examples and explanations, for it allows them to make some sense out of the bewildering array of forms and usages of a language that is strange to them. These understandings provide the basis for practice in a relaxed, safe grammar classroom that encourages risk-taking as the students experiment with ways to communicate their ideas in a new language.

Teaching grammar does not mean lecturing on grammatical patterns and terminology. It does not mean bestowing knowledge and being an arbiter of correctness. Teaching grammar is the art of helping students make sense, little by little, of a huge, puzzling construct and engaging them in activities that enhance language acquisition in all skill areas.

The aims of this text are to acquaint the learners with fundamental structures of high frequency in English and to provide ample opportunities for practicing those structures. Perhaps the most important aim, however, is to supply a wealth and variety of material for teachers to adapt to their individual teaching situations. The text seeks to be interesting and easy to understand and to provide myriad learning opportunities, but in truth, grammar comes alive only with a teacher.

Classroom Techniques

Following are some techniques that have proven useful. *Suggestions for Presenting the Grammar Charts* are discussed first. Next are some notes on *Degrees of Teacher and Student Involvement*. Then *Techniques for Exercise Types* are outlined.

Suggestions for Presenting the Grammar Charts

A chart is a concise visual presentation of the structures to be learned in one section of a chapter. Some charts may require particular methods of presentation, but generally any of the following techniques are viable.

Technique #1: Use the examples in the chart, add your own examples to explain the grammar in your own words, and answer any questions about the chart. Elicit other examples of the target structure from the learners. Then go to the accompanying exercise immediately following the chart.

Technique #2: Elicit oral examples from the students before they look at the chart in the textbook. To elicit examples from the students, ask leading questions whose answers will include the target structure. (For example, for the present progressive, ask: "What are you doing right now?") You may want to write the elicited answers on the board and relate them to the examples in the chart. Then proceed to the exercises.

Technique #3: Assign the chart and accompanying exercise(s) for out-of-class study. In class the next day, ask for and answer any questions about the chart, and then immediately proceed to the exercises. (With advanced students, you might not need to deal with every chart and exercise thoroughly in class. With intermediate students, it is generally advisable to clarify charts and do most of the exercises.)

Technique #4: Lead the students through the accompanying exercise prior to discussing the chart. Use the material in the exercise to discuss the focus of the chart as you go along. At the end of the exercise, call attention to the examples in the chart and summarize what was discussed during the exercise.

Technique #5: Before presenting the chart in class, give the students a short written quiz on its content. Have the students correct their own papers as you review the answers. The quiz should not be given a score; it is a learning tool, not an examination. Use the items from the quiz as examples for discussing the grammar in the chart.

Presentation techniques often depend upon the content of the chart, the level of the class, and the students' learning styles. Not all students react to the charts in the same ways. Some students need the security of thoroughly understanding a chart before trying to use the structure. Others like to experiment more freely with using new structures; they refer to the charts only incidentally, if at all. Given these differing learning strategies, you should vary your presentation techniques and not expect students to "learn" or memorize the charts. The charts are just a starting point for class discussion and a point of reference.

Demonstration can be very helpful to explain the meaning of structures. You and the students can act out situations that demonstrate the target structure. Of course, not all grammar lends itself to this technique. For example, the present progressive can easily be demonstrated (e.g., "I *am writing* on the board right now."). However, the use of gerunds as the objects of prepositions (e.g., *instead of writing* or *thank you for writing*) is not especially well suited to demonstration techniques.

In discussing the target structure of a chart, use the chalkboard whenever possible. Not all students have adequate listening skills for "teacher talk," and not all students can visualize and understand the various relationships within, between, and among structures. Draw boxes and circles and arrows to illustrate connections between the elements of a structure.

The students need to understand the terminology, but don't require or expect detailed definitions of terms, either in class discussion or on tests. Terminology is just a tool, a useful label for the moment, so that you and the students can talk to each other about English grammar.

Most students benefit from knowing what is going to be covered in the following class session. The students should be assigned to read the charts at home so that they can become initially familiar with the target structure and, it is to be hoped, come to class with questions.

For every chart, try to relate the target structure to an immediate classroom or "real-life" context. Make up or elicit examples that use the students' names, activities, and interests. The here-and-now classroom context is, of course, one of the grammar teacher's best aids.

Degrees of Teacher and Student Involvement

Most of the exercises in the text are intended to be teacher-led, but other options are group work, pair work, and student-led work.

TEACHER-LED EXERCISES

In an eclectic text such as this, many approaches are possible, based on various sound theories of language learning and teaching. The teacher plays many roles and can employ a wide variety of techniques.

In essence, all exercises in the main text are "teacher-led." Even so, there is a wide range of possible teacher involvement: from explaining "rules" to eliciting deductive understandings, from supplying answers to eliciting responses, from being the focus of the students' attention to being solely an initiator and facilitator. Consider the students' goals and the time that is available, then decide whether to focus a lot of attention on every item in an exercise or to go through it quickly and spend time on related activities. It is beneficial for students to push hard and work intensively on English grammar, but it is also beneficial for the students to spend relaxed time in class exchanging ideas in structure-oriented conversations or similar pursuits.

GROUP WORK AND PAIR WORK

Many, but not all, exercises in the text are suitable for group or pair work. Suggestions for such alternatives are included in the comments on the exercises in the chapter notes.

Exercises done in groups or pairs may often take twice as much time as they would if teacher-led, but it is time well spent if you plan carefully and make sure that the students are speaking in English to each other. There are many advantages to student-student practice.

When the students are working in groups or pairs, their opportunities to use what they are learning are greatly increased. They will often explain things to each other during pair work, in which case both students benefit greatly. The students in group work are often much more active and involved than in teacher-led exercises.

Group and pair work also expands the students' opportunities to practice many communication skills at the same time that they are practicing target structures. In peer interaction in the classroom, the students have to agree, disagree, continue a conversation, make suggestions, promote cooperation, make requests, be sensitive to each other's needs and personalities, and the like—the kinds of exchanges that are characteristic of any group communication, whether in the classroom or elsewhere.

In addition, group and pair work helps to produce a comfortable learning environment. In teacher-centered activities, students may sometimes feel shy and inhibited or may experience stress. They may feel that they have to respond quickly and accurately and that *what* they say is not as important as *how* they say it—even though you strive to convince them to the contrary. If you set up groups that are non-competitive and cooperative, the students usually tend to help, encourage, and even joke with each other. This encourages them to experiment with the language and speak more.

Students should be encouraged to monitor each other to some extent in group work, especially when monitoring activities are specifically assigned. You shouldn't worry about "losing control" of the students' language production, and they shouldn't worry about learning each other's mistakes. (But perhaps you should remind them to give some *positive* as well as corrective comments to each other in order to maintain good feelings.) Not every mistake needs to be corrected, but you can take some time at the end of an exercise to call attention to mistakes that you heard frequently as you monitored the groups.

WAYS OF USING EXERCISES FOR GROUP OR PAIR WORK

1. Divide the class into groups of two to six, usually with one student as leader. You may appoint the students to the groups or sometimes let them divide themselves. You may appoint a leader or let the students choose one. Leadership can be rotated. Be sure that the leader understands what to do, and set a reasonable time limit for finishing the activity.

2. For ORAL (BOOKS CLOSED) exercises, only the leader has his/her text open. If these exercises are used for pair work, one student has an open text and the other doesn't. Halfway through an exercise, the pair may change roles.

3. For ORAL or some other types of exercises, the students can discuss completions, transformations, etc. among themselves prior to, or instead of, class discussion. You can move about the classroom answering questions as necessary.

4. For exercises that require writing in the textbook, each group should produce one paper with answers that all (or at least a majority) of the members agree are correct. The leader can present the group's answers for class discussion or hand in a collaborative paper for your correction (and sometimes even for a grade). Similarly, pairs of students can compare their answers prior to class discussion and come to an agreement on their correctness.

STUDENT-LED EXERCISES

Once in a while you may wish to ask a student to assume the teacher role in some of the ORAL or ORAL (BOOKS CLOSED) exercises; the student conducts the exercise by giving the cues and determining the appropriateness of the response, while you retire to a corner of the room. It is helpful, but not essential, for you to work with the student leader outside of class in preparation for his/her role as teacher. Generally, a student-led oral exercise will take twice as much class time as it would if teacher-led, but if the time is available, it can be a valuable experience for the student-teacher and fun for the class as a whole.

Techniques for Exercise Types

Some of the exercises in the text have specific labels: ORAL (BOOKS CLOSED), ORAL, WRITTEN, ORAL/WRITTEN, ERROR ANALYSIS, PREPOSITIONS, PHRASAL VERBS. It is important to note that the "oral" and "written" labels on particular exercises are only suggestions to the teacher. If you deem it appropriate, you can have the students write out an oral exercise or discuss a written exercise.

Exercise: ORAL (BOOKS CLOSED)

a. For exercises of this type, which range from simple manipulation to open-ended communicative interaction, the students are to have their books closed. These exercises are not intended as drills to be completed rapidly without interruption. You are not "drilling" grammar into the students; rather, you are giving them the chance to practice speaking and to experiment with target structures. You are providing a good opportunity for the students to develop their listening and speaking skills while expanding their ability to use the structures. With their books closed, they can concentrate on what you and others are saying and can practice speaking without relying on written words.

b. Be flexible in handling these exercises. You don't have to read the items aloud as though reading a script from which there should be no deviation. Modify the format to make it more workable for your particular class. Try to add more oral-aural items spontaneously as they occur to you. Change the items in any way you can to make them more relevant to your students. (For example, if you know that some students plan to watch the World Cup soccer match on TV soon, include a sentence about that.) Omit irrelevant items. Sometimes an item will start a spontaneous discussion of, for example, local restaurants or current movies or certain experiences the students have had. These spur-of-the-moment dialogues are very beneficial to the students. Encourage and facilitate the discussion, and then, within a reasonable length of time, bring attention back to the grammar at hand.

c. To initiate an ORAL (BOOKS CLOSED) exercise, give the class an example or two of the format. Sometimes you will want to give explicit oral directions. Sometimes you will want to use the chalkboard to write down key words to help the students focus on the target structure or consider the options in their responses.

d. Repeat a cue in ORAL (BOOKS CLOSED) exercises as often as necessary. Start out with normal spoken English, but then slow down and repeat as needed. You may want to write on the board, do a pantomime, demonstrate, draw a picture—whatever may help the students understand what you're saying. One of your goals is to convince students that they *can* understand spoken English. They shouldn't feel failure or embarrassment if they don't understand a spoken cue immediately. If an exercise is too difficult for your class as a whole or for particular students, let them do it with their books open.

e. In general, ORAL (BOOKS CLOSED) exercises follow a chart or an open-book exercise. First, students should build up their understanding of the structure and practice using it. Then they will feel more confident during these oral exercises, which for most students are riskier and far more difficult than written work.

Essentially, in the ORAL (BOOKS CLOSED) exercises, the teacher is saying to the students, "Okay, now you understand such-and-such (for example, word order in noun clauses), so let's play with it a bit. With any luck, you'll be happily surprised by how much you already know. Mistakes are no big problem. They're a natural part of learning a new language. So just give it a try and let's see what happens."

f. Sometimes ORAL (BOOKS CLOSED) exercises precede a chart or open-book exercises. The purpose of this order is to elicit student-generated examples of the target structure as a springboard to the discussion of the grammar. If you prefer to introduce any particular structure to your students orally, you can always use an ORAL (BOOKS CLOSED) exercise prior to the presentation of a chart and written exercises, no matter what the given order is in the textbook.

Exercise: ORAL

Exercises of this type are intended to be done with books open but require no writing and no preparation. In other words, the students can read what is in the text, but they don't have to write in their books. You don't have to assign these exercises ahead of time; they can be done directly in class. These exercises come in many forms and are often suitable for group or pair work.

Exercise: ORAL / WRITTEN

This label indicates that the material can be used for either speaking practice or writing practice. Sometimes it indicates that the two are combined: for example, a speaking activity may lead to a writing activity.

Exercise: WRITTEN

In this type of exercise, the intention is for the students to use their own paper and submit their writing to you. Some of the WRITTEN exercises require sentence completion, but most are designed to produce short, informal compositions. In general, the topics or tasks concern aspects of the students' lives in order to encourage free and relatively effortless communication as they practice their writing skills. While a course in English rhetoric is beyond the scope of this text, many of the basic elements are included and may be developed and emphasized according to your purposes.

For best results, whenever you make a writing assignment, let your students know what you expect: "This is what I suggest as content. This is how you might organize it. This is how long I expect it to be." If at all possible, give your students composition models, perhaps taken from good compositions written by previous classes, perhaps written by you, perhaps composed as a group activity by the class as a whole (e.g., you write on the board what the students tell you to write, and then you and the students revise it together).

In general, WRITTEN exercises should be done outside of class. All of us need time to consider and revise when we write. And if we get a little help here and there, that's not unusual. The topics in the exercises are structured so that plagiarism should not be a problem. Use in-class writing if you want to appraise the students' unaided, spontaneous writing skills. Tell your students that these written exercises are simply for practice and that—even though they should, of course, always try to do their best—mistakes will be considered only as tools for learning.

Encourage the students to use their dictionaries whenever they write. Point out that you yourself never write seriously without a dictionary at hand. Discuss the use of margins, indentation of paragraphs, and other aspects of the format of a well-written paper.

Ask your students to use lined paper and to write on every other line so that you and they have space to make corrections. APPENDIX 3 presents a system for marking errors so that students may make their own corrections and so that you may mark papers quickly and efficiently. (See p. xvi of this *Guide* for information about using APPENDIX 3.)

Exercise: ERROR ANALYSIS

ERROR ANALYSIS exercises focus on common mistakes made in typical student use of the target structures of a chapter. The main purpose of these exercises is to sharpen the students' self-monitoring skills. The exercises are challenging and fun, as well as a good way to summarize the grammar in a unit. If you wish, tell the students they are either newspaper editors or English teachers; their task is to locate all mistakes and write corrections.

The recommended technique is to assign an ERROR ANALYSIS for in-class discussion the next day. The students benefit most from having the opportunity to find the errors themselves prior to class discussion. These exercises can, of course, be handled in other ways: seatwork, written homework, group work, pair work.

You can make up your own error analysis exercises by presenting to the class student errors collected from their written completion exercises and compositions. It is usually best at this level to keep the focus on one or maybe two errors in one sentence. Adapt the mistakes in the students' writing to suit your purposes. The errors in such an exercise should be ones students can correct from their knowledge of English grammar. Awkward, convoluted sentences full of errors of many kinds are usually not suitable for class discussion; a wide-ranging discussion of numerous grammar points tends to confuse more than elucidate.

Some teachers may object to allowing students to see errors written in a textbook. There is little chance, however, that any harm is being done. Students look at errors all the time in their own writing and profit from finding and correcting them. The benefits of doing ERROR ANALYSIS exercises far outweigh any possible (and highly unlikely) negative results. Mistakes are a natural part of learning a new language, and indeed all language users make mistakes sometimes. Even native speakers or highly proficient non-native speakers—including you yourself—have to scrutinize, correct, and revise what they write. This is a normal part of the writing process.

Exercise: PREPOSITIONS

Exercises of this type focus on prepositions that are combined with verbs and adjectives. The intention is that the students simply make their "best guess" according to what "sounds right" to them when completing each item, then get the correct answers from class discussion and learn the ones they missed. They can refer to the list of combinations in APPENDIX 1 if they want to.

To reinforce the prepositions in an exercise, you can make up quick oral reviews (books closed) by rephrasing the items and having the students call out the prepositions. When you want the students to add onto a sentence you have begun, don't let your voice drop as it normally would at the end of speaking. Indicate with your voice that the sentence isn't complete yet. For example:

> TEXT entry: Are you ready __*for*__ the test?

Made-up oral reinforcement exercise:
> TEACHER: "We're having a test tomorrow. Are you ready . . . ?"
> STUDENTS call out: "for"
> TEACHER: "Good. Ready **for**. Are you ready **for** the test?"

> TEXT entry: Kathy was absent __*from*__ class yesterday.

Made-up oral reinforcement exercise:
> TEACHER: "Where was (Roberto) yesterday? He was absent . . . ."
> STUDENTS call out: "from"
> TEACHER: "Right. Absent **from**. (Roberto) was absent **from** class yesterday."

Exercise: PHRASAL VERBS

These contain two- and three-word verbs and can be handled in the same ways as the PREPOSITIONS exercises, adding increased emphasis on discussion of the phrases as vocabulary items.

As with the PREPOSITIONS exercises, the PHRASAL VERBS exercises are interspersed throughout the text at the ends of chapters. The intention is that the students review and/or learn a few of the most common of these expressions at a time. The scope and length of the text do not allow for an intensive treatment of the hundreds of phrasal verbs in the English language.

Additional Techniques

Most of the exercises in the textbook do not have specific labels. The following section outlines additional techniques, not only for labeled exercises but also for other activities.

The majority of the exercises in the text require some sort of completion, transformation, combination, sentence construction, or a combination of such activities. They range from those that are tightly controlled and manipulative to those that encourage free responses and require creative, independent language use. The techniques vary according to the exercise type.

FILL-IN-THE-BLANKS AND CONTROLLED COMPLETION EXERCISES

The label "fill-in-the-blanks" refers to those exercises in which the students complete the sentences by using words given in parentheses. The label "controlled completion" refers to those exercises in which the students complete cloze sentences according to directions. The possible ways of completing a sentence are limited. The directions may ask the students to use the words in a given list, to use the appropriate forms of a given structure such as *be going to* or *used to*, or to select the completion from multiple choices. All of these types of exercises call for similar techniques.

Technique A: A student can be asked to read an item aloud. You can say whether the student's answer is correct or not, or you can open up discussion by asking the rest of the class if the answer is correct. For example:

TEACHER: "Mr. Wah, would you please read Number 2?"
STUDENT: "Right now I'm in class. I *am sitting* at my desk I usually *sit* at the same desk in class every day."
TEACHER (to the class): "Do the rest of you agree with Mr. Wah's answer?"

The slow-moving pace of this method is beneficial for discussion not only of grammar items but also of vocabulary and content. The students have time to digest information and ask questions. You have the opportunity to judge how well they understand the grammar.

However, this time-consuming technique doesn't always, or even usually, need to be used.

Technique B: You, the teacher, read the first part of the item, then pause for the students to call out the answer in unison. For example:

TEXT entry: Right now I'm in class. I (*sit*)_____ at my desk.
TEACHER (with the students looking at their texts): "Right now I'm in class. I . . . . "
STUDENTS (in unison): "am sitting"(plus possibly a few incorrect responses scattered about)
TEACHER: "am sitting at my desk. *Am sitting.* Do you have any questions?"

This technique saves a lot of time in class, and is also slow-paced enough to allow for questions and discussion of grammar, vocabulary, and content. It is essential that the students have prepared the exercise by writing in their books, so it must be assigned ahead of time as homework or seatwork.

Technique C: If a particular exercise is little more than a quick review, you can simply give the answers so the students can correct their own previously prepared work in their textbooks. ("Number 2: Right now I'm in class. *I'm sitting* at my desk.") You can give the answers to the items one at a time, taking questions as they arise, or give the answers to the whole exercise before opening it up for questions. As an alternative, you can have one of the students read his/her answers for parts or all of an exercise and have the other students ask questions if they disagree.

Technique D: Divide the class into groups (or pairs) and, before the exercise is discussed in class, have each group prepare one set of answers that they all agree is correct. The leader of each group can present their answers.

Another option is to have the groups (or pairs) hand in their set of answers for correction and possibly a grade.

It's also possible to turn these exercises into games wherein the group with the best set of answers gets some sort of reward (perhaps applause from the rest of the class).

Of course, you can always mix Techniques A, B, C, and D—with the students reading some aloud, with you prompting unison response for some, with you simply giving the answers for others, or with the students collaborating on the answers for others. Much depends on the level of the class, their familiarity and skill with the grammar at hand, their oral-aural skills in general, and how flexible or limited your available class time is.

Technique E: When an exercise item has a dialogue between two speakers, A and B, ask one student to be A and another B and have them read the entry aloud. Then, occasionally, say to A and B: "Without looking at your text, what did you just say to each other?" (If necessary, let them glance briefly at their texts before they repeat what they've just said in the exercise item.) The students may be pleasantly surprised by their own fluency.

OPEN COMPLETION AND SEMI-CONTROLLED COMPLETION EXERCISES

The term "open completion" refers to those exercises in which the students use their own words to complete the sentences. "Semi-controlled completion" exercises allow for limited variations in the possible responses, permitting some independent input from the students.

Technique A: Exercises where the students must supply their own words to complete a sentence should usually be assigned for out-of-class preparation. Then in class, one, two, or several students can read their sentences aloud; the class can discuss the correctness and appropriateness of the completions. Perhaps you can suggest possible ways of rephrasing to make a sentence more idiomatic. Students who don't read their sentences aloud can revise their own completions based on what is being discussed in class. At the end of the exercise discussion, you can tell the students to hand in their sentences for you to look at, or simply ask if anybody has questions about the exercise and not have the students submit anything to you.

Technique B: If you wish to use an open or semi-controlled completion exercise in class without having previously assigned it, you can turn the exercise into a brainstorming session in which students try out several completions to see if they work. As another possibility, you may wish to divide the students into small groups and have each group come up with completions that they all agree are correct and appropriate. Then use only these completions for class discussion or as written work to be handed in.

Technique C: Some open or semi-controlled completion exercises are designated WRITTEN, which usually means the students need to use their own paper, as not enough space has been left in the textbook. It is often beneficial to use the following progression: (1) assign the exercise for out-of-class preparation; (2) discuss it in class the next day, having the students make corrections on their own papers based on what they are learning from discussing other students' completions; (3) then ask the students to submit their papers to you, either as a requirement or on a volunteer basis.

TRANSFORMATION AND COMBINATION EXERCISES

In transformation exercises, the students are asked to change form but not substance (e.g., to change the active to the passive). In combination exercises, the students are asked to combine two or more ideas or sentences into one sentence that contains a particular structure (e.g., an adjective clause).

In general, these exercises, which require manipulation of a form, are intended for class discussion of the form and meaning of a structure. The initial stages of such exercises are a good opportunity to use the chalkboard to draw circles and arrows to illustrate the characteristics and relationships of a structure. Students can read their answers aloud to initiate the class discussion, and you can write on the board as problems arise. Another possibility is to have the students write their sentences on the board. Also possible is to have them work in small groups to agree upon their answers prior to class discussion.

SENTENCE CONSTRUCTION AND DIALOGUE CONSTRUCTION EXERCISES

In sentence construction exercises, the students have to incorporate certain structures in sentences of their devising based on given information or situations. In dialogue construction, the students create situational conversations that include certain target structures. These exercises can be used for class discussion and/or written homework. In class discussion, students learn from what others have created. They can make corrections in their own work as the class discusses what other students have written. Often the dialogue construction can be done in pairs and then role-played before the class.

STRUCTURE IDENTIFICATION EXERCISES

Identifying structures does not play a large role in *Fundamentals of English Grammar,* but it is a useful technique in some instances, for example, in clarifying terminology such as separable vs. nonseparable phrasal verbs or gerunds vs. infinitives. Having the students identify structures such as subjects and verbs also helps them focus on underlying sentence patterns: simple, compound, complex. In many respects, punctuation exercises on commas and periods are structure identification exercises; asking the students to punctuate sentences requires that they understand the sentence structure.

Almost any exercise can involve structure identification, if the teacher chooses, by asking the students to point out or name whatever the target structure may be: adjective clause, adverb clause, noun, verb tense, etc.

PRONUNCIATION EXERCISES

A few exercises focus on pronunciation of grammatical features, such as endings on nouns or verbs and contracted or reduced forms. Most of the pronunciation exercises for *Fundamentals of English Grammar* are in the *Workbook.*

Some phonetic symbols are used in these exercises to point out sounds that should not be pronounced identically; for example, /s/, /əz/, and /z/ represent the three predictable pronunciations of the grammatical suffix that is spelled *-s* or *-es.* It is not necessary for students to learn a complete phonetic alphabet; they should merely associate each symbol in an exercise with a sound that is different from all others. The purpose is to help students become more aware of these final sounds in the English they hear to encourage proficiency of use in their own speaking and writing.

In the exercises on spoken contractions, the primary emphasis should be on the students' hearing and becoming familiar with spoken forms rather than on their production of these forms. The students need to understand that what they see in writing is not exactly what they should expect to hear in normal, rapid spoken English. The most important part of most of these exercises is for the students to listen to your oral production and become familiar with the reduced forms.

Language learners are naturally conscious that their pronunciation is not like that of native speakers of the language. Therefore, some of them are embarrassed or shy about speaking. In a pronunciation exercise, they may be more comfortable if you ask groups or the whole class to speak in unison. After that, individuals may volunteer to speak alone. The learners' production does not need to be "perfect," just understandable. You can encourage the students to be less inhibited by having them teach you how to pronounce words in their languages (unless, of course, you're a native speaker of the students' language in a monolingual class). It's fun—and instructive—for the students to teach the teacher.

SEATWORK

Many exercises can and should be assigned for out-of-class preparation, but sometimes it's necessary to cover an exercise in class that you haven't been able to assign previously. In "seatwork," you have the students do an unassigned exercise in class immediately before discussing it. Seatwork allows the students to try an exercise themselves before the answers are discussed so that they can discover what problems they may be having with a particular structure. Seatwork may be done individually, in pairs, or in groups.

HOMEWORK

The textbook assumes that the students will have the opportunity to prepare most of the exercises by writing in their books prior to class discussion. Students should be assigned this homework as a matter of course.

The use of the term "written" in this *Guide* suggests that the students write out an exercise on their own paper and hand it in to you. The amount generally depends upon such variables as class size, class level, available class time, your available paper-correcting time, not to mention your preferences in teaching techniques. Most of the exercises in the text can be handled through class discussion without the necessity of the students' handing in written homework. Most of the written homework that is suggested in the text and in the chapter notes in this *Guide* consists of activities that will produce original, independent writing.

CORRECTING WRITING ERRORS

APPENDIX 3 in *Fundamentals of English Grammar* (pp. A6–A7 in the back of the text) presents a system for marking errors in students' written work. It uses a numbering scheme for the purpose of signaling errors. This system is quite flexible, intended only to give the students hints when they set about correcting their own writing.

Some of the numbers have multiple uses. For example, 2 (Wrong Form) can signal that an adjective has been used instead of an adverb, a noun instead of an adjective, a gerund instead of an infinitive, incorrect *has being done* instead of *has been done*, incorrect *would has* instead of *would have*, etc. Other numbers have more limited uses. For example, 13 is intended only for run-on sentences or comma splices.

Some errors could be marked by either of two numbers. For example, *to*, as in *The weather is to cold*, could be marked by either 3 (Wrong Word) or 8 (Spelling). The word "beautifuls," as in *I saw some beautifuls pictures*, could be marked by either 1 (Singular-Plural) or 2 (Wrong Form). Simply choose the number that you think will give the student the best help in correcting and learning from the mistake in that context.

For some errors, it is necessary to use two numbers in the same circle. For example, the word "interesting," as in *I am interesting in that subject*, could be marked by both 8 (Spelling) and 2 (Wrong Form).

Write the full correction for any error that you are sure the student would be unable to correct him/herself. When necessary, write a more idiomatic phrase. Use 12 (Meaning Not Clear) when you want the student to find a different way to express what he/she is trying to say, or when the handwriting is illegible.

Using the numbers soon becomes automatic, and marking papers proceeds quickly and efficiently.

Reviewing the corrections made later by the students also proceeds smoothly, especially if they have written the original composition on every other line, have left adequate margins, and have used a pen or pencil of a different color to make the corrections. Compositions with numerous errors should be rewritten entirely.

You may wish to add numbers to the list to specify particular problems with structure or style. For example, 14 could suggest Parallel Structure; 15 could denote Repetitiveness. The numbers given in APPENDIX 3 have been distilled from many to a few through years of experimentation, but the system is still adaptable.

Using the *Workbook*

The *Workbook* contains two kinds of exercises: Selfstudy and Guided Study. The answer key for the Selfstudy practices is found at the end of the *Workbook* on perforated pages. Encourage your students to remove this answer key and put it in some sort of folder. It's much easier for the students to correct their own answers if they make their own answer key booklet. For the teacher's convenience, the answers to both the Selfstudy and the Guided Study practices are in this *Guide*.

The *Workbook* mirrors the main text. Exercises are called "exercises" in the main text and "practices" in the workbook to minimize confusion when you make assignments. Each practice in the *Workbook* has a content title and refers the students to appropriate charts in the main text or chartbook.

In any given grammar unit in this *Teacher's Guide*, the exercises in the main text are discussed first and then followed by the related group of practices from the *Workbook*. It's up to you to decide exactly how you would prefer to integrate and order the two sets of material. For example, students can be assigned to work at home on certain Selfstudy practices from the *Workbook* while the class is covering certain exercises in class. Guided Study practices can be included in lesson plans at your discretion.

SELFSTUDY PRACTICES (ANSWERS GIVEN IN THE *WORKBOOK*)

Answers to the Selfstudy practices are included in the *Workbook* so that students can immediately check their understanding and accuracy. The primary purpose of the Selfstudy practices is to give the students ample opportunity to understand and use the target structures on their own. They should be encouraged to bring any questions about the Selfstudy practices to class.

Selfstudy practices can be assigned by you or, depending upon the level of maturity or sense of purpose of the class, simply left for the students to use as they wish. They may be assigned to the entire class or only to those students who need further practice with a particular structure. They may be used as reinforcement after you have covered a chart and exercises in class or as introductory material prior to discussing a chart in class.

In addition, the students can use the Selfstudy practices to acquaint themselves with the grammar of any units not covered in class. Earnest students can use the *Workbook* to teach themselves.

GUIDED STUDY PRACTICES (ANSWERS NOT GIVEN IN THE *WORKBOOK*)

Answers to the Guided Study practices are given only in this *Teacher's Guide;* they are not available to the students. Guided Study practices can be used as supplementary teaching materials for class use, written homework, individualized instruction, or possibly as tests. It would also be possible for the teacher to photocopy the answers to certain practices and give them to the class, thus turning Guided Study practices into Selfstudy practices. A number of the Guided Study practices, however, don't have answers; they depend on creative language use.

Notes on American vs. British English

Students should be aware that the differences between American and British English are minor. Any students who have studied British English (BrE) should have no trouble adapting to American English (AmE) and vice-versa. In addition to American and British English, there are other varieties: Canadian English, Australian/New Zealand English, Scottish English, Irish English, West Indian English, West African English, Indian English, etc. Although some differences exist among these various Englishes in grammar, spelling, vocabulary, and pronunciation, their speakers can communicate with each other with relatively little difficulty.

DIFFERENCES IN USAGE AND SPELLING

Differences in usage or spelling can be found in notes to the answers in this *Guide*. Differences in article and preposition usage in certain common expressions follow. These differences are not noted in the text; they are given here for the teacher's information.

AmE	BrE
be in **the** hospital	be in **Ø** hospital
be at **the** university	be at **Ø** university
go to **a** university/go to **Ø** college	go to **Ø** university
go to **Ø** class/be in **Ø** class	go to **a** class/be in **a** class
in **the** future	in **Ø** future (OR in **the** future)
did it **the next** day	did it **Ø** next day (OR **the** next day)
haven't done something **for/in** weeks	haven't done something **for weeks**
ten minutes **past/after** six o'clock	ten minutes **past** six o'clock
five minutes **to/of/til** seven o'clock	five minutes **to** seven o'clock

Differences in spelling of certain common words follow. British spellings should not be marked as incorrect in the students' writing. The students should simply be made aware of the variant spellings.

AmE	BrE	AmE	BrE
jewelry, traveler, woolen	jewellry, traveller, woollen	curb	kerb
skillful, fulfill, installment	skilful, fulfil, instalment	forever	for ever/forever
color, honor, labor, odor	colour, honour, labour, odour	jail	gaol
realize, analyze, apologize	realise, analyse, apologise	program	programme
defense, offense, license	defence, offence, licence (n.)	specialty	speciality
theater, center, liter	theatre, centre, litre	story	storey (of a building)
check	cheque (bank note)	tire	tyre

DIFFERENCES IN VOCABULARY

Differences in vocabulary usage usually do not significantly interfere with communication. Students should know that when American and British speakers read each other's literature, they encounter very few differences in vocabulary usage. A few differences follow:

AmE	BrE	AmE	BrE
attorney, lawyer	barrister, solicitor	hood (of a car)	bonnet (of a car)
bathrobe	dressing gown	living room	sitting room, drawing room
can (of beans)	tin (of beans)	raise in salary	rise in salary
cookie, cracker	biscuit	rest room	public toilet, WC (water closet)
corn	maize	schedule	timetable
diaper	nappy	sidewalk	pavement, footpath
driver's license	driving licence	sink	basin
drug store	chemist's	soccer	football
elevator	lift	stove	cooker
eraser	rubber	truck	lorry, van
flashlight	torch	trunk (of a car)	boot (of a car)
gas, gasoline	petrol	be on vacation	be on holiday

Key to Pronunciation Symbols

THE PHONETIC ALPHABET (Symbols for American English)

CONSONANTS

Most consonant symbols are used phonetically as they are in normal English spelling. However, a few additional symbols are needed, and some other letters are more restricted in their use as symbols. These special symbols are presented below. (Note that slanted lines indicate that phonetic symbols, not the spelling alphabet, are being used.)

/ θ /	(Greek theta) = voiceless *th* as in **th**in, **th**ank
/ ð /	(Greek delta) = voiced *th* as in **th**en, **th**ose
/ ŋ /	= *ng* as in si**ng**, thi**nk** (but not in *danger*)
/ š /	= *sh* as in **sh**irt, mi**ss**ion, na**t**ion
/ ž /	= *s* or *z* in a few words like plea**s**ure, a**z**ure
/ č /	= *ch* or *tch* as in wa**tch**, **ch**urch
/ ǰ /	= *j* or *dge* as in **j**ump, le**dge**

The following consonants are used as in *conventional spelling:*

/b, d, f, g, h, k, l, m, n, o, p, r, s, t, v, w, y, z/

Spelling consonants that are <u>not</u> used phonetically in English: c, q, x

VOWELS

The five vowels in the spelling alphabet are inadequate to represent the 12-15 vowel sounds of American speech. Therefore, new symbols and new sound associations for familiar letters must be adopted.

Front	**Central**	**Back** (lips rounded)
/i/ or /iy/ as in b**ea**t		/u/, /u:/, or /uw/ as in b**oo**t
/ɪ/ as in b**i**t		/ʊ/ as in b**oo**k
/e/ or /ey/ as in b**ai**t		/o/ or /ow/ as in b**oa**t
		/ɔ/ as in b**ou**ght
/ɛ/ as in b**e**t	/ə/ as in b**u**t	
/æ/ as in b**a**t	/a/ as in b**o**ther	

Glides: /ai/ or /ay/ as in b**i**te
/ɔi/ or /ɔy/ as in b**oy**
/au/ or /aw/ as in ab**ou**t

British English has a somewhat different set of vowel sounds and symbols. You might want to consult a standard pronunciation text or BrE dictionary for that system.

COMMON FIRST NAMES USED IN THE TEXT

FEMALE

Alice	Ingrid	Nadia
Alicia	Irene	Nancy
Alison	Ivonne	Nicole
Amanda		
Amy	Jackie	Olga
Angela	Jan	Olivia
Anita	Jane	
Ann(e)	Janet	Pam
Anna	Janice	Pat
Annie	Jean	Paula
Anya	Jennifer	Peggy
	Jenny	
Barbara	Jessica	Rebecca
Beth	Jo Ann	Rita
Betsy	Joanna	Rosa
Bonnie	Joy	
	Juanita	Sally
Carla	Judy	Sandra
Carol	Julia	Sandy
Carmella	Julie	Sara(h)
Carmen		Shannon
Chris	Karen	Sharon
Cindy	Kate	Shelley
Colette	Kathy	Sitara
	Kay	Sonya
Debbie	Kim	Stacy
Debra		Stella
Della	Laura	Sue
Denise	Laurie	Susan
Dian(n)e	Linda	Susie
Donna	Lisa	Suzanne
	Liz	
Elaine	Lizzy	Tina
Elena	Louise	
Elizabeth	Lynn	Yoko
Ella		Yvette
Ellen	Margaret	
Emily	Marge	
Erica	Maria	
Erin	Marie	
	Marika	
Fatima	Marilyn	
Fumiko	Marti	
	Mary	
Gina	Martha	
Gloria	Maureen	
Graziela	Michelle	
Heidi		
Helen		
Hillary		

MALE

Abdul	Hamid	Pablo
Abdullah	Hank	Pat
Adam	Harry	Paul
Ahmed	Hiroki	Pedro
Akihiko	Howard	Pete
Al		Peter
Alan	Jack	Philip
Alex	Jake	Pierre
Ali	James	Po
Andy	Jason	
	Jeffrey	Ralph
Ben	Jerry	Ricardo
Benito	Jim	Richard
Bill	Jimmy	Rick
Billy	Jin Won	Rob
Bob	Joe	Robby
Bobby	John	Robert
Boris	Johnny	Roberto
Brian	Jonas	Rod
Bud	Jonathan	Rodney
	Jose	Ron
Carl	Josh	Ronald
Carlos	Juan	Ryan
Charlie		
Chris	Keith	Sam
Claudio	Ken	Sarosh
	Kevin	Scott
Dan	Khalid	Sergio
Danny	Kim	Simon
David	Kirk	Spiro
Dennis	Kunio	Spyros
Dick		Steve
Don	Larry	Surasuk
	Louie	
Ed	Luigi	Tarik
Eddie	Luis	Ted
Edward		Teddy
Eric	Mark	Tim
Ernesto	Masako	Timmy
Estefan	Matt	Tom
	Michael	Tommy
Frank	Mike	Tony
Fred	Mikhail	Toshi
	Mustafa	Toshiro
Gary		
George	Nick	William
Georgio	Nicky	Willy
Greg		
Guido	Olive	
	Omar	
	Oscar	
	Otto	

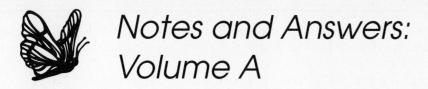

Notes and Answers: Volume A

Chapter 1: PRESENT TIME

ORDER OF CHAPTER	CHARTS	EXERCISES	WORKBOOK
First day of class: talking and writing		Ex. 1	Pr. 1 → 2
Simple present/present progressive	1-1 → 1-2	Ex. 2 → 6	Pr. 3 → 5
Spelling: final -s vs. -es	1-3	Ex. 7	Pr. 6 → 7
Cumulative review			Pr. 8 → 14
Nonprogressive verbs	1-4	Ex. 8	Pr. 15
Yes/no questions and short answers	1-5	Ex. 9	Pr. 16
Cumulative review		Ex. 10 → 11	Pr. 17 → 22
Prepositions		Ex. 12 → 13	Pr. 23

General Notes on Chapter 1

• OBJECTIVE: This chapter includes some of the most fundamental and useful structures in everyday English. Students learn to ask and answer questions that are useful in getting and giving information, describing, and keeping a conversation moving along.

• APPROACH: The book emphasizes everyday English, a style and register acceptable in most situations. The first exercise models a simple dialogue for an interview to help classmates get acquainted. Then the charts and exercises focus on important details of a few fundamental verb structures.

• TERMINOLOGY: The text does not differentiate between verb "tenses" and "aspects." The usual student understanding of the term "tense" is a verb form that expresses time relationships; most students are comfortable with the term. The goal is always to present and explain structures with a minimum of technical terminology. The hope is that the students will one day leave their formal study of English with good control of its structures; most terminology can and probably will be soon forgotten.

The "present progressive" is also called the "present continuous" in some texts.

☐ EXERCISE 1, p. 1. *Getting to know each other the first day of class.*

First explain the purpose of the task: pairs of students are going to interview each other and then introduce their partners to the rest of the class. If your students already know each other, you might ask them to pretend to be other people—famous film stars, historical figures, etc. The example of the conversation between Kunio and Maria is intended to show the learners what they are supposed to do.

Before they begin the task, ask the class to suggest some questions that will elicit information on the topics in italics in the text: *name, native country*, etc. Write their questions on the chalkboard, then call attention to the same or similar questions in the dialogue between Kunio and Maria as you go through it in class.

The expected questions are:

> *What's your name?*
> *Where are you from? | What country are you from?*
> *Where are you living? | Where do you live?*★
> *What's your field of study? | What's your major? | What's your major field of study? |*
> *What are you studying? | What's your field?*
> *Where do you work?*
> *What do you like to do in your free time? | Do you have any hobbies? | What do you enjoy*
> *doing in your spare time?*

1. Have two students read the dialogue aloud. Stop them at important points, and discuss briefly with the class.

   SUGGESTIONS:

   • Model some parts of the dialogue. For example, you could model how a native speaker might say "Hi. My name's (. . .)." and have the students try to imitate your intonation. You could model any of the sentences and have the whole class repeat.

   • Point out everyday contracted speech. For example: *Where are* becomes *Where're*. Model some of the contractions and encourage students to use them when they speak.

   • Point out phrases that keep a conversation moving along. Discuss their meanings and functions: *And you?* (meaning "And where are you living now?" referring to the immediately preceding question) and *How about you?* (meaning the speaker is asking the other person the same question that immediately preceded).

2. After going through the dialogue with the class, have one student play Kunio's part and another play Maria's. Ask "Kunio" to use the written introduction in the text to introduce "Maria." The purpose is to show the students what they're supposed to do when they make their introductions. Be sure "Kunio" writes "Maria's" name on the board. You could have him write the name of her country, too.

3. Have the students, working individually or in small groups, write Maria's introduction of Kunio. Have various students present their introductions; discuss them with the class.

★*Where are you living?* (present progressive) is the usual form of a question about a current but probably temporary residence: a dormitory, an apartment, etc. *Where do you live?* (simple present) is more often the question about the resident's permanent home. In addition to a street address, the question *Where do you live?* can elicit a response of a city or state/province (e.g., *I live in Kansas City, Kansas.*). The distinction between these forms is subtle. In this interview, either question is appropriate and will elicit the desired information.

POSSIBLE INTRODUCTION:

I would like to introduce you to Kunio. His last name is Akiwa. He is from Japan. Kunio, please stand up. Kunio lives in an apartment on Fifth Avenue. His major is chemistry. His hobby is collecting stamps from all over the world.

The next step is to divide the students into pairs, mixing language groups in a multilingual class or mixing proficiency levels in a monolingual class. Give the pairs ten minutes or so to do the interviews and prepare their introductions. Allow the students to read from their notes during the introductions. Encourage the class to write down the names of their classmates as a way of getting to know each other.

As a follow-up to the in-class activity, you could ask the students to write the information from their interviews in a short descriptive composition (in class or out of class) and hand it in.

◊ WORKBOOK PRACTICE 1, p. 1.   *Interview questions and answers.*

Completion. [Selfstudy]

This practice echoes the first exercise in the main text. It is intended to reinforce material discussed in class on the first day.

ANSWERS:

A: Hi. My name _is_ Kunio.

B: Hi. My _name_ is Maria. I '_m_ glad to meet you.

KUNIO: I '_m_ glad to _meet_ you, too. Where _are you from_ ?

MARIA: I '_m_ from Mexico. Where _are you from_ ?

KUNIO: I '_m_ from Japan.

MARIA: Where _are you_ living now?

KUNIO: On Fifth Avenue in _an_ apartment. And you?

MARIA: I '_m_ living in a dorm.

KUNIO: _What's (What is)_ your field of study?

MARIA: Business. After I study English, I '_m_ going to attend the School of Business Administration. How _about_ you? _What's_ your major?

KUNIO: Chemistry.

MARIA: _What do_ you like to do in your free time? _Do_ you have any hobbies?

KUNIO: I _like_ to swim. How _about_ you?

MARIA: I read a lot and I _collect_ stamps from all over the world.

KUNIO: Really? _Would_ you like some stamps from Japan?

MARIA: Sure! That would be great. Thanks.

KUNIO: I have _to_ write your full name on the board when I introduce _you_ to the class. _How_ do you spell your name?

MARIA: My first _name_ is Maria. M-A-R-I-A. My last _name_ is Lopez. L-O-P-E-Z.

KUNIO: My _first_ name is Kunio. K-U-N-I-O. My _last_ name is Akiwa. A-K-I-W-A.

MARIA: Kunio Akiwa. _Is_ that right?

KUNIO: Yes, it _is_ . It's been nice talking with you.

MARIA: I enjoyed it, too.

◊ WORKBOOK PRACTICE 2, p. 2.   *Introducing yourself.*

Written. [Guided Study]

This practice allows you to get to know your students and evaluate their proficiency. Students using this text should have no trouble answering these questions clearly and appropriately in written English. Students who can't may need a lower-level text.

◇ WORKBOOK PRACTICE 3, p. 2. *Present verbs. (Charts 1-1 → 1-3)*

Error analysis. [Guided Study]

This practice alerts students to common problems in using present verb forms. The intention is to use it as a preview of some of the grammar in this chapter. You might want to ask the students to write out and hand in the corrected sentences in order to evaluate their level of understanding and usage ability. Group or pair work would be another possibility.

ANSWERS: **1.** I'm not living at home right now. **2.** I'm living in this city. **3.** I'm a student at this school. **4.** I'm studying English. **5.** I don't know my teacher's name. **6.** *(Teacher's name)* teaches our English class. **7.** She/He expects us to be in class on time. **8.** We always come to class on time. **9.** Does Tom go to school? **10.** Tom doesn't go to school. **11.** My sister doesn't have a job. **12.** Does Sara have a job? **13.** Do you have a job? **14.** Is Canada north of the United States? **15.** I never go to my office on Saturday. **16.** Ahmed, Toshi, Ji, Ingrid, and Pedro eat lunch together every day.

**CHARTS 1-1 and 1-2: SIMPLE PRESENT AND
PRESENT PROGRESSIVE**

• It is assumed that the students are already acquainted with these two present tenses, their negative and question forms, and contractions with *am, are, is,* and *not.* It is not assumed that the students have full control of these forms and their uses, however.

• The time-line diagram below is used to demonstrate tenses throughout the text, with the vertical crossbar representing "now" or the "moment of speaking."

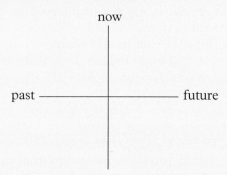

• The other tenses in the text are presented with the same time-line diagram. See Chart 2-6 for the diagrams for the simple past and past progressive; Chart 3-1 for the simple future; Chart 7-3 for the present perfect; Chart 7-10 for the past perfect.

NOTES on presenting the grammar in Charts 1-1 and 1-2.★

• One option in presenting Chart 1-1 is to draw the diagrams on the board, relate them to the examples, then proceed immediately to the exercises, reviewing all the relevant grammar points as they arise.

★See the INTRODUCTION: Classroom Techniques (pp. ix) for suggestions for presenting grammar charts.

• As another option, you could review all the grammar points in Charts 1-1 and 1-2 before turning to the exercises. Elicit examples from the class, write them on the board, discuss differences in meaning, manipulate forms, and orally model the contractions. You might, for example, use the verb "sit" and have the students make sentences about themselves and their classmates in statements, negatives, and questions such as these:

> *(Pedro) sits in class every day. (Pedro) is sitting*
> *(in that seat) right now.*
> *He doesn't sit in the back row every day. He isn't sitting*
> *in the back row right now.*
> *Does he usually sit in the center row? Is he sitting*
> *in the center row?*

Ask leading questions so that the students will answer variously with *I, s/he,* and *they* as the subjects. Ask other questions so that students give short answers. For example, *Is (Talal) sitting next to (Janko)? Who is sitting in front of (Somchart)?*

• To get across the idea that the simple present expresses daily habits, ask the class to give you examples of their daily habits. To contrast with the present progressive, ask them if they are doing these things right now. An example of a daily habit: *I eat breakfast every day.* Contrast: *Are you eating breakfast right now?* Just a few examples should suffice to help the students understand the chart. The exercises that follow give them many opportunities to use the target structures.

• To emphasize that one use of the simple present is to express general statements of fact, ask the class to give you examples: *Rain falls. Birds fly. The earth is round.* Try to elicit truths that exist past, present, and future.

• To emphasize the meaning of the present progressive, have students perform a few actions such as standing up or holding a pen for other students to describe. (Exercise 3 that follows has a list of actions that students can perform.)

☐ EXERCISE 2, p. 4.   *Simple present and present progressive. (Charts 1-1 and 1-2)*

Fill-in-the-blanks. ∗
The intention of this exercise is call attention to the grammar points presented in Charts 1-1 and 1-2. Students could work in pairs or small groups before the whole class discusses the correct answers.

   Model contracted speech, using nouns (e.g., the **baby's** *sleeping*) as well as pronouns (**I'm** *sitting*).

ANSWERS: **2.** am sitting . . . sit   **3.** speaks . . . is speaking   **4.** is not (isn't) standing . . . is sitting [Note: A teacher sitting on the corner of a desk may be considered rude or guilty of inappropriate behavior in some cultures.]   **5.** is eating . . . eats   **6.** is not (isn't) raining . . . is shining . . . is   **7.** Does it rain   **8.** Is it raining   **9.** is sitting . . . is reading . . . reads . . . is pouring . . . drinks . . . goes . . . are not (aren't) watching . . . are playing . . . watch . . . are not (aren't) paying . . . are not (aren't) watching . . . do not (don't) like   **10.** does not (doesn't) take . . . walks . . . Do you take . . . do you walk

---

∗See the INTRODUCTION: *Classroom Techniques* (pp. ix–xix) for descriptions of possible techniques to use in the various kinds of exercises: *written, oral (books closed), fill-in-the-blanks, completion,* etc., and ways of handling teacher and student involvement: *teacher-led, student-led, group work, pair work.*

□ **EXERCISE 3, p. 5.** *Oral survey of the present progressive. (Charts 1-1 and 1-2)*

Oral (books closed), teacher-led. ★

If the vocabulary is difficult for your class, let them keep their books open. Try to elicit definitions or demonstrations of meaning from the class before you supply them. Vocabulary that may be difficult: *whistle, hum, bite, fingernails, rub, palms, kick, knock, shake, scratch.* (NOTE: In India and some other cultures, whistling may be considered rude.)

The words in the text in a books-closed exercise are not intended as a script for the teacher. They are suggestions. For the first item, for example, the teacher would probably say to a student, "Would you please stand up? Thank you," and then elicit the present progressive from another student.

You might mention that short answers (Maria [is].) are more natural than complete sentences in response to conversational questions (e.g., *Who is standing there?*). A complete sentence is more natural in response to a question with *doing* (e.g., *What is Maria doing?*). Point out that the complete sentence responses are designed to provide practice with the target structures.

The cues in this exercise could be written on slips of paper and handed to pairs of students, who could then perform the actions as a pair while the rest of the class describes the action using the present progressive. This would encourage the use of plural pronouns *(they, their, them)* and plural verb forms.

EXPANSION: Suggest to the learners that they talk to themselves, either silently or aloud. For example, if they are entering their apartment: *I'm turning the doorknob. I'm opening the door. I'm walking into my apartment. I'm closing the door.* They can get a lot of valuable practice with English by themselves. Ask them if they ever talk to themselves in their own language. They may or may not admit it. Assure them that most people *do* talk to themselves and that it's a good language-learning technique.

EXPANSION: Here are some other ideas for eliciting present verbs:

(1) Ask a student to pretend to be a television reporter. S/he is covering an event live. The event is an exciting ESL or EFL English class at *(name of your school)*. The TV audience doesn't know much about this kind of class. The reporter needs to tell the audience the nature of the class and describe what is happening at the moment during the live broadcast. The reporter could also interview some of the class members. Students can take turns being the reporter. You should demonstrate being the reporter first, then ask for a volunteer to continue.

(2) Use a video camera to make a movie of the class. Perhaps you could videotape pantomimes or some other predetermined activity. Show the movie in class and ask the students to describe what is happening on the screen.

(3) Show a videotape in class without the sound. Have the students describe the actions using present verbs. They will need to guess what is going on in addition to describing the physical activities.

(4) Set up a pretend microphone. Ask one student at a time (preferably volunteers) to pretend to be a radio news reporter reporting on important events in the world today. (The reporters will probably need to use past verbs as well. This role-play could be postponed until Chapter 2.)

★Throughout this *Teacher's Guide,* see the INTRODUCTION for descriptions of suggested techniques, pp. ix–xix.

ANSWERS: **1.** is standing   **2.** is smiling   **3.** is whistling   **4.** is opening/is closing   **5.** is humming   **6.** is biting   **7.** is reading   **8.** is erasing   **9.** is looking   **10.** is holding   **11.** is rubbing   **12.** is kicking   **13.** is knocking   **14.** is sitting   **15.** is shaking hands   **16.** is looking   **17.** is counting   **18.** is shaking   **19.** is scratching   **20.** Etc.

☐ EXERCISE 4, p. 6.   *The simple present and frequency adverbs. (Charts 1-1 and 1-2)*

Oral, discussion of meaning, teacher-led and/or group work.

Discuss the meaning of the frequency adverbs first. (The text includes no chart presentation of the meaning of frequency adverbs; however, midsentence placement is dealt with in Chart 7-8, p. 181). Perhaps present to the students the actual frequency of some activity and ask them which adverb would be best. Examples:

> *I drink coffee every morning of the week.* = **always**
> *I drink coffee six mornings a week.* = **usually**
> *I drink coffee four or five mornings a week.* = **often**
> *I drink coffee two, three, or four mornings a week.* = **sometimes**
> *I drink coffee once every two weeks.* = **seldom**
> *I drink coffee once or twice a year.* = **rarely**

Other possible points to discuss:

• *Usually* and *often* are close in meaning. If any students want to pursue a distinction, you might say that *usually* is 95% of the time and *often* is 90% of the time. Or you might say that *usually* means "most of the time, regularly" and *often* means "many times, repeated times, frequently."

• *Often* can be pronounced /ɔfən/ or /ɔftən/.

• In discussing the difference between *seldom* and *rarely,* you might assign *seldom* 5% of the time and *rarely* 1% of the time. (For more advanced learners, you might note that *seldom* and *rarely* are negatives; the word "not" cannot be used in the same clause. Refer students to Chart 7-8 for more information.)

  The exercise can be teacher-led and can also be done in groups of three to six. The roles of A, B, and C should rotate among the group during the exercise. The purposes in having Student C summarize what Students A and B have said are (1) to include practice with verbs that end in final *-s/-es* for a third person singular subject; (2) to further help the students learn each other's names; and (3) to encourage everyone to pay attention to what everyone else is saying.

☐ EXERCISE 5, p. 6.   *The simple present and frequency adverbs. (Charts 1-1 and 1-2)*

Oral (books closed), teacher-led.

This exercise is intended for teacher-student interaction to elicit creative language use. This is an ideal exercise to use with native-speaker teaching helpers if they are available. The next exercise is more suitable for group work than this exercise.

  The intention is for you to engage the students in conversation about their daily activities. Then Student B summarizes the conversation. Tell all the class to listen carefully for final *-s/-es* in Student B's summary.

  With a very large class, you could divide the room into sections. Appoint a helper or a very good student to lead the exercise for each section of the room.

□ EXERCISE 6, p. 7. *The simple present and frequency adverbs. (Charts 1-1 and 1-2)*

> *Oral (books closed), group work or teacher-led.*
> This exercise can be done in small groups. Appoint a leader or have each group elect their leader. (See the INTRODUCTION, p. xi, for suggestions on setting up group work.) The leader can change for Parts II and III. In Parts II and III, the questioner should choose only one of the frequency adverbs for each question. With luck, you'll have a room full of students enjoying conversations with each other and using the target structure.
>
> NOTE ON USAGE: In the example, the question is "take *a* bus," which implies that someone might use another form of transportation. This question could also be "take *the* bus," which may imply the bus that goes to the school or the usual bus the person takes. The difference between these phrases is minor, but alert students may ask about it.

◇ WORKBOOK PRACTICE 4, p. 3. *Present verbs. (Charts 1-1 → 1-3)*

> *Fill-in-the-blanks.* [Selfstudy]
>
> ANSWERS: **1.** am sitting **2.** am reading **3.** am looking **4.** am writing **5.** am doing **6.** sit . . . am sitting **7.** read . . . am reading **8.** look . . . am looking **9.** write . . . am writing **10.** do . . . am doing

◇ WORKBOOK PRACTICE 5, p. 3. *Forms of the simple present. (Chart 1-1)*

> *Fill-in-the-blanks.* [Selfstudy]
>
> ANSWERS:
> **PART I:** **1.** speak **2.** speak **3.** speaks **4.** speak **5.** speaks
> **PART II:** **1.** do not (don't) speak **2.** do not (don't) speak **3.** does not (doesn't) speak **4.** do not (don't) speak **5.** does not (doesn't) speak
> **PART III:** **1.** Do you speak **2.** Do they speak **3.** Does he speak **4.** Do we speak **5.** Does she speak

CHART 1-3: SPELLING: FINAL -*S* vs. -*ES*

- Give additional examples of the points made in the chart and have students supply the correct endings. Suggestions of verbs to use:

(a) *begin* → *begins*; (b) *move* → *moves*; (c) *watch* → *watches, push* → *pushes, guess* → *guesses, mix* → *mixes, fizz* → *fizzes* [very few verbs end in -z]; (d) *goes* and *does* are oddities; (e) *worry* → *worries*; (f) *play* → *plays*.

- A common error is adding -*es* when only -*s* is needed. Emphasize when -*es* is and is not added.

- Discuss the pronunciation of *does* /dəz/ and *goes* /gowz/. Tell them you know that they look like they should be pronounced similarly, but that English has some funny little oddities, just as any other language. In fact, some of the most common short words in English are the most unusual in spelling and pronunciation (e.g., *their, says, was, has*). As with most things, frequent use has caused them to change shape.

- The pronunciation of final -*s*/-*es* is dealt with in the *Workbook* in conjunction with plural nouns, Chapter 4, Practice 3, p. 62. You may want to present a similar unit on pronunciation at this time. If not, simply model the pronunciation for your students. (A summary of the pronunciation of final -*s*/-*es* follows:

  It is pronounced /s/ after voiceless sounds, e.g., *meets*.
  It is pronounced /z/ after voiced sounds, e.g., *needs*.
  It is pronounced /əz/ after -*sh*, -*ch*, -*s* [including -*ks*], -*z*, and -*ge*/*dge* sounds, e.g., *wishes, watches, passes, mixes, sizes, judges*.)

☐ EXERCISE 7, p. 8. *Final -S vs. -ES. (Chart 1-3)*

   Structure identification and error analysis.
   The focus of this exercise is on (1) identification of subjects and verbs in simple sentences; (2) the use of final -*s*/-*es* in the simple present; and finally (3) the spelling of final -*s*/-*es*. Ask the students to find the subjects and verbs in the sentences. The ability to recognize subjects and verbs is essential to their successful use of this textbook. If necessary, refer the students to Charts 4-2 (Subjects, Verbs, and Objects) and 4-3 (Objects of Prepositions) on pp. 70 and 71.
   EXPANSION: a spelling test. Give the simple form of a verb and ask students to write the correct -*s*/-*es* form. They can correct each other's papers. Possible verbs to use: *carry, buy, enjoy, kiss, wish, taste, disappear, break, catch, cry, enter, explain, finish, exist, occur, marry, stay.*

   ANSWERS: **3.** floats   **4.** flow   **5.** worries   **6.** buys   **7.** fly   **8.** teaches
   9. asks   **10.** watches   **11.** consists   **12.** [pesticides = /pəstə saidz/] destroy
   13. travels   **14.** contains   **15.** freezes . . . boils   **16.** [Ms. = /mɪz/] crosses . . . walks
   . . . uses   **17.** [Subject = *parts. Of the world* is a prepositional phrase, not the subject of the sentence. The subject here can also be called the "head of the noun phrase."] enjoy . . . [Subject = *each season*. Note that *each* is always immediately followed by a singular noun and a singular verb.] lasts . . . brings [Point out the parallel verbs: one subject (*each season*) has two verbs connected by *and*. The second verb needs to agree with the singular subject also.]

◊ WORKBOOK PRACTICE 6, p. 4.   *Simple present. (Charts 1-1 → 1-3)*

Controlled completion. [Selfstudy]

ANSWERS: **1.** like **s**   **2.** watch **es**   **3.** do **es** n't like **/**   **4.** climb **/**   **5.** Do **/** ...
like **/**   **6.** Do **es** ... like **/**   **7.** like **s**   **8.** wash **es**   **9.** go **es**   **10.** make **/**
11. visit **s**   **12.** get **s**   **13.** get **/**   **14.** Do **es** ... get **/**   **15.** do **es** n't get **/**
16. carr **ies**   **17.** play **s**   **18.** catch **es**   **19.** live **/**   **20.** live **s**

◊ WORKBOOK PRACTICE 7, p. 5.   *Final forms with -S/-ES. (Charts 1-1 → 1-3)*

Sentence construction. [Guided Study]
Students can work in pairs or groups to prepare the written sentences. Then the correct sentences can be discussed in class, along with pronunciation and vocabulary.

The vocabulary in this practice will be difficult for many of the students; vocabulary development is one of the intentions. You could ask for and answer questions about the meanings of words prior to the students doing the practice, or you could leave them on their own as they explain to each other the meanings of the words with the aid of their dictionaries. Both approaches to vocabulary discussion have their own advantages. A teacher can give quick and accurate information; in peer teaching, the students have the chance to practice various communication skills.

ANSWERS: **1.** (D) A star shines in the sky at night.   **2.** (L) A hotel supplies its guests with clean towels.   **3.** (H) Newspaper ink stains my hands when I read the paper.
4. (J) Bees gather nectar from flowers.   **5.** (A) Do automobiles cause air pollution?
6. (G) Does physical exercise improve your circulation and general health?
7. (B) A rubber band stretches when you pull on it.   **8.** (K) A river flows downhill.
9. (C) Oceans support a huge variety of marine life.   **10.** (I) Brazil produces one-fourth of the world's coffee.   **11.** (F) Does an elephant use its long trunk like a hand to pick things up?
12. (E) A hurricane causes great destruction when it reaches land.

◊ WORKBOOK PRACTICE 8, p. 5.   *Forms of the present progressive. (Charts 1-1 and 1-2)*

Fill-in-the-blanks. [Selfstudy]

ANSWERS:
PART I: **1.** am speaking   **2.** are speaking   **3.** is speaking   **4.** are speaking
PART II: **1.** am not speaking   **2.** are not (aren't) speaking   **3.** is not (isn't) speaking
4. are not (aren't) speaking
PART III: **1.** Are you speaking   **2.** Are they speaking   **3.** Is she speaking   **4.** Are we speaking

◊ WORKBOOK PRACTICES 9 & 10, p. 6.   *Simple present and present progressive. (Charts 1-1 → 1-3)*

Controlled completion. [Selfstudy and Guided Study]
Students have to be aware of many grammar points in these two practices. Congratulate them on their alertness and breadth of understanding of English grammar.

PR. 9 ANSWERS: **1.** does   **2.** Do   **3.** /   **4.** is   **5.** Are   **6.** are   **7.** Is   **8.** Do
9. /   **10.** is   **11.** is   **12.** are   **13.** /   **14.** /   **15.** Do   **16.** Does   **17.** Is
18. Are   **19.** are   **20.** /   **21.** are   **22.** is

PR. 10 ANSWERS: **1.** is   **2.** are   **3.** /   **4.** Does   **5.** do   **6.** /   **7.** /   **8.** do
9. /   **10.** does   **11.** does   **12.** /   **13.** is   **14.** /...**/**   **15.** is   **16.** /...are
17. Do   **18.** Does

◇ WORKBOOK PRACTICE 11, p. 7.   *Frequency adverbs. (Charts 1-1 and 1-2)*

Controlled completion. [Selfstudy]

ANSWERS: **1.** often   **2.** rarely/seldom   **3.** always   **4.** usually/often   **5.** sometimes
6. usually   **7.** rarely/seldom   **8.** rarely/seldom   **9.** never   **10.** always   **11.** often
12. rarely/seldom [also possible: sometimes]

◇ WORKBOOK PRACTICE 12, p. 8.   *Simple present: frequency adverbs. (Charts 1-1 and 1-2)*

Sentence construction. [Guided Study]

◇ WORKBOOK PRACTICES 13 & 14, pp. 9 –10.   *Present progressive. (Charts 1-1 and 1-2)*

Sentence construction. [Selfstudy and Guided Study]
The term "progressive" comes from the idea of an activity being "in progress." The emphasis
in these two practices is on connecting the use of the progressive with the idea of an activity in
progress. All of the pictures show activities in progress.
   EXPANSION: Ask students to come up with miscellaneous vocabulary suggested by the
pictures. For example, in item 1 of Practice 13: *palm tree, tropical island, drops of water, splash,
kick, elbow.*

PR. 13 EXPECTED RESPONSES: **1.** He is (He's) swimming. / He's doing the crawl.   **2.** He's
cutting her hair. / He's using scissors. / She's getting a haircut.   **3.** She's sleeping. / She's
dreaming. / She's having a pleasant dream.   **4.** He's crying. / He's wiping his tears with his
hand.   **5.** She's kicking a ball. / She's playing soccer.   **6.** He's hitting a golf ball. /
He's playing golf. / He's golfing. / He's swinging a golf club.   **7.** She's riding a motorcycle. /
She's wearing a helmet.   **8.** They're dancing. / They're smiling. / They're having a good time.

PR. 14 EXPECTED RESPONSES: **1.** He's cooking. / He's frying something. / He's burning the food.
2. She's tying her shoe. / She's tying her shoelaces. / She's getting ready to go jogging.
3. They're jogging. / They're running. / They're sweating. / They're exercising.   **4.** He's
climbing a mountain. / He's pounding a spike into the side of the mountain.
5. They're laughing. / They're having a good time. [In English, the sounds of laughter are often
represented by "ha ha" and "hee hee." Ask your students how the sounds of laughter are represented in
their languages.]   **6.** He's kissing the baby. / He's getting ready to leave for the office. / He's just
getting home from his office.   **7.** She's pouring milk into a glass. / She's pouring a glass of
milk.   **8.** He's whistling. / He's driving a taxi.

CHART 1-4: NONPROGRESSIVE VERBS

- The key point is the difference between "states" and "activities." The intention of this chart and its terminology is simply to inform the students that certain common verbs are usually not used in the progressive form.

- The list of nonprogressive (i.e., stative) verbs is by no means complete. It presents only a few common verbs.

- Remind students about negative verb forms:
  Progressive: *I'm studying English now.*   ***I'm not*** *studying French.*
  Nonprogressive: *I like tea.*   *I **don't** like coffee.*

- Vocabulary:
  look at = focus attention on sights   vs.   *see* = notice, become aware of
  listen to = pay attention to sounds   vs.   *hear* = notice, be aware of
  Looking and listening are conscious, deliberate acts. Seeing and hearing happen by chance; they are not planned acts.

☐ EXERCISE 8, p. 10.   *Simple present vs. present progressive. (Chart 1-4)*

Fill-in-the-blanks.
This exercise emphasizes nonprogressive (i.e., stative) verbs. They describe a state that exists now, not an activity that is in progress now.

ANSWERS: **2.** am looking . . . see   **3.** need . . . do not (don't) know   **4.** like . . . prefer
5. are . . . are having . . . have . . . are playing . . . like . . . are sunbathing [Note the correct spelling with no *e*. Pronunciation: /sᵊnbeyðiŋ/] . . . are trying . . . are listening . . . hear   **6.** am thinking
7. think   **8.** think . . . know . . . forget . . . remember   **9.** is sitting . . . is writing . . . is using
. . . does not (doesn't) belong . . . belongs . . . is looking . . . wants   **10.**   A: Do you believe
B: are you talking . . . exist   **11.**   A: do you prefer   B: like   A: am reading . . . prefer . . .
are . . . value . . . means . . . is . . . loves   B: sounds

◇ WORKBOOK PRACTICE 15, p. 11.   *Simple present and present progressive. (Charts 1-1 → 1-4)*

Controlled completion. [Selfstudy]

ANSWERS: **1.** is snowing   **2.** takes   **3.** drive   **4.** am watching   **5.** prefer
6. need   **7.** are playing   **8.** is looking . . . sees   **9.** sings   **10.** bite   **11.** writes
12. understand   **13.** belongs   **14.** is shining . . . is raining

---

CHART 1-5: SIMPLE PRESENT AND PRESENT PROGRESSIVE: SHORT ANSWERS TO QUESTIONS

- Students need to understand that auxiliary verbs can substitute for verb phrases. For example, in the first short answer in the chart (*Yes, he does*), *does* means "likes tea."

☐ EXERCISE 9, p. 12.   *Simple present vs. present progressive: questions and short answers. (Chart 1-5)*

Fill-in-the-blanks.

Discuss the full meaning of the short answers. For example, in item 1: *Yes, she does* means "Yes, she has a bicycle."

   Note that it may seem impolite to give only a short answer and then stop talking. A short answer is often followed by more detailed information or another question that keeps the conversation open. A short answer might cut off the dialogue and appear a bit rude in everyday conversational situations.

   Refer students to Chart 6-2, p. 128, if they need more information about the forms of *yes/no* questions.

ANSWERS: **2.** A: Is it raining   B: It isn't/it's not raining . . . don't think [Note: *so* substitutes for the noun clause "that it is raining." See Chart 14-6.]   **3.** A: Do you like   B: I don't. . . . like   **4.** A: Do your friends write   B: they do . . . get   **5.** A: Are the students taking   B: they aren't/they're not . . . are doing [*Do* is the main verb, not an auxiliary, in this sentence.]   **6.** A: Do you know   B: I don't   **7.** A: Does your desk have   B: it does . . . has   **8.** A: Is Jean studying   B: she isn't/she's not . . . is [*Is* is the main verb in this sentence.] . . . is playing   A: Does Jean play   B: she doesn't . . . studies   A: Is she   B: she is . . . plays   A: Do you know   B: I do . . . am not

◇ WORKBOOK PRACTICE 16, p. 12.   *Simple present and present progressive. (Charts 1-1 and 1-2)*

Controlled completion. [Selfstudy]

ANSWERS:

1. A: Are	B: I am	OR	I'm not
2. A: Do	B: they do	OR	they don't
3. A: Do	B: I do	OR	I don't
4. A: Does	B: she does	OR	she doesn't
5. A: Are	B: they are	OR	they aren't
6. A: Do	B: they do	OR	they don't
7. A: Is	B: he is	OR	he isn't
8. A: Are	B: I am	OR	I'm not
9. A: Is	B: it is	OR	it isn't
10. A: Does	B: it does	OR	it doesn't

☐ EXERCISE 10, p. 14.   *Simple present vs. present progressive. (Charts 1-1 and 1-2)*

Fill-in-the-blanks.

This is a cumulative review exercise of the simple present and present progressive (statements, negatives, questions, short answers) and progressive vs. nonprogressive verbs.

   This is a good exercise for pair work before or while you review it with the whole class. Two students can agree on the responses before they present them to the rest of the class, thus avoiding possible solo embarrassment.

ANSWERS: **1.** A: Are they watching   B: they aren't/they're not . . . are playing   **2.** A: hear . . . Do you hear   B: I do   **3.** A: has   B: Do you have   A: I don't   **4.** B: Is the baby sleeping   A: is taking   B: don't want   **5.** A: is   B: it isn't/it's not . . . doesn't belong . . . belongs   **6.** A: are you listening   B: want   **7.** A: do you think   B: think . . . don't think   **8.** ["A penny for your thoughts" is an idiom meaning roughly "You look like you're thinking seriously. What are you thinking about? I'd like to know."] ["Huh?" is an informal and possibly impolite way of saying "What?" or "Excuse me?"]   A: are you thinking   B: am thinking

. . . am not thinking   A: don't believe   **9.**   A: Do you see . . . am talking . . . is wearing . . .
Do you know   B: don't think [*So* means "I know him."]   A: don't know   **10.**   A: Do you
know   B: I do   A: is   B: doesn't make   A: know [Students may have fun playing around with
the tongue-twisters. Ask them to see how fast they can say *She sells seashells down by the seashore*, an old
and familiar English tongue-twister. The second one is simply made up and contains sounds that many
ESL/EFL students have difficulty distinguishing between: /s/ vs. /sh/; /s/ vs. /z/; /č/ vs. /š/. It's intended as a
fun pronunciation activity.]

☐ EXERCISE 11, p. 16.   *Present progressive. (Charts 1-1 and 1-2)*

Oral/written.
Ask half the class to perform activities. Each member of the group can perform a different
action; several students can perform the same action if they wish. Then ask students in the other
half of the class to identify a person or persons in the activity group and describe the activity,
using the present progressive.
      EXPANSION: After the groups have performed their activities, ask individual students to
perform an activity of their choice while the rest of the class describes it in writing, using their
classmates' names and the present progressive.

◇ WORKBOOK PRACTICE 17, p. 13.   *Present progressive. (Charts 1-1 and 1-2)*

Oral. [Guided Study]
NOTE: Pantomine /pæntəmaym/ means to pretend to be doing something, using no words, only
actions. You yourself should demonstrate the art of pantomime for the class before breaking the
students into groups. Pretend to comb your hair, blow up a balloon, be asleep, etc. Your relaxed
manner and willingness to perform publicly will encourage shy students to at least try a
pantomime themselves. You might want to put suggestions for actions to pantomime on note
cards and hand them out. If not, help the class brainstorm some ideas in addition to the
suggestions in the text. Additional suggestions: brushing your hair, typing, talking on the phone,
swimming, laughing, drinking through a straw, erasing something, shaking hands with someone,
reading a newspaper. Almost any usual activity is suitable for pantomime.

◇ WORKBOOK PRACTICE 18, p. 14.   *Present progressive. (Charts 1-1 and 1-2)*

Oral. [Guided Study]
This is a variation on the use of pantomime to elicit the present progressive. In a longer and
more involved pantomime, sometimes a student's detailed actions can seem a bit arcane and
bewildering to the rest of the group, so it helps to have the performer describe these actions
her/himself.

◇ WORKBOOK PRACTICE 19, p. 14.   *Present verbs. (Charts 1-1 → 1-5)*

Fill-in-the-blanks. [Selfstudy]

ANSWERS: **1.** is . . . is blowing . . . are falling   **2.** eats . . . don't eat . . . do you eat
3. A: Do you shop   B: don't . . . usually shop   A: are you shopping   B: am trying
4. am buying . . . buy   **5.** A: Do you read   B: do . . . read . . . subscribe . . . look
6. B: am . . . am trying   A: is resting   **7.** A: am I studying . . . do I want . . . need
8. lose . . . rest . . . grow . . . keep . . . stay . . . don't grow . . . don't have . . . Do trees grow

◇ WORKBOOK PRACTICE 20, p. 15.   *Present verbs. (Charts 1-1 → 1-4)*

Fill-in-the-blanks. [Guided Study]

ANSWERS: **1.** goes . . . likes . . . is preparing   **2.** A: are you reading   B: think
A: see   B: is   **3.** A: am leaving . . . Do you want   B: am waiting   **4.** is trying . . . is
travel(l)ing . . . (is) talking . . . knows   **5.** B: spins . . . is spinning   A: don't feel . . . Are you
trying   B: Do you really think   B: Do you believe . . . are growing . . . are getting [also possible:
get] . . . are taking . . . are speaking   **6.** A: is she going . . . is she walking   B: is rushing . . .
submits . . . presents   A: usually hear   B: rewrites . . . takes . . . reads . . .
acts   A: doesn't seem   B: isn't

◇ WORKBOOK PRACTICE 21, p. 17.   *Present verbs. (Charts 1-1 → 1-4)*

Transformation and sentence structure. [Guided Study]
Essentially you are asking the students to create new contexts when they change the verb forms.
Most of these new contexts can be created through use of different adverbial phrases of time.
Contexts can also be created by the addition of another idea within the sentence or in a second
sentence.

POSSIBLE RESPONSES:
PART I: **1.** I'm studying English right this very minute.   **2.** The sun is shining this morning.
3. While we are talking, the earth is rotating on its axis.   **4.** Today Dr. Li is talking to the
students at Jefferson High School in Foxton.   **5.** Ted is sleeping in class right now because he
is very tired.
PART II: **6.** Sue and her husband often travel in South America.   **7.** Sam plays the piano
beautifully.   **8.** Our physics professor runs in a marathon at least twice a year.   **9.** Adam
wears jeans almost every day. He says they're comfortable.   **10.** We work hard in our
grammar class. I do a lot of grammar exercises in this class.

◇ WORKBOOK PRACTICE 22, p. 17.   *Present verbs. (Charts 1-1 → 1-4)*

Open completion. [Guided Study]
Some of the items in this practice require the students to use adverb clauses of time, which they
have not yet been introduced to in this text. Adverb clauses of time are first presented in the
next chapter in Chart 2-8. Most students at this level already have a fair usage ability of simple
adverb clauses, but some students may have trouble with or questions about the sentence
structure suggested in items 1, 2, 8, and 9.

☐ EXERCISE 12, p. 16.   *Prepositions. (Chapter 1)*

Oral, teacher-led; sentence construction.
The teacher's function in this exercise is to make sure the students understand the meaning of
these prepositions of place. Use objects and people in the classroom to illustrate meanings. Ask
the students to do the same. Stay with simple, basic meanings related to physical relationships.
Many of these prepositions have several different meanings and many different usages.
    After practicing simple sentences with the verb *be*, students may want to try some with
progressive and nonprogressive verbs (e.g., *My book is lying on the corner of my desk. His friend is
waiting for him on the corner of High Street. The teacher usually stands in the front of the room in
front of us. Yoshi is sitting behind Hei-Huei.* Etc.).

NOTES on particular items:

3. As prepositions describing physical relationships, *under* and *below* can have identical meanings (e.g., *I can place my right hand under/below my left hand*); however, *under* can indicate that two things are touching, whereas *below* usually indicates a space between two items (e.g., *My notebook is under my textbook.* = the two items are touching. *My notebook is below my textbook.* = the two items are not touching).

4. *Beside* means "next to," not to be confused with *besides*, which means "in addition."

5. *Against* implies that two items are touching (e.g., *He's standing against the wall*). *Next to* and *beside* can describe two items that may or may not be touching (e.g., *He's standing next to/beside his wife*).

8. *Between* describes the space from one point to another (e.g., *It's a long distance between this city and that city*) or the position of something in relation to two other objects (e.g., *I can put my book between my feet*).

9. *Among* describes the position of something in relation to more than two other objects (e.g., *There are five pens and one pencil on the desk. The pencil is among the pens*).

18. *In back of*, meaning "behind," may have to be distinguished from *in the back of*. *In the back of* describes the relative position of something within a given space, such as a book, a room, a car. For example: *The index is in the back of the book*, not *in back of the book*. *In the back of* does not mean "behind."

21. and **22.** *In the corner* describes the position of something within a given space, such as a piece of paper, a room, a box. *On the corner* describes the position of something atop a corner (e.g., *My book is on the corner of the desk*). A person can stand in the corner of the room, but not on the corner of the room. For a person to stand *on the corner* would probably mean on a sidewalk at a crossroads.

EXPANSION: You can make a quick game out of these prepositions. Note the location of things in the classroom and near the building. Divide the class into teams. Ask a question of one team (e.g., *Where's the clock?*). The team must answer with a complete, correct sentence (e.g., *It's on the wall*). Accept only the first answer that you hear. Permit no corrections. Repeat their answer to the other team. If they accept it as correct, Team 1 gets a point; if they do not accept it, they must answer correctly to win the point. They lose the point, however, if they reject a correct answer from Team 1.

☐ EXERCISE 13, p. 16.   *Prepositions. (Chapter 1)*

Controlled completion.
Follow up class discussion of the correct answers with a quick oral drill in which you give the first part of the sentence and the students call out the preposition:

    TEACHER: *Mr. Porter is nice . . . .*
    STUDENTS: *to*
    TEACHER: *to everyone.*

ANSWERS: **2.** from   **3.** for   **4.** at/with   **5.** at   **6.** of   **7.** to   **8.** to   **9.** for   **10.** to   **11.** with   **12.** of

◇ WORKBOOK PRACTICE 23, p. 18.   *Prepositions. (Chapter 1)*

Controlled completion. [Selfstudy]

ANSWERS: **1.** of   **2.** to   **3.** to   **4.** with   **5.** for   **6.** to   **7.** with/at   **8.** of   **9.** from   **10.** to   **11.** at   **12.** for

Chapter 2: PAST TIME

ORDER OF CHAPTER	CHARTS	EXERCISES	WORKBOOK
Simple past	2-1 → 2-2	Ex. 1 → 3	Pr. 1 → 3
Irregular verbs	2-3 → 2-4	Ex. 4 → 10	Pr. 4 → 7
Pronunciation of *-ed*			Pr. 8 → 9
Spelling of *-ing* and *-ed* forms	2-5	Ex. 11 → 13	Pr. 10 → 11
Cumulative review			Pr. 12
Simple past and past progressive	2-6 → 2-7	Ex. 14 → 16	Pr. 13 → 14
Time clauses	2-8	Ex. 17 → 18	Pr. 15 → 16
Cumulative review		Ex. 19 → 21	Pr. 17 → 18
Past habit (*used to*)	2-9	Ex. 22 → 24	Pr. 19 → 21
Cumulative review			Pr. 22 → 24
Prepositions of time	2-10	Ex. 25	Pr. 25 → 26

General Notes on Chapter 2

• OBJECTIVE: In Chapter 2, students learn to use the simple past and the past progressive verb tenses. They learn to associate the simple past with actions that were completed at a specific time before the present, and the past progressive with actions that co-occurred with other actions at some time before the present. They also practice some of the irregular forms and the spellings that arise in these verb tenses.

• APPROACH: Chapter 2 begins with a quick review of the simple past in affirmative, negative, question, and short answer forms. Each of these is used in several exercises. A list of common irregular verbs is presented, as well as the spelling of *-ing* and *-ed* verb forms. Some repetition and memorization are necessary at this stage.

   The limited meaning of the past progressive is compared with the simple past, and the "time clause" (subordinate or adverbial clause) is introduced. This greatly expands the learner's ability to express fairly complex ideas in English. Thus, some exercises in this chapter use longer sequences of spoken or written discourse than in Chapter 1.

   The very common past phrase "used to" is introduced in both questions and statements. The chapter ends with an exercise on the usage of some common prepositions in time expressions.

• TERMINOLOGY: The term "verb tense" is used more broadly here than in some other grammar books. A progressive verb form is often called an "aspect" instead of a tense, but that distinction is not made here in order to keep terminology to a minimum.

   An "irregular" verb form is one that does not follow the common pattern (e.g., adding *-ed* to the present form to signal the past form or past participle).

□ EXERCISE 1, p. 18. *Simple present and simple past. (Charts 2-1 and 2-2)*
Oral (books closed).

Exercise 1 is an oral introduction to the chapter. It is assumed that the students are acquainted with the simple past forms and can speak about their past activities. Use the sentences generated by the students to discuss the forms of the simple past: statements, negatives, questions, short answers; and regular vs. irregular verbs. The grammar points in Charts 2-1 and 2-2 are covered in this exercise.

Item 6 can be used in various ways:

• You can give the class about five minutes to write, then collect their papers. When you mark them, you could use the Guide for Correcting Writing Errors in APPENDIX 3, p. A6. You may want to mark all or most of the errors, or you may wish to mark only mistakes in the verb forms.

• EXPANSION: Select some of the errors for class discussion; keep the authors anonymous and only choose errors that the students are probably able to correct given their level of proficiency. For example, a student might have written: *I didn't went to the library yesterday* or *A bad thing happend yesterday.* Reproduce these sentences for the class, making your own error analysis exercise. (See the INTRODUCTION, p. xiv.)

• As an alternative, don't collect the papers immediately but have the students exchange them. Then you could ask them to do one or more of these activities:
Underline all the simple past verbs on their classmate's paper.
Read the other student's paper silently and then report orally what that student did yesterday.
Find mistakes and talk about them with the writer of the paper, meaning that two students will work on each paper before it is handed in to you.

• If the class is small enough, you could talk with individuals or pairs while the rest of the students are discussing their papers with each other. After discussing their papers with another student and with you, the students should be asked to rewrite them (preferably on every other line).

CHARTS 2-1 and 2-2: SIMPLE PAST

• Spelling of *-ed* forms is covered in Chart 2-5.

• Pronunciation of *-ed* forms is covered in the *Workbook*, Chapter 2, Practice 8, p. 24.
A summary of the pronunciation of *-ed*:
It is pronounced /t/ after voiceless sounds: *stopped = stop/t/*
It is pronounced /d/ after voiced sounds: *rubbed = rub/d/*
It is pronounced /əd/ after /t/ and /d/: *waited = wait/əd/*; *needed = need/əd/*

• Learners usually have lots of trouble with *did* in questions. They often neglect to change the main verb form, so they produce incorrect sentences like these:
INCORRECT: *Did he worked yesterday?*
INCORRECT: *Did you ate breakfast?*
On the chalkboard, you might show a statement and a question:
He worked yesterday.
Did he work yesterday?
Then make a circle around *-ed* and draw an arrow from *-ed* to *did*. Point out that *-ed* has moved away from *work* and has now become the word "did" in a new position. (The same change can be illustrated for the simple present, where the *-s* moves away from the main verb and joins *do* to become *does* at the beginning of a question. You could use the sentence "He works every day" to show this.)

☐ EXERCISE 2, p. 19. *Negative and affirmative verb forms. (Charts 2-1 and 2-2)*

Transformation and sentence construction.
This is a review of the negative and statement (i.e., affirmative) forms of the simple present, present progressive, and simple past. It is also intended to prepare the students for the oral work in the next exercise.

Students can do this exercise as seatwork (individually, in pairs, or in groups) prior to class discussion. Before they begin, you might need to preview the vocabulary in this exercise: *float* = stay on the surface of water; *sink* = fall below the surface of water; *a sofa* = a kind of furniture for two to four people to sit on.

Ask the students to name the tenses in each item. In this textbook, terminology is not intended to be memorized or tested. But it does help teacher-student communication considerably if the students learn such basic terminology as the names of these three tenses.

As they name the tense in each sentence, you might also ask them to explain why that tense is the best one for the sentence. (See Chart 1-1 for uses of the simple present and the present progressive.)

Students should, by this time, be clear on the use of *do/don't, does/doesn't,* and *did/didn't.*

POSSIBLE RESPONSES: **3.** (a) Wood doesn't sink.   (b) It floats. [A miscellaneous note: There is one kind of wood that sinks (lignum vitae, from tropical American guaiacum trees), and certain volcanic rocks actually float. Sometimes a knowledgeable student with a scientific bent might challenge the statements in the text about wood floating and rocks sinking; it is possible to explain that the simple present often gives the idea of "as a rule or generally speaking."]   **4.** (a) I didn't take a taxi to school today.   (b) I walked to school today.   **5.** (a) I'm not sitting on a soft, comfortable sofa.   (b) I'm sitting on a hard chair.   **6.** (a) I didn't stay home all day yesterday.   (b) I went to school yesterday.   **7.** (a) Spiders don't have six legs.   (b) They have eight legs.   **8.** (a) The population of the world isn't getting smaller.   (b) It's increasing. / It's getting larger.   **9.** (a) Our teacher didn't write *Romeo and Juliet*.   (b) Shakespeare wrote *Romeo and Juliet*.

☐ EXERCISE 3, p. 20. *Present and past: negative and affirmative. (Charts 2-1 and 2-2)*

Oral (books closed).
This exercise is intended for teacher-student communicative interaction with tense forms as the target structures. It can also be done in groups with a leader. This exercise is not a drill. Get the students talking and enjoying themselves. Repeat the cue sentences as often and as slowly as necessary. For a more natural-sounding discourse, begin the example cues with something like: "I think that . . . ." or "Someone told me that . . . ." and then add "Is that right?" or "Is that true?" Allow students to peek in their books if that makes them feel more comfortable.

Items 2, 3, and 4 are intended for a review of forms as necessary.

NEGATIVE RESPONSES ONLY: **1.** didn't get up   **2.** isn't standing   **3.** doesn't stand
4. didn't stand   **5.** doesn't have   **6.** didn't write   **7.** doesn't flow   **8.** don't cook
9. didn't teach   **10.** don't have   **11.** didn't drive   **12.** doesn't take   **13.** don't speak   **14.** doesn't have   **15.** didn't study   **16.** didn't go

◊ WORKBOOK PRACTICE 1, p. 19. *Simple past. (Charts 2-1→2-3)*

Controlled completion. [Selfstudy]
This practice compares the simple present and the simple past, with an emphasis on present and past time words. Point out that *yesterday* is used with *morning* and *afternoon,* but *last* is used with the other time expressions listed.

ANSWERS: **1.** walked . . . yesterday   **2.** talked . . . last   **3.** opened . . . yesterday
4. went . . . last   **5.** met . . . last   **6.** Yesterday . . . made . . . took   **7.** paid . . . last
8. Yesterday . . . fell   **9.** left . . . last

◇ WORKBOOK PRACTICE 2, p. 20. *Simple past: regular and irregular verbs. (Charts 2-1→2-4)*

> *Fill-in-the-blanks.* [Selfstudy]
> The main point of this introductory practice is for the students to identify regular and irregular verbs.

> ANSWERS: **1.** started   **2.** went   **3.** saw   **4.** stood   **5.** arrived   **6.** won
> **7.** had   **8.** made   **9.** finished   **10.** felt   **11.** fell   **12.** heard   **13.** sang
> **14.** explored   **15.** asked   **16.** brought   **17.** broke   **18.** ate   **19.** watched
> **20.** built   **21.** took   **22.** paid   **23.** left   **24.** wore

◇ WORKBOOK PRACTICE 3, p. 20. *Simple past forms. (Charts 2-1→2-4)*

> *Controlled completion.* [Selfstudy]

> ANSWERS: **1.** A: Did you answer   B: I did . . . I answered   OR   I didn't . . . I didn't
> answer   **2.** A: Did he see   B: he did . . . He saw   OR   he didn't . . . He didn't see
> **3.** A: Did they watch   B: they did . . . They watched   OR   they didn't . . . They didn't
> watch   **4.** A: Did you understand   B: I did . . . I understood   OR   I didn't . . . I didn't
> understand   **5.** A: Were you   B: I was . . . I was   OR   I wasn't . . . I wasn't

---

**CHARTS 2-3 and 2-4: PRINCIPAL PARTS AND IRREGULAR
VERBS**

- You may wish to discuss or model pronunciation of *-ed* endings for your class:

finished = finish/t/	*waited = wait/əd/*
stopped = stop/t/	*played = play/d/*
hoped = hope/t/	*tried = try/d/*

- Point out that the present participle is always regular: the simple form + *ing*. (See Chart 2-5 for spelling rules.)

- Point out the variations in patterns of irregular verbs in the simple form, simple past, and past participle:
  All three parts may be different *(see, saw, seen)*.
  The second two parts may be the same *(make, made, made)*.
  All three parts may be the same *(put, put, put)*.★

- Students may question why *see*, presented as a nonprogressive verb in Chapter 1, has an *-ing* form. Explain that *see* has more than one meaning. When it means "visit" or "consult," it can be used in the progressive: *Bob is seeing his doctor this afternoon.* You might also explain that the *-ing* form of verbs has uses other than in progressive verb tenses. *-Ing* participles can be used as adjectives (e.g., *a confusing book*), and *-ing* verbs are also used as gerunds (e.g., *I enjoyed seeing my friends*).

★See the *Understanding and Using English Grammar Workbook* (Chapter 1, Practice 8, p. 10) for the subcategories of vowel and consonant changes within these three categories of irregular verb patterns.

- There are about 250 irregular verbs in English. Many of them are high frequency. Chart 2-4 contains 100 common irregular verbs.

Should or shouldn't the students be encouraged to memorize irregular verbs? The text tries to provide practice opportunities, but it seems equally beneficial to the ESL/EFL student and the native speaker to simply know these forms by memory. Most educated speakers of English can recite the principal parts of most of the irregular verbs. It's like a memory checklist they have to call on when needed.

The students should already know many of the more common irregular verbs. It would seem profitable for the students to memorize a few new ones every day. And of course practice is essential. Verbs not used as often as others come less readily to mind (just as a native speaker may have to pause and rummage through her/his memory for the correct forms for *slay, forebear,* or *stride*). You might take three minutes a day to conduct a quick drill: say the simple form and have the class say the other forms from memory, developing a kind of rhythmic chant. Choose new verbs each day and include a few that were difficult from earlier days. Answer questions about meanings as necessary.

The irregular verb emphasis in this chapter is on the simple past form. In memory work, the students should start learning the past participles, too, even though they won't need to use them until Chapter 7, where particular exercises help students learn and practice them.

- Some verbs that are regular in AmE have variant spellings with *-t* in BrE: *burnt, dreamt, leant, leapt, learnt, spelt, spilt, spoilt.*

□ EXERCISES 4, 5, AND 6, pp. 23-25. *Simple past of irregular verbs. (Chart 2-3)*

Controlled completion.
These three exercises should be assigned as homework before class discussion, or they could be done as seatwork prior to discussion. In this kind of controlled cloze, the students need to read for meaning, then supply the appropriate word and form. Preparation time is important; remind them that it's not helpful if they simply write down what other students say.

After class discussion of each of these, you might conduct an oral review, books open or closed. For example: *What did Sue drink before class this morning?* Response: *She drank a cup of coffee (or tea or juice:* the exact answer is far less important than the correct verb form). Other examples of questions for an oral review: *Where did you and your friend eat a delicious dinner last night? What did you do to the windows in your apartment when it began to rain yesterday afternoon? Do you remember that Chris had an accident while he was fixing dinner? He hurt his finger. What happened?* Etc. (Obviously, an oral review is not a normal conversation, but it does force students to get their noses out of their books and listen carefully to your questions.)

EX. 4 ANSWERS: **2.** ate   **3.** began . . . shut   **4.** cut   **5.** spent [A *dime* is a small silver coin equal to ten cents (ten pennies) or one-tenth of a dollar. *Flat broke* is an idiom meaning completely without money.]   **6.** kept   **7.** read [Note the pronunciation of /rɛd/.]   **8.** lost . . . went . . . found [*Glad* means "happy."]   **9.** held   **10.** met   **11.** spoke   **12.** shook [You might discuss greeting customs and who shakes hands with whom: in most Western cultures, two men almost always shake hands when introduced. Two women usually shake hands, but not always. Etiquette says that a woman should offer her hand to a man first, but, like other rules of polite behavior, this one is not always followed.]

EX. 5 ANSWERS: **1.** rode . . . took   **2.** fell . . . hurt   **3.** lent   **4.** fed   **5.** stole   **6.** left . . . forgot   **7.** drew   **8.** felt   **9.** heard . . . got   **10.** bit

EX. 6 ANSWERS: **1.** broke [Note: In English we can say either *I broke it* (transitive) or *It broke* (intransitive).]   **2.** bought   **3.** brought   **4.** came   **5.** rang . . . woke   **6.** rose   **7.** wrote [*My folks* means "my parents."]   **8.** taught [Women have three formal titles: *Miss* (meaning an unmarried woman and pronounced /mɪs/); *Mrs.* (meaning a married woman and pronounced /mɪsəz/); and *Ms.* (which has no reference to marital status and is pronounced /mɪz/). Also of note: A period is used after such title abbreviations in AmE, but no period (or full stop) is used in BrE: e.g., Mrs Smith; Mr Jones.] **9.** caught **10.** slept **11.** wore [*Has on* means "wears."] **12.** froze **13.** thought **14.** dug [pronunciation: dog /dɔg/; dug /dəg/]

☐ EXERCISE 7, p. 26. *Simple past forms.* (Chart 2-4)

Controlled completion.
This exercise covers the simple past forms for statements, negatives, questions, and short answers.

ANSWERS: **2.** A: Did you sleep B: I did . . . slept **3.** A: Did Tom's plane arrive B: it did . . . got in [*On the dot* means "exactly."] **4.** A: Did you stay . . . (did you) study B: I didn't . . . I went A: Did you like **5.** A: Did Mary study B: she didn't . . . watched **6.** A: Did Mark Twain write B: he did . . . wrote **7.** A: Did the children go B: they did . . . had **8.** A: Did you eat B: I didn't . . . didn't have [also possible in BrE: hadn't] . . . didn't ring.

☐ EXERCISE 8, p. 27. *Simple past: irregular verbs.* (Chart 2-4)

Oral.
This exercise can be like a game for the students. They should just relax and get in the conversational rhythm of question, short answer, full answer. The purpose is to provide comfortable practice using the simple past of irregular verbs. The students should understand that they can get valuable experience using target structures in exercises such as this, even with other learners who sometimes make mistakes. Their goal of fluency in English comes closer every time they use the language.

ANSWERS:
PART I: **1.** slept **2.** woke up **3.** ate **4.** took **5.** drove **6.** rode **7.** brought **8.** lost **9.** heard **10.** said **11.** did **12.** gave **13.** caught **14.** felt **15.** saw **16.** read **17.** found **18.** went **19.** had **20.** thought
PART II: **21.** came **22.** bought **23.** flew **24.** ran **25.** wrote **26.** sent **27.** lent **28.** wore **29.** went **30.** fed **31.** made **32.** left **33.** drank **34.** fell **35.** hurt **36.** broke **37.** understood **38.** spoke **39.** met **40.** shook

☐ EXERCISE 9, p. 28. *Simple past: regular and irregular verbs.* (Chart 2-4)

Oral (books closed).
This exercise can be teacher-led or done in groups with a leader.
    To keep the class alert, you should call on students in an unpredictable order. You might begin your requests with *please* to avoid sounding too dictatorial. Keep the pace lively.

ANSWERS: **1.** gave **2.** opened **3.** shut **4.** stood **5.** blew **6.** put **7.** bent **8.** touched **9.** spelled [BrE: spelt] **10.** shook **11.** bit **12.** hid **13.** left **14.** spoke **15.** tore **16.** told **17.** threw **18.** drew **19.** turned **20.** held **21.** chose **22.** invited **23.** thanked **24.** stole **25.** sold **26.** hit **27.** stuck **28.** read [/rɛd/] **29.** repeated **30.** hung **31.** took **32.** wrote

☐ EXERCISE 10, p. 28. *Simple past: regular and irregular verbs. (Chart 2-4)*

> *Oral (books closed).*
> This exercise is good for pair work. Some of the questions should encourage free conversation between the two students in the pair. The purpose of this exercise is to get the students talking while using the target structures. With some pairs it works; with others it doesn't.
>
> *ANSWERS:*   **1.** began   **2.** rose   **3.** got up   **4.** left   **5.** had   **6.** drank
> **7.** put   **8.** wore   **9.** woke up   **10.** grew up   **11.** bought   **12.** ate . . . cost
> **13.** sat   **14.** met   **15.** flew

◇ WORKBOOK PRACTICE 4, p. 21. *Regular and irregular verbs. (Charts 2-1→2-4)*

> *Controlled completion.* [Selfstudy]
>
> *ANSWERS:*   **1.** shook   **2.** stayed   **3.** swam   **4.** jumped   **5.** held   **6.** fought
> **7.** taught   **8.** froze [*Solid* functions as an intensifier here in the idiomatic phrase *to freeze solid* or *be frozen solid.*]   **9.** thought   **10.** called   **11.** rode   **12.** sold

◇ WORKBOOK PRACTICE 5, p. 21. *Regular and irregular verbs. (Charts 2-1→2-4)*

> *Controlled completion.* [Guided Study]
>
> *ANSWERS:*   **1.** rang   **2.** stole   **3.** built   **4.** played   **5.** dug   **6.** talked
> **7.** chose   **8.** asked   **9.** lost   **10.** quit [also possible in BrE: quitted]   **11.** spent
> **12.** forgave

◇ WORKBOOK PRACTICE 6, p. 22. *Simple past: irregular verbs. (Charts 2-1→2-4)*

> *Semi-controlled completion.* [Selfstudy]
> Students may come up with other possible responses. Possible regular verbs should be discussed if they arise.
>
> *EXPECTED RESPONSES:*   **1.** swept   **2.** flew   **3.** caught/held/took   **4.** taught
> **5.** froze   **6.** felt   **7.** drew/got/made   **8.** heard   **9.** fell . . . broke   **10.** won
> **11.** drove/took   **12.** fought   **13.** sold   **14.** hid/put   **15.** shut   **16.** ran
> **17.** led   **18.** paid   **19.** drank/had   **20.** bought/chose   **21.** wore   **22.** gave/lent

◇ WORKBOOK PRACTICE 7, p. 23. *Simple past: irregular verbs. (Charts 2-1→2-4)*

> *Semi-controlled completion.* [Guided Study]
> Students may come up with other possible responses. Possible regular verbs should be discussed if they arise.
>
> *EXPECTED RESPONSES:*   **1.** ate   **2.** did   **3.** rose   **4.** hung   **5.** slept   **6.** built
> **7.** found   **8.** cut   **9.** met   **10.** began . . . put . . . left   **11.** wrote   **12.** tore . . .
> threw   **13.** kept   **14.** gave . . . spoke   **15.** grew   **16.** forgot   **17.** read
> **18.** shook   **19.** stole   **20.** swam   **21.** rang   **22.** told . . . knew   **23.** lit . . . blew

◇ WORKBOOK PRACTICES 8 AND 9, pp. 24-25. *Pronunciation of -ED endings. (Chart 2-3)*

> *Pronunciation.* [Guided Study]
> Explain voiceless vs. voiced sounds by having the students touch their throats to feel whether their voice box vibrates. Model the sounds and ask the class to repeat. Encourage the students to exaggerate the final sounds during the exercises.
>   PRACTICE 9, ITEM NOTE: Crossing one's fingers is a gesture that represents a person's hope for good luck. In North America, when children want something to come true, they cross their

fingers and make a wish. If a person says "I'm crossing my fingers for you," it expresses a wish for good luck. Ask your students if the gesture of crossing their fingers has any meaning in their cultures.

CHART 2-5: SPELLING OF *-ING* and *-ED* FORMS

• The students will need your assistance in understanding this chart. Demonstrate the rules on the board and relate them to the examples in the text. Suggestions for additional examples: (a) *use, phone*; (b) *count, turn*; (c) *join, shout, need*; (d) *drop, grab*; (e) *open, order*; (f) *refer, permit*; (g) *stay, annoy*; (h) *marry, pity*; (i) *lie* [*Die, tie, lie*, and *belie* are the only common verbs that end in *-ie*.].

• Two-syllable verbs that end in *-l* (e.g., *control, cancel, travel*) are not dealt with in the chart. *Control* follows rule (f): the second syllable is stressed so the consonant is doubled: *controlled, controlling*. *Cancel* and *travel* follow rule (e) in American English: the first syllable is stressed, so the consonant is not doubled: *canceled, canceling* and *traveled, traveling*. But the *-l* is doubled in British spelling: *cancelled, cancelling* and *travelled, travelling*. Another similar spelling variation is *worshiped, worshiping* in American English and *worshiped, worshipping* in British English. You can tell the students that they are correct whether they double the consonant or not in these particular words. Always consult a dictionary when necessary!

☐ EXERCISES 11-13, pp. 30-31. *Spelling of -ING and -ED. (Chart 2-5)*

Transformation.
Immediately follow up the discussion of the chart with individual seatwork. Discussion of the correct answers can be done in groups or pairs. One or two students could work at the chalkboard, then everyone could check the correct spelling.

The students will not know the meaning of some of the words. Tell them they can figure out the spelling without knowing the meaning. Discuss the meanings only after discussing the spelling.

Exercise 11 includes the rules illustrated by examples (a) through (d) in the chart.
Exercise 12 covers the rules illustrated by examples (e) through (i) of the chart.
Exercise 13 is a summary.

EX. 11 ANSWERS: **2.** waiting, waited   **3.** hitting   **4.** writing   **5.** shouting, shouted   **6.** cutting   **7.** meeting   **8.** hoping, hoped   **9.** hopping, hopped   **10.** helping, helped   **11.** sleeping   **12.** stepping, stepped   **13.** taping, taped   **14.** tapping, tapped   **15.** raining, rained   **16.** running   **17.** whining, whined   **18.** winning   **19.** explaining, explained   **20.** burning, burned [BrE: burnt]   **21.** swimming   **22.** aiming, aimed   **23.** charming, charmed   **24.** cramming, crammed   **25.** taming, tamed   **26.** choosing   **27.** riding   **28.** reminding, reminded

EX. 12 ANSWERS: **1.** opening, opened   **2.** beginning   **3.** occurring, occurred   **4.** happening, happened   **5.** referring, referred   **6.** offering, offered   **7.** listening, listened   **8.** admitting, admitted   **9.** visiting, visited   **10.** omitting, omitted   **11.** hurrying, hurried   **12.** studying, studied   **13.** enjoying, enjoyed   **14.** replying, replied   **15.** staying, stayed   **16.** buying   **17.** trying, tried   **18.** tying, tied   **19.** dying, died   **20.** lying, lied

1. lifting, lifted   **2.** promising, promised   **3.** slapping, slapped
4. waving, waved   **5.** carrying, carried   **6.** mapping, mapped   **7.** moping, moped
8. smiling, smiled   **9.** failing, failed   **10.** filing, filed   **11.** dragging, dragged
12. using, used   **13.** preferring, preferred   **14.** praying, prayed   **15.** pointing,
pointed   **16.** appearing, appeared   **17.** relaxing, relaxed   **18.** borrowing, borrowed
19. crying, cried   **20.** shipping, shipped

◊ WORKBOOK PRACTICE 10, p. 26. *Spelling of -ING and -ED. (Chart 2-5)*

Controlled completion. [Selfstudy]
It is hoped that the spelling rules in Chart 2-5 will become clearer if students can fill out this
chart on their own. This chart mirrors Chart 2-5 exactly.

ANSWERS:

END OF VERB	DOUBLE THE CONSONANT?	SIMPLE FORM	*-ING*	*-ED*
-e	**NO**	*excite*	***exciting***	***excited***
Two Consonants	**NO**	*exist*	***existing***	***existed***
Two Vowels + One Consonant	**NO**	*shout*	***shouting***	***shouted***
One Vowel + One Consonant	**YES**	ONE-SYLLABLE VERBS *pat*	***patting***	***patted***
	NO	TWO-SYLLABLE VERBS (STRESS ON **FIRST** SYLLABLE) *visit*	***visiting***	***visited***
	YES	TWO-SYLLABLE VERBS (STRESS ON **SECOND** SYLLABLE) *admit*	***admitting***	***admitted***
-y	**NO**	*pray* *pry*	***praying*** ***prying***	***prayed*** ***pried***
-ie	**NO**	*tie*	***tying***	***tied***

◊ WORKBOOK PRACTICE 11, p. 26. *Spelling of -ING. (Chart 2-5)*

Spelling. [Selfstudy]

ANSWERS:

1. wai **t** ing . . . wait
2. pa **tt** ing . . . pat
3. bi **t** ing . . . bite
4. si **tt** ing . . . sit
5. wri **t** ing . . . write
6. figh **t** ing . . . fight

7. wai **t** ing . . . wait
8. ge **tt** ing . . . get
9. star **t** ing . . . start
10. permi **tt** ing . . . permit
11. lif **t** ing . . . lift
12. ea **t** ing . . . eat

13. tas **t** ing . . . taste
14. cu **tt** ing . . . cut
15. mee **t** ing . . . meet
16. visi **t** ing . . . visit

◇ WORKBOOK PRACTICE 12, p. 27. *Simple present vs. simple past. (Charts 2-1 → 2-4)*

  Fill in the blanks. [Selfstudy]

  ANSWERS: **1.** A: Did you hear B: didn't . . . didn't hear . . . was **2.** A: Do you hear
  B: don't . . . don't hear **3.** A: Did you build B: didn't . . . built **4.** A: Is a fish
  B: it is A: Are they B: they are B: don't know **5.** A: want . . . look . . . Do you
  want B: have . . . bought . . . don't need **6.** offer . . . is . . . offered . . . didn't accept
  7. took . . . found . . . didn't know . . . isn't . . . didn't want . . . went . . . made . . . heated . . .
  seemed . . . am not **8.** likes . . . worry . . . is . . . trust . . . graduated [also possible: was
  graduated] . . . went . . . didn't travel . . . rented . . . rode . . . was . . . worried [also possible: were
  worried] . . . were . . . saw . . . knew

CHARTS 2-6 AND 2-7: SIMPLE PAST AND PAST PROGRESSIVE

• Compare the past progressive to the present progressive: e.g., *I am sitting in this chair right now. At this same time yesterday, I was sitting in this chair.* Show that both tenses give the idea of "in progress at a particular time."

• The distinction between *when* and *while* is not always as clear as the chart indicates. Sometimes, in fact, *when* can mean *while: When I was living in Nepal, I ate rice every day.* However, for students at this level, making a sharp distinction between *when* and *while* can help them learn the differences in meaning between the simple past and the past progressive. The text uses *when* as a cue for the simple past in an adverb clause and *while* as a cue for the past progressive in an adverb clause.

• Adverb clauses of time are presented in Chart 2-8. You can refer the students to that chart if you want to use the term "time clause," or you can simply use terms such as "the *when* part of the sentence" and "the *while* part of the sentence."

☐ EXERCISE 14, p. 33. *Simple past and past progressive. (Charts 2-6 and 2-7)*

  Fill-in-the-blanks.
  This exercise is intended as an extension of Chart 2-6. It provides further examples for
  discussion of the form and meaning of the past progressive compared to the simple past.

  ANSWERS: **1.** was eating **2.** was eating . . . came **3.** came . . . was eating **4.** was
  sleeping **5.** was sleeping . . . rang **6.** rang . . . was sleeping **7.** began . . . was walking
  . . . saw **8.** saw . . . was standing . . . was holding . . . waved . . . saw

☐ EXERCISE 15, p. 34. *Simple past and past progressive. (Charts 2-6 and 2-7)*

  Oral (books closed).
  This exercise requires a teacher to organize and conduct it. You need to get two students doing
  two things at the same time. One has to begin an activity and continue it as the other begins
  and ends an activity. When they both finish, other students describe these activities using the
  simple past and the past progressive.

  EXPECTED RESPONSES: **1.** While (A) was writing a note to (. . .), (B) knocked on the door.
  2. While (A) was walking around the room, (B) clapped her/his hands once. **3.** While (A)
  was talking to (. . .), (B) came into the room. **4.** While (A) was reading a book, (B)
  tapped (A)'s shoulder. **5.** While (A) was looking out the window, (B) asked (A) a question.
  6. While (A) was whistling, (B) left the room. **7.** While (A) was looking at her/his watch,

(B) asked (A) a question.   **8.** While (A) was eating, (B) sat down next to (A).   **9.** While (A) was sleeping, (B) took (A)'s grammar book.   **10.** While (A) was drinking a glass of water, (B) came in the room.

☐ EXERCISE 16, p. 34. *Simple past and past progressive. (Charts 2-6 and 2-7)*

Fill-in-the-blanks.

ANSWERS: **1.** was eating . . . knocked   **2.** came . . . was studying . . . came   **3.** was studying . . . dropped by [*Drop by* means "to visit without planning or announcing ahead of time."]   **4.** called . . . were watching   **5.** came . . . was talking   **6.** went . . . got . . . was . . . was planting . . . was . . . was working . . . was changing . . . were playing . . . was fixing . . . were playing   **7.** went . . . saw . . . had . . . were walking . . . began . . . ran . . . dried . . . were passing . . . lowered . . . started . . . stretched . . . tried . . . didn't let . . . was standing . . . pointed . . . said [*Shoo!* is a word that is said loudly to chase away an animal, insect, or even a person.]   **8.** A: Did your lights go out   B: was . . . was taking . . . found . . . ate . . . tried . . . went . . . slept   A: was reading . . . went out . . . was studying . . . got up

◇ WORKBOOK PRACTICE 13, p. 28. *Past progressive. (Charts 2-6 → 2-7)*

Controlled completion. [Selfstudy]
These items present typical situations in which the past progressive is used. If you discuss this practice in class, relate the items to the tense diagram, pointing out how one activity began first and was in progress when another event occurred.

ANSWERS: **1.** was standing   **2.** was eating   **3.** was answering   **4.** was singing   **5.** was walking   **6.** were climbing   **7.** was beginning   **8.** was counting   **9.** was melting   **10.** was looking . . . was driving

◇ WORKBOOK PRACTICE 14, p. 29. *Present and past progressives. (Charts 1-2, 2-6, 2-7)*

Open completion. [Guided Study]
Point out the similarity between the two progressives: they both describe events in progress in relation to another time or event. The only difference is the time frame.

SAMPLE RESPONSES: **1.** was waiting for my brother's plane.   **2.** am waiting for my brother's plane.   **3.** was walking to the newsstand.   **4.** am walking to the market on the corner.   **5.** are watching a comedy on T.V.   **6.** were watching a man who was trying to peel a banana with one hand.   **7.** are travel(l)ing in the south of France.   **8.** were travel(l)ing to California to visit relatives.   **9.** were describing the coat Maria wore to the party.   **10.** is describing the color of her new car.

CHART 2-8: EXPRESSING PAST TIME: USING TIME CLAUSES

• Be sure to emphasize that examples (a) and (b) have no difference in meaning. Discuss punctuation. Point out that a time clause is not a complete sentence. It cannot stand alone. It must be connected to a main or independent clause. *I visited my uncle* is a complete sentence. *When I went to Chicago* is not a complete sentence. (In speaking, the voice drops low at the end of a sentence, but it tends to drop a little then rise a little at the end of a time clause before a main clause. You might want to demonstrate this.)

• *When, after, before,* and *while* are subordinating conjunctions, but the text does not use that terminology. They can be called "words that introduce time clauses" or "time clause words."

• Examples (c) and (d) illustrate a difficulty students might have with pronoun usage in an adverb clause. Usually a noun comes before a pronoun: e.g. *After **Mary** ate dinner, **she** went to the library.* But when an adverb clause precedes the main clause, a pronoun may be used before a noun: *After **she** ate dinner, **Mary** went to the library.* This particular pronoun usage, where the pronoun precedes the noun, is not taught in the text, but the question may arise in class discussion.

• Example (k) needs some special attention. Perhaps demonstrate the time relationship expressed when both the *when*-clause and the main clause are in the simple past. For example, drop your pen and have a student pick it up for you. *When I dropped my pen, Ali picked it up for me.* (INCORRECT: *When I dropped my pen, Ali was picking it up for me.*) The act of dropping the pen occurs before picking it up.

☐ EXERCISE 17, p. 37. *Time clauses.* (Chart 2-8)

Sentence construction.
This is an exercise on complex sentence structure and punctuation. It is intended to provide further examples for discussion of the grammar in Chart 2-8. It can be done as seatwork leading to boardwork.

ANSWERS: **2.** (a) <u>After I washed the dishes,</u> I watched TV.   (b) I watched TV <u>after I washed the dishes.</u>   **3.** (a) <u>Before I left my apartment this morning,</u> I unplugged the coffee pot.   (b) I unplugged the coffee pot <u>before I left my apartment this morning.</u>
4. (a) <u>While I was eating dinner,</u> Jim came.   (b) Jim came <u>while I was eating dinner.</u>
5. (a) <u>When it began to rain,</u> I stood under a tree.   (b) I stood under a tree <u>when it began to rain.</u>

☐ EXERCISE 18, p. 38. *Time clauses.* (Chart 2-8)

Sentence construction.
This exercise can be done in groups or pairs, oral or written or both.

ANSWERS: **1.** <u>Before I went to bed,</u> I did my homework. OR I did my homework <u>before I went to bed.</u>   **2.** <u>After Bob graduated,</u> he got a job. OR Bob got a job <u>after he graduated.</u>
3. <u>While I was studying,</u> Amanda called me on the phone. OR Amanda called me on the phone <u>while I was studying.</u>   **4.** <u>When my alarm clock rang,</u> I woke up. OR I woke up <u>when my alarm clock rang.</u>   **5.** <u>While I was falling asleep last night,</u> I heard a strange noise. OR I heard a strange noise <u>while I was falling asleep last night.</u>   **6.** <u>When I heard a strange noise,</u> I turned on the light. OR I turned on the light <u>when I heard a strange noise.</u>   **7.** <u>When Eric came,</u> I was eating lunch. OR I was eating lunch <u>when Eric came.</u> [also possible: *Eric came when I was eating lunch*—but it is probably better not to confuse the students at this point. *When* and *while* are not always interchangeable, and the past progressive cannot always be used in a *when*-clause.]
8. <u>Before I went to the hospital to visit my friend,</u> I bought some flowers. OR I bought some flowers <u>before I went to the hospital to visit my friend.</u>

◇ WORKBOOK PRACTICE 15, p. 30. *Past time using time clauses. (Charts 2-1 → 2-8)*

Sentence construction. [Selfstudy]
Like Exercises 17 and 18 in the main text, this practice focuses on manipulation of form. Students should get a good idea of how the two parts of the sentence (the main clause and the dependent clause) can change places.

ANSWERS:
1. While I was climbing the stairs, the doorbell rang. OR The doorbell rang while I was climbing the stairs.
2. I gave Alan his pay after he finished his chores. OR After Alan finished his chores, I gave him his pay.
3. The firefighters checked the ashes one last time before they went home. OR Before the firefighters went home, they checked the ashes one last time.
4. When Mr. Novak stopped by our table at the restaurant, I introduced him to my wife. OR I introduced Mr. Novak to my wife when he stopped by our table at the restaurant.
5. While the kitten was sitting on the roof, an eagle flew over the house. OR An eagle flew over the house while the kitten was sitting on the roof.
6. My father was listening to a baseball game on the radio while he was watching a basketball game on television. OR While my father was watching a basketball game on television, he was listening to a baseball game on the radio.

◇ WORKBOOK PRACTICE 16, p. 30. *Simple past vs. past progressive. (Charts 2-1 → 2-8)*

Fill-in-the-blanks. [Selfstudy]

ANSWERS: **1.** began [also possible: was beginning] . . . were walking **2.** was washing . . . dropped . . . broke **3.** hit . . . was using **4.** was walking . . . fell . . . hit **5.** knew . . . were attending . . . mentioned . . . were . . . were staying [also possible: stayed] **6.** was looking . . . started/was starting . . . took . . . was taking . . . (was) enjoying . . . came . . . asked . . . told . . . thanked . . . went . . . came . . . covered . . . went

☐ EXERCISE 19, p. 39. *Time clauses. (Charts 2-1 → 2-8)*

Oral/Written.
Sometimes a talkative Student A can overwhelm a somewhat timid Student B, so it's a good idea to have exact time limits. A few minutes is sufficient to describe a few things one did or didn't do yesterday. The students don't have to describe exactly five things they did and two or three things they didn't do. The purpose of the directions is to get them to think about various things they did.

☐ EXERCISE 20, pp. 39–41. *Verb tense review. (Charts 2-1 → 2-8)*

Homework, fill-in-the-blanks.
The emphasis in this exercise is on the simple past of irregular verbs. Just a reminder: See the INTRODUCTION, pp. xv, for suggestions on handling fill-in-the-blanks exercises.
    EXPANSION: Have the students describe, in writing or orally, what the two people in the story did last Friday. For example, after you finish discussing the exercise, you could ask the class to close their books and tell you anything they can remember about the story. You could note key words from their statements on the board, so everyone can check the completeness of their recall, or you could ask them to write a summary.

ANSWERS: **(1)** was **(2)** slept **(3)** came **(4)** packed **(5)** took **(6)** spent **(7)** got **(8)** found **(9)** fed **(10)** threw **(11)** swam **(12)** caught **(13)** hit **(14)** stole **(15)** were feeding . . . met **(16)** comes **(17)** sat

(18) spoke **(19)** ate (had eaten) . . . took **(21)** was sleeping **(22)** bit **(24)** woke
(26) heard **(28)** looked **(29)** saw **(31)** flew **(32)** did **(33)** took . . . got
(34) read **(35)** is . . . drew **(36)** were playing **(37)** won . . . won **(38)** taught
(39) played **(40)** fell **(41)** found **(42)** joined **(43)** were **(44)** were
(45) hurt **(46)** was . . . left **(47)** was

☐ EXERCISE 21, p. 41. *Past time. (Charts 2-1 → 2-8)*

Written.
Students should be asked to write at least six sentences in their compositions. Longer papers similar to the story in Exercise 20 could also be encouraged. When you mark them, reward successful use of verb forms and their spellings. This is intended as a simple writing task on simple topics for the purpose of practicing past verbs. Show your students that you are thoroughly delighted by correctly used irregular verbs, correctly spelled *-ed* verbs, appropriately used past progressives, and correctly punctuated time clauses. Perfection or rhetorical complexity is not expected.

EXPANSION: Make up an error analysis exercise from mistakes taken from the students' papers.

EXPANSION: Have the students sit or stand in two facing lines. One line is designated the talkers, and the other is the listeners. The talkers are given 60, 90, or 120 seconds to tell their story non-stop. Then time is called, and the talkers shift to the next listeners in line and tell the same story again. Once more time is called, and the talkers move to the next listeners and tell the same story. Through all this, the listeners say nothing. At the end of three rounds, it's time for the listeners to talk. They are asked to summarize the three stories they heard. Other listeners will of course have heard some of the same stories, so it's interesting to see if they heard the same information. Open discussion can ensue. The next day, the listeners can be the talkers and the exercise repeated. All of this speaking activity elicits lots of past verbs.

◇ WORKBOOK PRACTICE 17, p. 31. *Simple past vs. past progressive. (Charts 2-1 → 2-8)*

Fill-in-the-blanks. [Guided Study]
A day or two after discussing this practice in class, hand out photocopies of the illustration and ask the class to write the story as best they can remember. It is hoped that the descriptions will contain properly used past progressive verbs.

ANSWERS: **1.** was preparing **2.** rang **3.** put **4.** rushed **5.** opened
6. smiled **7.** was holding **8.** was telling **9.** rang **10.** excused **11.** reached
12. tried/was trying **13.** ran **14.** was trying **15.** swam/was swimming **16.** said
17. shut **18.** said **19.** hung **20.** yelled **21.** shooed **22.** sat **23.** caught
[*To catch one's breath* means "to rest for a minute in the middle of some sort of physical exertion."]
24. was sitting **25.** rang **26.** rang **27.** didn't move

◇ WORKBOOK PRACTICE 18, p. 32. *Present and past verbs. (Chapters 1 and 2)*

Fill-in-the-blanks. [Guided Study]
The purpose of this practice is to compare present and past verbs. Part I is told from a present-time perspective; the students are given a present-time setting and a dialogue. Part II reports the same events from a past perspective.

ANSWERS:

PART I: **1.** is sitting   **2.** is writing   **3.** is sitting   **4.** isn't studying   **5.** is staring
6. wants   **7.** is looking   **8.** are you looking   **9.** am watching   **10.** don't know
11. admire   **12.** is steering   **13.** is drinking [also possible: drinks]   **14.** is weaving
15. seems   **16.** isn't   **17.** looks   **18.** had   **19.** was   **20.** was   **21.** tried
22. laughed   **23.** tried   **24.** was

PART II: **25.** was sitting [also possible: sat]   **26.** was writing [also possible: wrote]
27. was sitting [also possible: sat]   **28.** wasn't studying [also possible: didn't study]   **29.** was
staring [also possible: stared]   **30.** was watching [also possible: watched]   **31.** walked
32. pointed   **33.** was steering [also possible: steered]   **34.** was drinking [also possible: drank]
35. was weaving [also possible: wove]   **36.** seemed   **37.** learned   **38.** was
39. offered   **40.** accepted

CHART 2-9: EXPRESSING PAST HABIT: *USED TO*

- *Be used to* is presented in Chapter 11 and compared to *used to*. *Be used to* doesn't need to be mentioned here.

- *Past habit* is also termed the "habitual past."

- The usual pronunciation of *used to* is /yustə/ or /yustuw/. The /s/ is lengthened slightly, and there is only one /t/ sound. Some students want to pronounce both the *-ed* and the *t*, but this is never done. Be careful in negatives and questions—many people are not aware that *use* (not *used*) is the correct written verb form with *did*: *Did you* **use** (NOT *used*) *to live in Paris?*

☐ EXERCISE 22, p. 42. *Past habit: USED TO. (Chart 2-9)*

Transformation.
Again, this exercise is an extension of the chart, intended to provide further examples for discussion. Statement, question, and negative forms are practiced.

Relate the items in the exercise to the students' own experiences by asking leading questions: Did you ever use to be shy? Where did you use to live? What did you use to do every weekend when you lived in your hometown? Where did you use to work? Etc.

ANSWERS: **3.** used to go [ERRATUM: *hometown* should be written as one word. The separation of *home* and *town* in the text is a mistake that is corrected in later editions.]   **4.** used to work
5. didn't use to wear   **6.** used to hate/didn't use to like . . . didn't use to have   **7.** did you use to do   **8.** used to wear   **9.** used to drink . . . didn't use to drink . . . Did you use to drink   **10.** used to watch . . . didn't use to watch . . . did you use to watch

☐ EXERCISE 23, p. 43. *Past habit: USED TO. (Chart 2-9)*

Semi-controlled and open completion.
Students have to read for meaning and think some of these items through, so they need time to prepare before class discussion. See the INTRODUCTION, pp. xvii, for notes on conducting open completion exercises.

Students need to deduce the correct form from the sentence contexts. Use the contexts to ask leading questions that occur to you in the course of the discussion in order to elicit creative, communicative use of *used to*.

ANSWERS: **4.** used to be   **5.** used to play   **6.** didn't use to do/get   **7.** did you use to go   **8.** used to eat   **9.** *(name of a person)* . . . I don't   **10.** did you use to do   **11.** never used to eat   **12.** used to have a *(kind of pet, e.g., dog, cat)*   **13.** used to go to *(name of a school)* . . . *(name of a school)*   **14.** *(name of a place)* . . . used to live . . . *(name of a place)*   **15.** *(do something)* . . . I do   **16.** did you use to do . . . in *(high school)*   **17.** I used to . . . I don't/I live *(by myself)*   **18.** I didn't use to be . . . *(name of a field of interest)*

☐ EXERCISE 24, p. 44. *Past habit: USED TO. (Chart 2-9)*

Oral and/or written.
This exercise can be done in pairs or groups or can be teacher-led. It can be oral or written or both. It is hoped that the topics will be springboards to open conversations or compositions that include the target structure.

SAMPLE RESPONSES:
1. I used to jump rope / play marbles / swim in a pond / play on swings / climb trees / eat junk food / play in a sandbox / play badminton / jump in piles of leaves / build snow forts / blow soap bubbles . . . .   **2.** I used to go to a lot of movies / go to parties with my friends / visit my relatives / go camping / cook my favorite foods . . . .   **3.** When I was in high school, I used to get up early. I used to eat toast and drink hot chocolate for breakfast. Later, I used to ride the bus to school. I used to spend the morning in class. At lunch, I used to sit with my friends in the school cafeteria. We used to talk about our teachers and our latest boyfriends. When I got older, I used to eat lunch with my boyfriend. If I couldn't eat everything, he used to eat it for me. After school, I used to go to the music room for choir practice. I used to catch a late bus home.   I used to eat supper with my family every night at 6:00 P.M.   Then I used to wash and dry the dishes. Afterward, I used to study in my room and then watch some TV with my family. I used to be in bed by 10:00 P.M.

◊ WORKBOOK PRACTICE 19, p. 33. *Past habit with USED TO. (Chart 2-9)*

Transformation. [Selfstudy]

ANSWERS: **1.** used to hate school   **2.** used to think   **3.** used to be a secretary   **4.** used to have a rat   **5.** used to go bowling   **6.** used to raise chickens   **7.** used to have fresh eggs   **8.** used to crawl under his bed . . . (used to) put his hands over his ears

◊ WORKBOOK PRACTICE 20, p. 34. *Past habit with USED TO. (Chart 2-9)*

Transformation. [Guided Study]
In this practice, the students take the given information and change it into a sentence with *used to* that gives the same meaning. It is an exercise on form and meaning.

ANSWERS:
1. I used to smoke two packs a day, but now I don't smoke at all.   **2.** Amanda used to stay up late when she was student, but now she goes to bed early.   **3.** My neighbor Bill used to drive his car to work, but now he rides the bus.   **4.** Eric used to work hard, but now he is too busy with his social life.   **5.** Dinosaurs used to rule the world, but now they are extinct.
6. The Allens used to have a large house, but now they live in a small three-room apartment.
7. Susan used to eat a balanced diet, but now she eats a lot of junk food.   **8.** I didn't use to stay up late, but now I'm up late every night.   **9.** Hiroki never used to wear cowboy boots, but now he wears cowboy boots every day.   **10.** I used to go swimming every day during the summer, but now I go swimming only on weekends.

◇ WORKBOOK PRACTICE 21, p. 34. *Past habit with USED TO. (Chart 2-9)*

Written/Oral. [Guided Study]
This practice requires independent, creative use of *used to* and some thought and insight on the part of the students. They might come up with ideas more easily in groups than in individual writing.

◇ WORKBOOK PRACTICE 22, p. 34. *Verb tense review. (Chapters 1 and 2)*

Completion. [Guided Study]
This practice concentrates on past verbs, with an emphasis on irregular verbs, but also includes present verbs.

    EXPANSION: Following class discussion, ask the students to write the story of Princess Tina and the Frog Prince in their own words.

    EXPANSION: Another possibility would be to have the class retell the story in a chain: one student begins the story with a sentence or two, then the next student says what happens next, then a third continues the story, etc.

ANSWERS: **(1)** lived . . . was thinking . . . had . . . formed **(2)** came . . . announced . . . meet **(3)** chose . . . took . . . held . . . walked . . . dropped . . . picked . . . spotted . . . bent . . . was **(4)** hopped . . . picked . . . brought . . . am **(5)** told . . . refused . . . heard . . . laughed . . . laughed . . . said **(6)** felt . . . am . . . sobbed . . . believed . . . loved . . . didn't understand . . . hid . . . kept . . . grew . . . had . . . rang **(7)** left . . . ran . . . went . . . ate . . . drank . . . cut . . . washed . . . swept . . . made . . . took . . . was **(8)** went . . . was . . . swam . . . became . . . was swimming . . . lost . . . quit [BrE: quitted] . . . was drowning . . . appeared . . . pushed . . . saved **(9)** did you save . . . are . . . have . . . don't . . . am **(10)** said . . . began . . . sat . . . listened . . . understood . . . told . . . shared . . . spent . . . talked . . . laughed . . . played . . . worked **(11)** were sitting . . . bent . . . kissed . . . turned . . . took . . . saved . . . looked . . . saw . . . found . . . am . . . saw . . . found **(12)** returned . . . got . . . were . . . ignored . . . didn't talk . . . made . . . gave . . . lived

◇ WORKBOOK PRACTICE 23, p. 38. *Past time. (Chapter 2)*

Oral. [Guided Study]
This practice requires teamwork involving numerous communication skills. Be sure students know that they can make up their own beginning for their story.

◇ WORKBOOK PRACTICE 24, p. 38. *Verb tense review. (Chapter 2)*

Written. [Guided Study]
This story-writing can take place over several days as the paper makes its way through the class. Its principal purpose is fun. Students should be encouraged to be humorous.

    Small classes (twelve or less) can all work on the same story. Larger classes should be divided into groups of eight to ten.

    When the story is completed, you can make many uses of it to encourage editing and revising skills. (1) Photocopy it and have each student proofread and rewrite it, being very careful about spelling and punctuation. (2) Photocopy it and proofread it together with the class. (3) Give the story to groups to put into good written shape. (4) Tell the students to rewrite the story the way <u>they</u> want it to happen.

CHART 2-10: PREPOSITIONS OF TIME: *IN, AT,* AND *ON*

- Your students might remember these prepositions with the help of a triangle written on the chalkboard or a large piece of heavy paper.

This triangle shows that *at* is related to the smallest, most specific point in time (*at 9:30, at noon,* etc.); *on* is related to a single day; and *in* is related to the longest, most general periods of time (*in the evening, in 1997,* etc.). Some phrases, however, do not fit as well into this scheme (e.g., *at present, in the present, in a few minutes, in the afternoon* vs. *on Monday afternoon*); special attention is necessary.

☐ EXERCISE 25, p. 45. *Time prepositions. (Chart 2-10)*

    Controlled completion.
    In items 3, 4, and 5, you may have to explain the difference between *in the present* (meaning *not in the past or in the future*), and *at present/at the present time* (meaning *now, nowadays, for the time being, temporarily*). Using the triangle, show that *in* is more general than *at* in these phrases.

    ANSWERS:　**1.** in　**2.** in　**3.** in　**4.** At　**5.** at　**6.** at　**7.** in　**8.** in
    9. in　**10.** at　**11.** at　**12.** at　**13.** in　**14.** in　**15.** in　**16.** on　**17.** on
    18. in　**19.** in . . . In　**20.** On . . . On　**21.** On　**22.** at

◇ WORKBOOK PRACTICE 25, p. 38. *Prepositions of time. (Chart 2-10)*

    Controlled completion. [Selfstudy]

    ANSWERS:　**1.** on　**2.** at . . . in　**3.** in . . . on . . . At . . . In　**4.** In . . . at . . . in
    5. in . . . at　**6.** at　**7.** In . . . In . . . on . . . on　**8.** in [also possible: during]

◇ WORKBOOK PRACTICE 26, p. 39. *Prepositions. (Chapters 1 and 2)*

    Controlled completion. [Selfstudy]

    ANSWERS:　**1.** at . . . in　**2.** for . . . in　**3.** on . . . at . . . in . . . from . . . at/with . . . at
    4. with . . . in [also possible: during]　**5.** on . . . of . . . on . . . in　**6.** of . . . in

Chapter 3: FUTURE TIME

ORDER OF CHAPTER	CHARTS	EXERCISES	WORKBOOK
Forms: present, past, future			Pr. 1 → 3
Be going to and *will*	3-1 → 3-4	Ex. 1 → 8	Pr. 4 → 12
Future time in time clauses and *if*-clauses	3-5	Ex. 9 → 14	Pr. 13 → 16
Parallel verbs	3-6	Ex. 15 → 16	Pr. 17 → 18
Cumulative review			Pr. 19
Present verbs to express future time	3-7 → 3-9	Ex. 17 → 20	Pr. 20 → 24
Be about to	3-10	Ex. 21	Pr. 25
Cumulative review		Ex. 22	Pr. 26 → 30
Prepositions		Ex. 23	Pr. 31 → 32

General Notes on Chapter 3

- OBJECTIVE: Students learn common spoken and written forms of expressing future plans, predictions, promises, and hypotheses.

- APPROACH: The chapter begins by comparing *be going to* and *will* as markers of future meaning. Then time clauses and simple *if*-clauses are presented for expressing possible conditions and results in the future. A short section on parallel verbs introduces a common way of connecting ideas. Next, attention is focused on the use of present tenses with future meaning. Finally, a special verb phrase with a future meaning, *be about to*, is introduced and practiced.

- TERMINOLOGY: English has no verb ending that signals future time. Instead, it relies on verb phrases (with modal auxiliaries and periphrastic modals) and/or time expressions to refer to the future. Since there are various ways of expressing future time, this textbook generally just uses the phrase "expressing future time" instead of referring specifically to **will** + *a simple form of the verb* as "the future tense." For pedagogical ease and convenience, however, the traditional term "future tense" can be used in the classroom for verb phrases that include *will, shall,* or *be going to.*

◇ WORKBOOK PRACTICE 1, p. 40. *Present, past, and future. (Chapters 1, 2, and 3)*

Controlled completion. [Selfstudy]
This is a review of verb forms.

ANSWERS: **1.** a. arrives   b. arrived   c. is going to arrive   OR   will arrive
2. a. Does . . . arrive   b. Did . . . arrive   c. Is . . . going to arrive   OR   Will . . . arrive
3. a. does not (doesn't) arrive   b. did not (didn't) arrive   c. is not (isn't) going to arrive
O R   will not (won't) arrive   **4.** a. eats   b. ate   c. is going to eat   OR   will eat
5. a. Do . . . eat   b. Did . . . eat   c. Are . . . going to eat   OR   Will . . . eat   **6.** a. do
not (don't) eat   b. did not (didn't) eat   c. am not going to eat   OR   will not (won't) eat

◇ WORKBOOK PRACTICE 2, p. 41. *Present, past, and future. (Chapters 1, 2, and 3)*

Controlled completion. [Selfstudy]
This is a review of verb forms: questions, short answers, and statements.

ANSWERS: **1.** B: Do . . . get   A: do . . . get   B: Did . . . get   A: did . . . got   B: Are
. . . going to get   A: am . . . am going to get   **2.** B: Do . . . study   A: do . . . study
B: Did . . . study   A: did . . . studied   B: are . . . going to study   A: am . . . am going to
study

◇ WORKBOOK PRACTICE 3, p. 41. *Present, past, and future. (Chapters 1, 2, and 3)*

Open completion. [Guided Study]
Students can write this out quickly and you can check on their verb forms. Students who have
trouble writing this dialogue will need special assistance before continuing in the chapter.

SAMPLE DIALOGUE:
   A: *I went to my English class yesterday.*
   B: *Oh? Do you go to your English class every day?*
   A: *Yes, I do. I go there every day.*
   B: *Did you go there two days ago?*
   A: *Yes, I did. I went there two days ago.*
   B: *Are you going to go to your English class tomorrow?*
   A: *Yes, I am. I'm going to go there tomorrow.*

CHART 3-1: EXPRESSING FUTURE TIME: *BE GOING TO*
AND *WILL*

- Both *be going to* and *will* are presented in this chart. They are often, but not always, interchangeable. Their differences in meaning are presented in Chart 3-4.

- The text emphasizes *be going to* first in the exercises and relates it to present and past verbs. Then the text deals with *will*.

- The use of *will* is sometimes called "the simple future tense," but, as noted above, *will* is actually only one of several modals and periphrastic modals used to express future time. What you could point out here is that *be going to* and *will* are used to express that an event is, in the speaker's mind, 100% certain to occur at a future time, as in examples (a) through (d). We can't, of course, always be certain about future events, so other auxiliaries (see Chapter 5) are frequently used for future time.

- Some cultures resist the notion that any person can see into the future or dare to make predictions. Chart 3-3 presents the word "probably" as a way to communicate less certainty, which might satisfy some objections. As a side note on cultural attitudes toward predicting the future, three hundred years ago in Great Britain, predicting the weather was a crime punishable by death (burning at the stake as a witch).

- *Going to* is sometimes pronounced /gɔnə/ or /gənə/, which—though not an accepted written form—may be represented in writing as "gonna." Model *gonna* for your students so that they will be aware of it, but don't insist on its use by learners at this level. When learners force *gonna*, it may sound as though they are speaking careless, nonstandard English. The appropriate use of *gonna* will develop as the students gain experience with the language.

- *Shall* is used with *I* and *we* in formal BrE, but in AmE and informal BrE, *will* is far more common. One use of *shall* is to show great determination, e.g., *We shall overcome.* or *I shall return!* Otherwise, *will* is used with all subjects to express simple future time.

    Historically, there was no "rule" about *shall* being used with the first person and *will* with the second and third persons until the mid-seventeenth century. For centuries, no distinction existed in actual usage. The "rule" was originally formulated by prescriptive grammarians and passed on through generations of grammars.

☐ EXERCISE 1, p. 47. *BE GOING TO.* (Chart 3-1)

> *Oral (books closed).*
> It is assumed that the students are already familiar with *be going to.* This exercise is intended as a fairly quick oral review during which you can discuss its typical meaning and use. Also possible is group work if you are fairly certain the students have few, if any, questions about the use of *be going to.* Students get more opportunity for oral practice in group work.
>   Take care that students who say *gonna* do not make the mistake of saying *gonna to.* Show them that *to* is included in the pronunciation of /gɔnə/.

☐ EXERCISE 2, p. 48. *BE GOING TO and verb tense review.* *(Chart 3-1)*

Oral (books closed), teacher-led.
Conduct a review of the simple present, present progressive, simple past, past progressive, and *be going to* (or *will* if a student wishes). Students may spontaneously use modal auxiliaries in the sentences they construct. That is fine and gives you the opportunity to mention to them what they'll be studying in Chapter 5.

Draw tense diagrams on the board to assist the review. Ask for more than one response to each item. Pursue interesting responses. To keep students alert and interested, occasionally ask one student what another student has said.

The items with asterisks can be used with various tenses. For example, item 5:
> simple present: *I'm in class* **today.**
> present progressive: *We're studying future verb forms* **today.**
> > [with a future meaning: *I'm meeting Carlos after class* **today.** (see Chart 3-7)]
> simple past: *I had a cup of coffee before class* **today.**
> future: *I'm going to have dinner with Nadia* **today.**

Other comments: In item 4, point out that *every day* (an adverbial expression) is spelled as two words. (It is spelled as one word when it is used as an adjective, e.g., *everyday activities.*) Items 9 and 10 are difficult for learners and may require a calendar written on the board to ensure clarity of understanding. In item 15, point out that **in** + *an expression of time* is frequently used to express a length of time from the present moment to a future moment: e.g., *I'm going to graduate* **in** *a month.*

ALTERNATIVE: *Group work.* If this exercise is used for group work, the students can discuss verbs among themselves and get in some practice, but they'll miss the survey and explanations a teacher can provide.

☐ EXERCISE 3, p. 48. *Pronoun and negative contractions with BE GOING TO.* *(Chart 3-1)*

Controlled completion.
This exercise is a quick check on the written forms of *be going to.* Try to avoid discussing the use of the present progressive to mean future time even though it is possible in some of the completions (e.g., items 4, 7, and 8).

This exercise also introduces *too* and *either* in one of their typical patterns: *I did something yesterday/today,* **and** *I'm going to do it tomorrow* **too.** *I didn't do something yesterday/today,* **and** *I'm not going to do it tomorrow* **either.** This exercise seeks to prepare the students for the oral exercise that follows. One possible difficulty that the learners might have with the grammar is the fact that *too* is used with affirmative sentences and *either* is used with negative sentences. Otherwise, they just have to put *too* or *either* at the end of their sentences in Exercise 4.

PUNCTUATION NOTE: A comma may precede *too* at the end of a sentence, but not precede *either.* The comma preceding *too* is optional.

ANSWERS: **2.** [Point out that *he's not going to be* is also possible.] **3.** they're going to take **4.** she's going to walk **5.** it's not/it isn't going to rain **6.** we're going to be **7.** you aren't/you're not going to hitchhike [pronounced /hĭčhaik/] **8.** I'm not going to get **9.** he's not/he isn't going to wear

☐ EXERCISE 4, p. 49. *BE GOING TO and TOO/EITHER.* *(Chart 3-1)*

Oral, teacher-led.

ANSWERS: **1.** I'm going to do . . . too **2.** I'm not going to be . . . either **3.** we're not/we aren't going to have . . . either **4.** she's/he's going to be . . . too **5.** it's going to be . . . too **6.** I'm not going to go . . . either **7.** I'm going to bring . . . too **8.** I'm not going to get . . . either   **9.** it's going to rise . . . too   **10.** we're not/we aren't going to have . . . either

◇ **WORKBOOK PRACTICE 4, p. 41.** *BE GOING TO.* (Chart 3-1)

Fill-in-the-blanks. [Selfstudy]
This a a review of the forms of *be going to:* statement, negative, question, short answer.

ANSWERS: **1.** A: are you going to do   B: am going to finish   **2.** A: is Ryan going to be
B: is going to be   **3.** A: Are you going to have   B: am not going to eat   **4.** A: Are you
going to finish   B: am going to finish   **5.** A: are you going to call   B: am not going to
call her . . . am going to write   **6.** A: is Laura going to talk   B: is going to discuss

◇ **WORKBOOK PRACTICE 5, p. 42.** *BE GOING TO.* (Chart 3-1)

Oral. [Guided Study]
The purpose here is oral practice with typical conversational questions and answers about the
future. Student B should be encouraged to answer truthfully, but some students enjoy using
their imaginations and making up funny answers.

EXPECTED QUESTIONS: **1.** Where are you going to go after your last class today?   **2.** Are
you going to have pizza for dinner tonight?   **3.** What are you going to do this evening?
4. When are you going to visit your family?   **5.** Who(m) are you going to play soccer with
on Saturday?   **6.** What are you going to do this coming Saturday?   **7.** Are you going to
look for a new place to live soon?   **8.** Where are you going to live next year?   **9.** What
time are you going to go to bed tonight?   **10.** What are you going to wear tomorrow?
11. Are you going to wear your raincoat tomorrow?   **12.** Are you going to take a trip
sometime this year or next?   **13.** Where are you going to go, and what are you going to do?
14. How long are you going to stay at this school?   **15.** Are you going to talk to your family
soon?   **16.** When are you going to see your family again?

◇ **WORKBOOK PRACTICE 6, p. 42.** *BE GOING TO.* (Chart 3-1)

Sentence construction. [Guided Study]
This is essentially an exercise on future time expressions. Point out, for example, that ***in*** + *a
length of time* often expresses future time; that future verbs can be used with expressions like
today, tonight, this week; that ***next*** and ***this coming*** + *a time expression* are used for future
meanings. This practice can be completed orally and discussed. It can also be written.

CHART 3-2: FORMS WITH *WILL*

- Model contractions with *will*. Include some examples of nouns and question words contracted with
will in speech: *Tom'll be here soon. Where'll you be around eight tonight?* Mention that contractions are
natural in conversations, both formal and informal. In fact, speakers with native fluency of English find it
impossible not to use them; speech without contractions sounds stilted or bookish.

- After a consonant, the contraction "'ll" is pronounced as an additional syllable: /əl/. For example,
Bob'll is pronounced like the word "bobble" or "bauble": /b̲a̲bəl/.

- The negative contraction *shan't (shall not)* occurs in BrE but rarely in AmE.

☐ EXERCISES 5 & 6, p. 50. *Pronouns and nouns contracted with WILL. (Chart 3-2)*

Pronunciation.
The sentences in both exercises are intended as models for everyday spoken English. Ask the students to repeat after you. Point out to them that the *ll* is unemphasized, its sound low and fast; it's hard to discern unless one knows it's supposed to be there by understanding the form and meaning of *will*. One of the reasons learners study grammar is to enable them to understand normal contracted speech, e.g., understand that *dinner'll* is two words spoken as one, not a new vocabulary word, and expresses future time, as in *Dinner'll be ready soon.* You might point out that a common mistake in student production is a statement such as *Bye. I see you tomorrow.* Errors such as this arise because learners don't hear "*ll*"; and they don't hear "*ll*" because they haven't learned to expect it.

EX. 5 ANSWERS: **2.** We'll **3.** You'll **4.** She'll **5.** He'll **6.** It'll **7.** They'll

EX. 6 ANSWERS: **1.** Rob'll **2.** Dinner'll **3.** Mary'll **4.** weather'll **5.** party'll
6. Sam'll **7.** friends'll **8.** sun'll

◇ WORKBOOK PRACTICE 7, p. 43. *WILL. (Chart 3-2)*

Fill-in-the-blanks. [Selfstudy]
This is a review of forms.

ANSWERS:

1. A: Will you help	B: I will	OR	I won't
2. A: Will Paul lend	B: he will	OR	he won't
3. A: Will Jane graduate	B: she will	OR	she won't
4. A: Will her parents be	B: they will	OR	they won't
5. A: Will I benefit	B: you will	OR	you won't

CHART 3-3: USING *PROBABLY* WITH *WILL*

- This unit is included for two reasons:

    (1) Adding *probably* to *will* is common because one cannot always be 100% certain about future activities and events. It is helpful for students to know how to qualify their statements about the future. In Chapter 5, they will learn other ways of qualifying their statements about the future by using other auxiliaries (*may, might, should, can,* etc.)

    (2) The placement of midsentence adverbs isn't dealt with until Chapter 7. If the students are going to use *probably* with *will,* they need some information now about where to put it.

- If the question arises, tell the class that it is also sometimes possible to use *probably* in front of *will* (*Ann probably will go to the park tomorrow*), but tell them that the usual position is between the auxiliary and the main verb, and suggest they use that placement in the exercise. At this level, the text asks students to gain mastery of typical, fundamental patterns of English. They can and will add variations as they gain experience and fluency.

☐ EXERCISE 7, p. 51. *PROBABLY with WILL/WON'T. (Chart 3-3)*

Controlled completion.
This is essentially a word order exercise. It can be covered quickly in class.

ANSWERS: **3.** I'll probably watch   **4.** I probably won't be [formal: I will probably not be]
5. he'll probably go   **6.** he probably won't hand [formal: he will probably not hand]   **7.** it'll
probably be   **8.** they probably won't come [formal: they will probably not come]   **9.** they'll
probably have   **10.** she probably won't ride [formal: she will probably not ride]

◇ WORKBOOK PRACTICE 8, p. 43. *WILL PROBABLY. (Chart 3-3)*

Controlled completion. [Selfstudy]
Students have to read for meaning and choose between affirmative and negative. Other than
that, this is a word order exercise.

ANSWERS: **1.** probably won't   **2.** will probably   **3.** will probably   **4.** probably
won't   **5.** will probably [*Skipped* = omitted, missed on purpose.]   **6.** probably won't
7. will probably [*Assembly line* = a line of workers that a product passes through as it is assembled.]
8. will probably

◇ WORKBOOK PRACTICE 9, p. 44. *WILL PROBABLY. (Chart 3-3)*

Sentence construction; open completion. [Guided Study]
This practice is intended to be done orally in class.

ANSWERS: **1.** He'll probably get wet. He probably won't stay outside for a long time.
2. He probably won't go to work. He'll probably stay home today.   **3.** He'll probably go to
bed early tonight. He probably won't stay up all night again tonight.   **4.** He probably won't
go by plane. He'll probably take a bus or a train.   **5.–8.** *Free response.*

◇ WORKBOOK PRACTICE 10, p. 44. *BE GOING TO and WILL. (Chart 3-3)*

Sentence construction; open completion. [Guided Study]
Divide the class into groups. Encourage the students to go beyond what is suggested in the
Workbook to discuss their ideas of what the future will be like. Perhaps each group could agree
upon two or three original predictions and report them to the rest of the class. The intention
here is to start the students talking about the future; it is hoped that future verb forms will occur
spontaneously and correctly.
   Note on item 5: Actually, videophones are already available commercially.
   Item 7: Many population experts do indeed predict that the population of the earth will
double in 35 years; it is questionable whether there will be enough fresh (and unpolluted) water
to support a population that large.
   Item 9: If you have a group interested in ecology, you might ask them to do some research
on the rate at which tropical rain forests are disappearing and the effect that will have on life on
earth. They could present a report to the rest of the class. In fact, each group could be
assigned to do research and present reports on environmental issues that will affect all future
life: other topics, in addition to the increasing population, the supply of fresh water, and the
disappearance of rain forests, could be global warming, the thinning of the ozone layer, the
effect of pesticides on health, the problem of what to do with nuclear waste, and the extinction
of plant and animal species.

┌───┐
│ **CHART 3-4:** *BE GOING TO* VS. *WILL* │
└───┘

• Explain the notion of a "preconceived plan." Ask the students about their future plans: "What do you plan to do tomorrow?" The question should generate examples of preconceived plans that require *be going to* rather than *will*.

• As a point of comparison, set up a situation that requires *will* rather than *be going to*: *I need some help. I need that piece of chalk. Who'll get it for me?* Have the students demonstrate volunteering by raising their hands and saying, "I'll get it for you."

• It is possible that some situations might be understood as either a prediction or a plan. In those cases, it makes little difference whether *be going to* or *will* is used as long as the students understand what they are saying. Don't waste time arguing with students about it.

☐ EXERCISE 8, p. 52. *BE GOING TO vs. WILL.* (Chart 3-4)

Fill-in-the-blanks.
Students can prepare the exercise in pairs as seatwork. Many students would find it difficult to prepare this one as homework before you discussed Chart 3-4 in class, so it might be best to have them do it in class immediately after you have demonstrated the difference in meaning.

ANSWERS: **3.** am going to   **4.** will ('ll)   **5.** will   **6.** am going to   **7.** am going to
8. will   **9.** are going to . . . will   **10.** are going to   **11.** will . . . will . . . will   **12.** will

◇ WORKBOOK PRACTICE 11, p. 45. *BE GOING TO vs. WILL.* (Chart 3-4)

Controlled completion. [Selfstudy]
The text intends that there be sufficient information here for the students to puzzle out the difference between *be going to* and *will* by themselves, but that can be difficult. You may want to discuss the situations in this practice in class.

ANSWERS: **1.** am going to   **2.** will   **3.** am going to   **4.** will   **5.** am going to
6. will   **7.** am going to . . . will

◇ WORKBOOK PRACTICE 12, p. 46. *BE GOING TO vs. WILL.* (Chart 3-4)

Controlled completion. [Selfstudy]
Enlarge and enrich the contexts as necessary to convey the meanings the speakers are trying to express. Emphasize that *be going to* is used to express preconceived plans and *will* to volunteer on the spur of the moment, without having made a prior plan.

ANSWERS: **1.** am going to   **2.** will   **3.** will   **4.** am going to   **5.** will   **6.** am going to   **7.** A: are . . . going to   B: am going to   **8.** will

CHART 3-5: EXPRESSING FUTURE TIME IN TIME CLAUSES
AND *IF*-CLAUSES

- Illustrate and identify a time clause. (See Chart 2-8, p. 37.)

- Compare a main clause verb with a time clause verb that expresses future time. For example, both of the following express the same action (going to class tomorrow):

> Main clause: *I am going to go to class tomorrow.*
> Time clause: *Before I go to class tomorrow, . . .*

Write the main clause on the board. Then add *Before* at the beginning to change it to a time clause and demonstrate how the verb has to change.

If students can't understand what a main clause is, demonstrate by pretending to come into the room and saying, "Before I go to class tomorrow, . . ." then stop as though you had finished your communication. They should feel that your statement is incomplete. Then say, "I am going to go to class tomorrow," and ask if they feel that that is a more complete statement. A main clause is a complete statement, but a time clause must be attached to a main clause.

Point out that with a verb in a time clause, the form is simple present, but the meaning is future. Emphasize that *will* and *be going to* are not used in a time clause. Mistakes such as *before I will go to class tomorrow* and *after I'm going to eat dinner* are common. The learners may have logic on their side, but they must accept and learn traditional usages that have developed as English has evolved.

- You may want to concentrate on time clauses first and leave (e), tense usage in *if*-clauses, for in-depth discussion when the class does Exercise 11. Presenting both time clauses and *if*-clauses at the same time may be confusing.

- There is a situation in which *will* is used in an *if*-clause. The text doesn't teach this use, but the question may arise. Sometimes when a person is making a deal or trying to reach an agreement about who will do what, *will* is used in the *if*-clause: *If you'll make the sandwiches, I'll pour the drinks.* *Will* in an *if*-clause is close to the meaning of a polite question with *will*: *Will you make the sandwiches? If you do, I will pour the drinks. Is that agreeable to you?*

☐ EXERCISE 9, p. 54. *Simple present in future time clauses. (Chart 3-5)*

    Oral; sentence construction and transformation.
Perhaps ask students to write the answers on the board. Ask them to identify the time clause. Maybe ask them to circle the comma.

    ALTERNATIVE: Students work in pairs. One gives one form of the answer, then the partner gives the other form. They should discuss any questions about punctuation, meaning, and verb forms.

    NOTE: The phrase "as soon as" is sometimes difficult for learners to understand. It means "immediately after" the first action.

    ANSWERS: **2.** <u>After I **write** a letter</u>, I'm going to go to bed.   OR   I'm going to go to bed <u>after I **write** a letter</u>.   **3.** <u>When I **go** to Chicago next week</u>, I'm going to visit the art museum.   OR   I'm going to visit the art museum <u>when I **go** to Chicago next week</u>.   **4.** <u>After I **go** to the drug store</u>, I'll go to the post office.   OR   I'll go to the post office <u>after I **go** to the drug store</u>.   **5.** <u>Before Ann **watches** TV tonight</u>, she'll finish her homework.   OR   Ann will finish her homework <u>before she **watches** TV tonight</u>. [A name or noun usually occurs before a pronoun that refers to it. (See the footnote in the textbook, page 54.) However, it is also possible to have the pronoun first in the time clause, and then the noun in the main clause: *Before she watches TV tonight, Ann will finish her homework.*]   **6.** <u>After Jim **gets** home this evening</u>, he's going to read the newspaper.   OR   Jim is going to read the newspaper <u>after he **gets** home this evening</u>. [also possible: *After he . . . , Jim . . . .*]   **7.** <u>When I **call** John tomorrow</u>, I'll ask him to my party.   OR I'll ask John to my party <u>when I **call** him tomorrow</u>.   **8.** <u>As soon as the rain **stops**</u>, the children are going to go outside and play.   OR   The children are going to go outside and play <u>as soon as the rain **stops**</u>.   **9.** <u>As soon as the teacher **gets** here</u>, class will begin.   OR   Class will begin <u>as soon as the teacher **gets** here</u>.   **10.** <u>Before the Robertsons **leave** on vacation</u>, they will get some travelers' checks.   OR   The Robertsons will get some travelers' checks <u>before they **leave** on vacation</u>. [also possible: *Before they . . . , the Robertsons . . . .*]   **11.** <u>As soon as I **get** home tonight</u>, I'm going to take a hot bath.   OR   I'm going to take a hot bath <u>as soon as I **get** home tonight</u>.   **12.** <u>When I **go** shopping tomorrow</u>, I'm going to buy a new pair of shoes.   OR   I'm going to buy a new pair of shoes <u>when I **go** shopping tomorrow</u>.

□ EXERCISE 10, p. 55. *Simple present in future time clauses. (Chart 3-5)*

Open completion.
Possible options:
• Ask the class to prepare sentences for class discussion the next day.
• Have the students write and submit their completed sentences.
• Divide the class into groups and ask that each member of the group invent a different possible completion. This should be done orally, not in writing.

□ EXERCISE 11, p. 55. *IF-clauses. (Chart 3-5)*

Sentence construction and transformation.
SUGGESTION: Have students write items 2 through 5 on the board for general class discussion. Include the ideas of "condition" and "result." Review the tense information in Chart 3-5. Discuss the use of commas. Then use items 6 through 10 for pair or group work.

ANSWERS: **2.** <u>If **it's** hot tomorrow</u>, I'm going to go swimming.   OR   I'm going to go swimming <u>if **it's** hot tomorrow</u>.   **3.** <u>If it **snows** tomorrow</u>, Betsy isn't going to ride her bike to school.   OR   Betsy isn't going to ride her bike to school <u>if it **snows** tomorrow</u>.   **4.** <u>If Adam **has** enough time</u>, he'll finish his composition tonight. [also possible: *If he has enough time, Adam will . . . .*]   OR   Adam will finish his composition tonight <u>if he **has** enough time</u>.   **5.** <u>If I **don't get** a letter tomorrow</u>, I'll call my parents.   OR   I'll call my parents <u>if I **don't get** a letter tomorrow</u>.   **6.** <u>If the weather **is** nice tomorrow</u>, we're going to go on a picnic.   OR We're going to go on a picnic <u>if the weather **is** nice tomorrow</u>.   **7.** <u>If Greg **doesn't study** for his test</u>, he'll get a bad grade. [also possible: *If he doesn't study for his test, Greg will get . . . .*]   OR Greg will get a bad grade <u>if he **doesn't study** for his test</u>.   **8.** <u>If I **have** enough money</u>, I'm going to go to Hawaii for my vacation.   OR   I'm going to go to Hawaii for my vacation <u>if I **have** enough money</u>.   **9.** <u>If I **don't study** tonight</u>, I probably won't pass the chemistry exam.   OR   I probably won't pass the chemistry exam <u>if I **don't study** tonight</u>.   **10.** <u>If I **study** for the test</u>, I'll probably get a good grade.   OR   I'll probably get a good grade <u>if I **study** for the test</u>.

☐ EXERCISE 12, p. 56. *IF-clauses. (Chart 3-5)*

Oral (books closed); transformation and open completion.
This can be teacher-led or group work. The example between items 8 and 9 simply suggests the possibility of including a second student in order to practice *-s/-es* as well as to add some variation to the transformation-completion format.

EXPANSION: Before Exercise 12, you can invite the students to play "What if" with you. This is a kind of mental exercise. It is used by computer programmers, statisticians, financial planners, weather forecasters, and ordinary people every day. They try to imagine various results from certain conditions. (This can be done before Exercise 12 because it is not necessary for the students to change the verb form that you give them.) For example:

TEACHER: *What if I can't come to class tomorrow?*
STUDENT A: *If you can't come, we won't have a lesson.*
STUDENT B: *Or maybe we'll have another teacher.*
TEACHER: (following B's idea): *What if you have another teacher tomorrow?*
STUDENT C: *If we have another teacher, he or she probably won't give us homework.*
TEACHER (following C's idea): *What if you don't do any homework?*
Etc.

Change the topic after two or three students participate.
Point out that a "what if" question is a shortened form of "What will happen if . . . ?"

SAMPLE RESPONSES: **1.** If it**'s** nice tomorrow, I'll go for a long walk / I'm going to take my nephew to the zoo. [OR I'll go for a long walk / I'm going to take my nephew to the zoo if it**'s** nice tomorrow.] **2.** If it**'s** hot tomorrow, I'm going to wear shorts / I'll stay out of the sun. If it**'s** cold tomorrow, I'll wear more clothing / I'll stay indoors / I'll build a fire in the fireplace, etc. **3.** If it **isn't** nice tomorrow, I won't go shopping / I'm not going to drive into the city. **4.** If it **rains** tomorrow, I'm going to go to a movie / I'll visit my aunt. **5.** If it **doesn't rain** tomorrow, I'll walk to work / I'm going to eat lunch outside. **6.** If I**'m** tired tonight, I won't cook supper / I'm going to go to bed early. **7.** If I**'m not** tired tonight, I'll go with you to the concert / I'm going to finish my research paper. **8.** If I **have** enough time tomorrow, I'm going to clean out my closet / I'll go shopping for new shoes. **9.** A: If I **have** some free time tomorrow, I'm going to go to a movie. B: If (. . .) goes to a movie, I'd like to go along. **10.** A: If I**'m not** in class tomorrow, I'll need to get the exercise answers from someone. B: If (. . .) isn't in class tomorrow, I'll give (. . .) my corrected answers. **11.** A: If I**'m** hungry after class, I'll go to the pizza shop across the street. B: If (. . .) **goes** to the pizza shop across the street, s/he can get a slice of pepperoni and pineapple pizza. **12.** A: If I **go** to *(name of a local place)* tomorrow, I won't be able to visit my aunt. B: If (. . .) **doesn't visit** her/his aunt tomorrow, her/his aunt will be disappointed. **13.** A: If I **don't have** enough money to buy *(something)* when I go shopping tomorrow, I won't buy it. B: If you don't buy *(something)*, I'll lend you one / buy you one. **14.** A: If (. . .) **calls** on the phone tonight, I'll talk with her/him. B: If you talk with (. . .) tonight, ask her/him if s/he will return my history notes tomorrow.

☐ EXERCISE 13, p. 56. *Verb tense review, time clauses and IF-clauses. (Chart 3-5)*

Fill-in-the-blanks.
(REMINDER: See the INTRODUCTION, p. xv, for suggestions on handling fill-in-the-blanks exercises.)
Some students will try to do this exercise quickly, and they may miss the time expressions that determine the verb tenses. This is also a problem when they are in a real conversation, thinking about their message but not monitoring its correct form.

ANSWERS: **1.** b. goes . . . is going to write/will write   c. went . . . took   d. was taking . . .
rang   e. rang . . . jumped   f. gets . . . is going to brush/will brush   g. brushes . . . gets
2. a. get . . . drink   b. get . . . am going to drink/will drink   c. got . . . drank   d. was
drinking . . . came . . . offered   e. is going to drop/will drop [*Drop over* means to come without an
invitation; so does *drop by*.] . . . comes . . . am going to make/will make   **3.** is going to meet/will
meet . . . arrives   **4.** see . . . am going to tell/will tell   **5.** am . . . see   **6.** am . . . am
going to stay/will stay   **7.** are going to go/will go . . . is   **8.** was [*Was over* means "it was
finished or had ended."] . . . left   **9.** is watching . . . is . . . is going to mow/will mow
10. get . . . run

☐ EXERCISE 14, p. 58. *Time relationships. (Chart 3-5)*

Written.
You could use this for quick practice with time clauses and verb forms, concentrating only on
these two areas when marking papers. You could also turn this exercise into a discussion of how
to connect ideas with time words other than "time clause words" (i.e., subordinating
conjunctions):
  Before, after, when, while, and *as soon as* introduce adverb clauses. *Next, then, later,* and *after
that* do not introduce adverb clauses. They show the time relationships between two
independent sentences: these words are sometimes followed by a comma. To distinguish *after*
and *after that*:
    Example: *I watched TV. After that, I went to bed.*
    In the example, *that* is a pronoun that refers to the entire preceding sentence. In this
     case, *after that* means "after I watched TV."
    INCORRECT: *I watched TV. After I went to bed.*
  REMINDER: In a paragraph-writing exercise, students will produce some sentences that can
be used for teacher-made error-analysis exercises.

◇ WORKBOOK PRACTICE 13, p. 46. *Time clauses. (Chart 3-5)*

Combination and structure identification. [Selfstudy]

ANSWERS: **1.** <u>When I call Mike tomorrow</u>, I'll tell him the good news.   OR   I'll tell Mike the
good news <u>when I call him tomorrow</u>.   **2.** Ann will lock all the doors <u>before she goes to bed</u>.
OR   <u>Before Ann goes to bed</u>, she'll lock all the doors.   OR   (<u>Before she goes to bed</u>, Ann will
lock all the doors.)   **3.** <u>When I am in London</u>, I'm going to visit the Tate Museum.   OR
I'm going to visit the Tate Museum <u>when I am in London</u>.   **4.** The show will start <u>as soon as
the curtain goes up</u>.   OR   <u>As soon as the curtain goes up</u>, the show will start.   **5.** Nick is
going to change the oil in his car <u>after he takes a bath</u>.   OR   <u>After Nick takes a bath</u>, he's going
to change the oil in his car.   OR   (<u>After he takes a bath</u>, Nick is going to change the oil in his
car.)   **6.** We'll call you <u>before we drive over to pick you up</u>.   OR   <u>Before we drive over to
pick you up</u>, we'll call you.   **7.** I'll call you <u>when I get an answer from the bank about the
loan</u>.   OR   <u>When I get an answer from the bank about the loan</u>, I'll call you.   **8.** I'll pay my
rent <u>as soon as I get my paycheck</u>.   OR   <u>As soon as I get my paycheck</u>, I'll pay my rent.

◇ WORKBOOK PRACTICE 14, p. 47. *Time clauses. (Chart 3-5)*

Controlled completion. [Selfstudy]

ANSWERS: **1.** will read . . . take   **2.** will call . . . returns   **3.** won't be . . . come
4. go . . . will prepare   **5.** visits . . . will take   **6.** will move . . . graduates . . . finds

◇ WORKBOOK PRACTICE 15, p. 47. *IF-clauses. (Chart 3-5)*

> *Controlled completion.* [Selfstudy]
>
> ANSWERS: **1.** is . . . won't go **2.** get . . . will pay **3.** will be . . . don't go **4.** will stop . . . tells **5.** gets . . . will eat . . . is . . . will be

◇ WORKBOOK PRACTICE 16, p. 48. *Time clauses and IF-clauses. (Chart 3-5)*

> *Combination and structure identification.* [Guided Study]
> This is a general review of adverb clauses of time or condition. To complete it successfully, the students will have to demonstrate an understanding of complex structures with subordinating adverbial conjunctions, the meaning of these conjunctions, the use of present verb forms to express future time in subordinate clauses, and correct punctuation and capitalization. It is hoped by this point in the chapter that this is an easy exercise for them.
>
> ANSWERS:
> **1.** My friends are going to come over <u>after I clean up my apartment</u>   OR   <u>After I clean up my apartment</u>, my friends are going to come over.
> **2.** <u>When/As soon as the storm is over</u>, I'm going to do some errands.   OR   I'm going to do some errands <u>when/as soon as the storm is over</u>.
> **3.** <u>If you don't learn how to use a computer</u>, you will have trouble finding a job.   OR   You will have trouble finding a job <u>if you don't learn how to use a computer</u>.
> **4.** <u>As soon as/When/After Joe finishes his report</u>, he will meet us at the coffeeshop.   OR   Joe will meet us at the coffeeshop <u>as soon as/when/after he finishes his report</u>.
> **5.** <u>After/As soon as Sue washes and dries the dishes</u>, she will put them away.   OR   Sue will put the dishes away <u>after/as soon as she washes and dries them</u>.
> **6.** <u>If they don't leave at seven</u>, they won't get to the theater on time.   OR   They won't get to the theater on time <u>if they don't leave at seven</u>.

CHART 3-6: PARALLEL VERBS

- This unit introduces the concept of parallelism; it calls attention to parallel verbs for all the tenses presented to this point: simple present, present progressive, simple past, past progressive, simple future, and *be going to.* Parallelism is revisited and expanded in Chapter 9 in units on connecting ideas with coordinating conjunctions.

- Errors in parallelism are common, with a second verb often found in the simple form.
  INCORRECT: *I opened the door and look around.*
  INCORRECT: *A good teacher prepares interesting lessons and explain everything clearly.*

☐ EXERCISES 15 AND 16, pp. 59-60. *Parallel verbs. (Chart 3-6)*

> *Fill-in-the-blanks.*
> Exercise 15 can be used for seatwork and class discussion of the concept of parallelism in Chart 3-6. Exercise 16 can be assigned as homework or group work for the next day.
>
> EX. 15 ANSWERS: **1.** walked . . . was reading . . . (was) smoking **2.** is going to/will move . . . look . . . graduates **3.** calls . . . complains **4.** is crying . . . laughing **5.** [*I'm beat* (slang) means "I am extremely tired or fatigued."] get . . . am going to/will take . . . go **6.** dug . . . buried **7.** comes . . . am going to/will play . . . jog

EX. 16 ANSWERS: **1.** go . . . am going to/will finish . . . write **2.** was making . . . spilled [BrE: *spilt*] . . . caught . . . started . . . ran . . . thought **3.** plays . . . cuts [*Cut class* means "to stay away from a scheduled class."] . . . isn't doing . . . doesn't study . . . (doesn't) go . . . is going to/will flunk [*Flunk out* means "to be dismissed because of poor marks."] **4.** cries . . . stamps . . . gets . . . got . . . picked . . . threw . . . didn't hit . . . felt . . . apologized . . . kissed **5.** is beginning . . . begins . . . don't like . . . think . . . are going to take . . . is . . . are going to drive . . . enjoy

◇ WORKBOOK PRACTICE 17, p. 48. *Parallel verbs. (Chart 3-6)*

Structure identification and fill-in-the-blanks. [Selfstudy]

ANSWERS: **1.** was listening . . . (and)(was) doing **2.** are going to meet . . . (and)(are going to) study **3.** will rise . . . (and)(will) set **4.** was carrying . . . (and)(was) climbing / flew . . . (and) sat / dropped . . . (and) spilled **5.** is going to meet . . . (and)(is going to) go **6.** moves . . . (and) starts **7.** slipped . . . (and) fell **8.** am getting . . . (and)(am) walking **9.** arrived . . . (and) started / was . . . (and) felt / was watching . . . (and)(was) feeling / knocked . . . (and) asked / see . . . (and) usually spend / are borrowing . . . (and)(are) going / are going to take . . . (and)(are going to) go

◇ WORKBOOK PRACTICE 18, p. 49. *Parallel verbs. (Chart 3-6)*

Fill-in-the-blanks. [Selfstudy]

ANSWERS: **1.** will retire . . . (will) travel OR are going to retire . . . (are going to) travel **2.** close . . . think **3.** is watching . . . (is) studying **4.** takes . . . buys **5.** go . . . tell **6.** will take . . . (will) forget OR am going to take . . . (am going to) forget **7.** will discover . . . (will) apologize OR is going to discover . . . (is going to) apologize **8.** saw . . . ran . . . caught . . . knocked . . . went . . . sat . . . was waiting . . . got . . . understood . . . put . . . took

◇ WORKBOOK PRACTICE 19, p. 50. *Past and future. (Chapters 2 and 3)*

Controlled completion. [Guided Study]
The students can look at Part I to find the verb they need to complete the blanks in Part II. Parallel verbs are emphasized in this practice, as well as the use of present verb forms in subordinate clauses. Have the students practice contracting *will*.
EXPANSION: Students can write about what they will do tomorrow morning.

ANSWERS: **1.** will be . . . will get . . . will wash . . . brush . . . will . . . put . . . will go . . . (will) start **2.** will walk . . . see . . . will watch . . . (will) make . . . destroys **3.** get . . . will pour . . . (will) open . . . will come . . . will talk . . . will help . . . (will) make . . . say . . . (will) eat . . . (will) finish **4.** will go . . . is . . . has . . . will work . . . will ring . . . will talk . . . will go . . . (will) make . . . will be

---

CHART 3-7: USING THE PRESENT PROGRESSIVE TO EXPRESS FUTURE TIME

• The use of the present progressive to express future time is common, especially with the verbs presented in the chart and other verbs that express planned activities. Some common ones are *bring, build, eat, call, finish, get, give, make, meet, move, send, start, visit.*

• In example (k), *am buying* is said loud and clear, for emphasis. The tense choice and the speaker's tone of voice indicate the speaker's strength of determination.

☐ EXERCISE 17, p. 61. *The present progressive to express future time. (Chart 3-7)*

Controlled completion.
This exercise contains further examples for discussion of the grammar in Chart 3-7. Point out the element of planning in each example.

ANSWERS: **2.** they're coming **3.** she isn't/she's not coming **4.** we're having
5. I'm not eating **6.** I'm taking **7.** he's not/he isn't going **8.** they're going

☐ EXERCISE 18, p. 62. *The present progressive to express future time. (Chart 3-7)*

Controlled completion.
Point out that the present progressive has a present meaning in the first two completions in item 2. All of the rest have a future meaning. Also point out the future time words or the context that gives a future meaning to the present progressive form.

ANSWERS: **1.** B: am going . . . am going . . . are . . . doing A: am going . . . are going
B: am meeting **2.** A: are . . . taking [present] B: am taking [present] A: are . . . taking
B: am taking **3.** A: am going B: are . . . going B: Are . . . flying . . . driving/taking
A: am flying A: am taking B: am staying **4.** are coming . . . am making/cooking . . .
am making B: Is . . . coming **5.** A: am calling [*And that's it!* means "That is my decision; I
am definitely going to do it."]

◇ WORKBOOK PRACTICE 20, p. 51. *The present progressive to express future time. (Chart 3-7)*

Controlled completion. [Selfstudy]

ANSWERS: **1.** is traveling (travelling) **2.** are arriving **3.** am meeting **4.** am
getting **5.** is . . . taking **6.** am studying **7.** am leaving **8.** is attending . . . am
seeing **9.** is speaking **10.** am spending . . . am visiting

◇ WORKBOOK PRACTICE 21, p. 52. *The present progressive to express future time. (Chart 3-7)*

Controlled completion. [Selfstudy]

POSSIBLE RESPONSES: **1.** Fred is eating/having dinner with Emily on Sunday. **2.** He is
seeing Dr. Wood at 1:00 P.M. on Monday. **3.** He is going to Jean's birthday party at 7:00
P.M. on Tuesday. **4.** He is probably eating lunch with Jack on Wednesday. **5.** He is
meeting Tom's plane on Thursday at 2:00 P.M. **6.** He is attending a financial seminar on
Friday. **7.** He is taking his children to the zoo on Saturday.

◇ WORKBOOK PRACTICE 22, p. 52. *The present progressive to express future time. (Chart 3-7)*

Open completion. [Guided Study]
Here students are asked to produce original sentences using the present progressive about their
actual plans for the coming week. Use this practice as a springboard for eliciting creative use of
the target structure.

◇ WORKBOOK PRACTICE 23, p. 53. *The present progressive to express future time. (Chart 3-7)*

Written. [Guided Study]
The purpose here is practice expressing future time using a present verb form. Perhaps think of
other situations in which native speakers would be likely to use the present progressive for future
time and ask the students to write about those, too: plans for this evening, plans for this
weekend, plans for a coming student party, etc.

CHART 3-8:	USING THE SIMPLE PRESENT TO EXPRESS FUTURE TIME

• The use of the simple present to express future time in an independent clause is limited to relatively few verbs, ones that deal with schedules and timetables.

• To help the students understand this special use of the simple present, tell them as a general rule to use it only when the activity is one that is written down, as on a schedule or timetable, and will occur at a definite time.

☐ EXERCISE 19, p. 64. *The simple present to express future time. (Chart 3-8)*

Fill-in-the-blanks.
Item 1: For a scheduled activity such as the time a game starts, it is possible to use the simple present, present progressive, or *be going to*. (In addition, *will* would be correct in all the items in this exercise, but the focus is on learning when one can use the simple present instead of the present progressive to express future time.)

Item 2: The simple present is not possible because having chicken and pasta is not on a schedule. The focus of the sentence is on what we're having for dinner, not a timetable for eating.

ANSWERS: **3.** am walking/am going to walk [The simple present is not possible; walking describes a planned activity but not one that is on a timetable or schedule, such as the bus leaving at 8:15 in the next item.] **4.** leaves **5.** begins . . . ends **6.** opens . . . closes **7.** are getting/are going to get [The simple present is not possible.] **8.** am watching/am going to watch [The simple present is not possible.] **9.** arrives . . . is taking/is going to take [The simple present is not possible.] **10.** is

◇ WORKBOOK PRACTICE 24, p. 53. *The simple present to express future time. (Chart 3-8)*

Semi-controlled completion. [Selfstudy]

ANSWERS: **1.** A: does . . . begin/start B: begins/starts **2.** opens **3.** arrives/gets in/lands **4.** B: begins/starts A: does . . . end/finish B: ends/finishes **5.** A: does . . . close B: closes **6.** begins/starts

CHART 3-9:	PRESENT PLANS FOR FUTURE ACTIVITIES: USING *INTEND, PLAN, HOPE*

• A fairly common problem occurs when students use *intend*, *plan*, and *hope* in future forms when they actually need a present form.

INCORRECT: *I will intend to graduate in two years.*

□ EXERCISE 20, p. 65. *intend, plan and hope. (Chart 3-9)*

> *Oral; transformation.*
> This is just a quick oral exercise to make the point that intentions, plans, and hopes are present
> expressions of future activities.
>
> *ANSWERS:*   **2.** I intend/am intending to be . . . .   **3.** Tom plans/is planning to buy . . . .
> **4.** Jane is hoping/hopes to get . . . .   **5.** I am planning/plan to stay . . . .   **6.** I intend/am
> intending to finish . . . .

CHART 3-10: IMMEDIATE FUTURE: USING *BE ABOUT TO*

- In the phrase *be about to*, *about* is considered a preposition in an idiomatic phrase by some analyses, but
in others it is labeled an adjective. Assuming *about* to be a preposition, the text treats *be about to* as an
idiom; that is, its meaning is not predictable from the usual rules of grammar or usual meaning of the
constituent vocabulary elements. In Chapter 10, the students are taught that gerunds, not infinitives,
immediately follow prepositions; that is why *be about* followed by an infinitive is treated as a special case,
i.e., an "idiom." However, if *about* is considered to be an adjective meaning "immediately ready," the
phrase *be about to* can be seen as consistent with a common grammatical structure; infinitives frequently
follow *be* + an adjective.

- *Be about to* is common in spoken English.

□ EXERCISE 21, p. 65. *Immediate future: BE ABOUT TO. (Chart 3-10)*

> *Oral; transformation.*
> This is for further discussion of the grammar in Chart 3-10.
>   EXPANSION: Pretend to be about to do things; ask the class what you are about to do.
> Examples: Pick up a piece of chalk and hold it next to the chalkboard. (You're about to write on
> the board.) Pretend to be about to open/close a window/door. Pretend to be about to sneeze,
> turn off the ceiling light, put on your sweater/coat/etc. Ask the students to pretend to be about
> to do something.
>
> *EXPECTED RESPONSES:*   **2.** She's about to open the door.   **3.** He's about to leave.
> **4.** She's about to wash her dirty hands at the bathroom sink.   **5.** He's about to finish the
> examination.   **6.** She's about to swat the fly on the kitchen table.

◇ WORKBOOK PRACTICE 25, p. 54. *BE ABOUT TO. (Chart 3-10)*

> *Sentence construction.* [Selfstudy]
> The pictures can elicit a few sentences with *be about to*. Students also need spontaneous
> situational practice. See the expansion activity suggested above for Exercise 21.
>
> *ANSWERS:*   **1.** The chimpanzee is about to eat a banana.   **2.** Sam is about to leave.
> **3.** The plane is about to land.   **4.** The woman is about to answer the phone.

☐ EXERCISE 22, p. 66. *Past and future verbs. (Chapters 2 and 3)*

> *Written.*
> Use this exercise for some quick writing practice with past and future verbs.
>   EXPANSION: Another possibility is for Student A to write what s/he did yesterday and give her/his paper to Student B. Student B should assume that Student A's day will be exactly the same tomorrow and rewrite the paper in future time.
>   For a more ambitious and wide-ranging summary writing practice, you could have the students make time lines of their lives, then give the time line to other students to make into a composition.
>   Example of a time line:

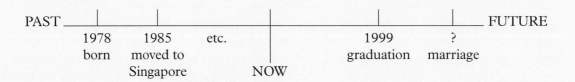

◇ WORKBOOK PRACTICE 26, p. 54. *Verb tense review. (Chapters 1, 2, and 3)*

> *Fill-in-the-blanks.* [Selfstudy]
>
> ANSWERS: **1.** don't need   **2.** is planning/plans . . . Are you coming/Are you going to come   **3.** A: do you usually get   B: take   **4.** was watching . . . became . . . stopped . . . found   **5.** A: am going/am going to go   B: are going/are going to go   **6.** will probably call/is probably going to call . . . go   **7.** A: is . . . are flashing   B: know . . . know . . . see   A: is going . . . Are you speeding   B: am going   A: is passing   **8.** is going to land/will land . . . think   **9.** ride . . . was raining . . . drove . . . arrived . . . discovered   **10.** will give   **11.** are you wearing/are you going to wear . . . am planning/plan . . . bought . . . is . . . will show . . . will get . . . (will) bring   **12.** B: is wearing   A: didn't lend   B: will be/is going to be

◇ WORKBOOK PRACTICE 27, p. 56. *Verb tense review. (Chapters 1, 2, and 3)*

> *Fill-in-the-blanks.* [Selfstudy]
> Practices 27 through 29 review present, past, and future verbs.
>
> ANSWERS: **(1)** made . . . did not have . . . were not . . . wore   **(2)** make . . . comes . . . buy   **(3)** is . . . wear . . . wear   **(4)** exist . . . wear . . . are   **(5)** will probably be/are probably going to be . . . will wear/are going to wear . . . Will we all dress/Are we all going to dress . . . show . . . do you think

◇ WORKBOOK PRACTICE 28, p. 56. *Verb tense review. (Chapters 1, 2, and 3)*

> *Fill-in-the-blanks.* [Guided Study]
>
> ANSWERS: **1.** went   **2.** had   **3.** learned   **4.** are working/work   **5.** eat   **6.** tell   **7.** remembered   **8.** were sitting/sat   **9.** was going/went   **10.** struck   **11.** spilled   **12.** was   **13.** apologized   **14.** left   **15.** remember   **16.** told   **17.** laughed   **18.** wasn't   **19.** is   **20.** are   **21.** are   **22.** get   **23.** get   **24.** are   **25.** are   **26.** will smile

◇ WORKBOOK PRACTICE 29, p. 57. *Verb tense review. (Chapters 1, 2, and 3)*

Fill-in-the-blanks. [Guided Study]

ANSWERS: **1.** was combing . . . broke . . . finished . . . rushed **2.** get . . . will read/am going to read . . . (will/am going to) watch . . . am not doing/won't do/am not going to do **3.** A: has . . . has B: does she have B: Do you have A: am not going to get/am not getting . . . don't have **4.** A: cut B: is bleeding B: will get **5.** A: Are you taking/Are you going to take [also possible: *Will you take,* asked as a polite request meaning "Would you please take the children?"] B: opens . . . leave . . . will probably get **6.** A: is ringing B: know A: Are you going to answer/Do you want to answer/Will you answer A: Do you want A: don't you want B: am expecting . . . don't want **7.** doesn't destroy . . . learn **8.** B: did you say/are you saying A: said . . . is **9.** B: does yours say A: will add . . . Are you planning/Do you plan B: will prove . . . like C: will overcome . . . don't understand . . . are speaking/speak . . . will just smile/am just going to smile D: will make A: looks . . . will have/are going to have **10.** A: The sun will keep/Is the sun going to keep . . . will it eventually burn/is it eventually going to burn B: will eventually burn/is eventually going to burn . . . won't happen/isn't going to happen

◇ WORKBOOK PRACTICE 30, p. 59. *Future time. (Chapter 3)*

Free response. [Guided Study]
The intention is that this practice be written, but you could change it into an oral exercise done in small groups. One student at a time could be a fortune-teller and tell fortunes for others in the group. Ask your students if there are fortune-tellers in their cultures. Ask them if they believe there are people who can predict their future. Talk about fortune-tellers in your experience, perhaps discussing the North American stereotype of a middle-aged or older woman wearing scarves, brightly colored clothes, and a lot of gold jewelry who reads palms or tea leaves, or gazes into a crystal ball.

☐ EXERCISE 23, pp. 66. *Prepositions. (Chapter 3)*

Controlled completion.

ANSWERS: **1.** from **2.** with **3.** to **4.** at **5.** to/in **6.** in **7.** at **8.** for **9.** with . . . about **10.** with **11.** to/at . . . for **12.** for

◇ WORKBOOK PRACTICE 31, p. 59. *Prepositions. (Chapter 3)*

Controlled completion. [Guided Study]

ANSWERS: **1.** at **2.** at **3.** in **4.** with **5.** for **6.** to . . . with **7.** for **8.** from **9.** about **10.** for

◇ WORKBOOK PRACTICE 32, p. 60. *Prepositions. (Chapters 1 and 3)*

Controlled completion. [Selfstudy]

ANSWERS: **1.** to **2.** from . . . for **3.** to . . . at **4.** to **5.** of **6.** from . . . for **7.** in . . . with **8.** for . . . with . . . to

Chapter 4: NOUNS AND PRONOUNS

ORDER OF CHAPTER	CHARTS	EXERCISES	WORKBOOK
Chapter introduction		Ex. 1	
Plural nouns	4-1	Ex. 2 → 3	Pr. 1 → 4
Structure of the simple sentence	4-2 → 4-3	Ex. 4 → 6	Pr. 5 → 7
Adjectives	4-4	Ex. 7	Pr. 8 → 10
Nouns as adjectives	4-5	Ex. 8	Pr. 11
Cumulative review		Ex. 9 → 10	Pr. 12 → 13
Personal pronouns	4-6	Ex. 11	Pr. 14 → 17
Possessive nouns	4-7	Ex. 12	Pr. 18 → 21
Possessive pronouns and adjectives	4-8	Ex. 13	Pr. 22
A friend of + possessive	4-9	Ex. 14	Pr. 23
Reflexive pronouns	4-10	Ex. 15 → 17	Pr. 24 → 25
Cumulative review			Pr. 26 → 27
Forms of *other*	4-11 → 4-13	Ex. 18 → 21	Pr. 28 → 31
Capitalization	4-14	Ex. 22 → 23	Pr. 32
Prepositions		Ex. 24	Pr. 33 → 34

General Notes on Chapter 4

• OBJECTIVE: Nouns are the basic tools for giving names to things and concepts; therefore, learners need to control a large vocabulary of nouns as well as associated words such as pronouns, adjectives, and prepositions. The exercises in this chapter build toward that control.

• APPROACH: To be sure the students have some terminology for talking about grammatical categories, the chapter begins with a brief pretest and a review of the "parts of speech." Common regular and irregular plural forms of nouns are listed. Then adjectives and several types of pronouns are associated with nouns. The chapter ends with basic rules for beginning nouns with capital letters.

• TERMINOLOGY: Some books use the term "noun adjunct" for the word "vegetable" in the phrase "vegetable garden," but this text simply calls it "a noun used as an adjective." A distinction is made between "possessive pronouns" (e.g., *my*) and "possessive adjectives" (e.g., *mine*). "Capitalization" refers to writing an upper-case (i.e., capital) letter at the beginning of a sentence or of certain nouns.

☐ EXERCISE 1, p. 67. *Basic grammar terminology. (Chapter 4)*

Structure identification.
This exercise is intended as seatwork followed by discussion in which you give the students an introductory understanding of the concepts these grammar terms represent. An alternative is to dictate Exercise 2 first, before the students open their books, and then tell them to look only at page 67 and write the answers to items 5 through 15. In this way, you will have both exercises ready for discussion. As an added bonus, an unexpected "quiz" at the beginning of a unit can get the attention of the class.

When you discuss Exercise 1, you might use the following explanations.

In item 1: *shirt* is a thing. The traditional definition of a noun as a "person, place, or thing" can be useful to students. A noun can also be defined as a word that functions as a subject or object in a sentence. In this item, *shirt* is grammatically the object of the verb *wear* in the basic structure of a simple sentence: subject + verb + object. (See Charts 4-2 and 4-3 for explanations of subjects and objects.)

Item 2: *in* is a "little word" called a preposition. Prepositions are usually placed in front of nouns (or pronouns) and give information about place, time, and other relationships. Ask the students how many prepositions they can name (without looking at Chart 4-3).

Item 3: a pronoun refers to, and has the same meaning as, a noun. *He* and *Steve* are the same person in this item.

Item 4: an adjective describes (i.e., gives information about) a noun or pronoun; *thirsty* describes the subject *I*. If you say *Ali is thirsty,* then *thirsty* describes *Ali.* (Note: some languages do not require a verb in this kind of statement, but English requires *be.*)

This pretest contains basic simple sentences. If your students want to analyze them, they will find:

- All three patterns with main verb *be:*
  be + prepositional phrase of place (items 2, 3, and 13)
  be + adjective (item 4)
  be + noun phrase (items 11 and 12)

- *Be* as auxiliary verb (item 3, second verb)

- Basic S+V+O = items 1, 5, 6, 9, 10, 14, 15

- Basic S+V (intransitive verb) = items 7 and 8

ANSWERS: **5.** noun [It is used as the object of the preposition *in.*]   **6.** noun [It is used as the object of the verb *know.*]   **7.** adjective [An adjective = a word that describes a noun or pronoun; here it describes the children.]   **8.** preposition [A preposition = a "little word" that shows relationships—though it may be easier to point to Chart 4-3 and tell the students that those words are prepositions than it is to define for them exactly what a preposition is.]   **9.** noun   **10.** adjective   **11.** noun   **12.** adjective   **13.** preposition   **14.** noun   **15.** pronoun

☐ EXERCISE 2, p. 68. *Plural nouns. (Chart 4-1)*

Written (books closed).
This exercise is a preparation for discussing Chart 4-1. It's not really a test. Students may pick up on some mistakes they tend to make, but the primary purpose here is to interest them in the information in a somewhat long chart.

Students can "correct" each other's papers. The correct answers should be written on the board. Discuss the chart at the same time you give the correct answers:
Items 1 through 6 correspond to examples (a) and (b) in the chart.
Items 7 through 9 correspond to example (c).
Items 10 through 12 correspond to example (d).
Items 13 through 15 correspond to example (e).

Items 16 through 20 correspond to example (f).
Items 21 and 22 correspond to examples (h) and (g) respectively.

ANSWERS: 1. glasses   2. problems [Emphasize that -es is added only in special cases.]
3. matches   4. bushes   5. animals   6. sexes [As in: *There are two sexes: female and male.*
Perhaps point out that many sorts of written application forms ask "sex: M or F."]   7. libraries
8. monkeys   9. families   10. wives   11. shelves   12. roofs [Some dialects of English
use *rooves* in speaking, but this is not an accepted written form.]   13. heroes   14. radios
15. zeroes/zeros   16. feet   17. mice   18. sheep   19. women   20. children
21. phenomena   22. offspring

CHART 4-1: PLURAL FORMS OF NOUNS

• Pronunciation of final -s/-es is presented in the *Workbook*, Practice 3, p. 62. You may wish to model
the nouns in (a) to illustrate the three different pronunciations of final -s/-es: *birds = bird + /z/; streets =
street + /s/; and roses = rose + /əz/.*

• In section (e), you may point out that -s, not -es, is added to nouns that end in -o when the noun is a
shortened form (e.g., *auto* instead of *automobile*), when the noun is related to a musical term, and when
the noun ends in two vowels. Or you can simply say that sometimes one adds -s and sometimes -es;
when in doubt, look it up. (Note: some dictionaries allow variant spelling for the plural of *mosquito:
mosquitoes* or *mosquitos*.)

• Section (h) is included simply to inform the students that some oddities in the formation of plural
nouns do exist. These words are not emphasized in this text; they are dealt with more fully in
Understanding and Using English Grammar. The four words in section (h) are difficult vocabulary for
most students at this level. They will encounter the word *phenomena* again in Chapter 8 in the
discussion of phenomena of nature that are used as noncount nouns. (You might want to note that
these rather unusual nouns are in the process of being Anglicized; that is, they are often spoken with
more regular forms: e.g., one bacteria, two cactuses, one phenomena. In formal writing, however, the
forms in this chart are still preferred.)

☐ EXERCISE 3, p. 69. *Plural forms of nouns. (Chart 4-1)*

Transformation; seatwork, pair work, or group work.

ANSWERS: 2. dormitories   3. children   4. leaves   5. wishes   6. fish
7. opinions   8. mice   9. sandwiches   10. men   11. women   12. flashes
13. tomatoes   14. teeth   15. halves   16. taxes   17. possibilities   18. thieves
19. volcanoes/volcanos   20. geese   21. attorneys   22. butterflies   23. categories
24. mosquitoes   25. sheep   26. wolves   27. stitches   28. feet   29. pianos
30. beliefs

◇ WORKBOOK PRACTICE 1, p. 61. *Plural nouns. (Charts 4-1 and 4-2)*

Structure identification. [Selfstudy]
This is an introductory practice intended to call students' attention to singular and plural nouns.
Students using this text are already familiar with much of the grammar in this practice, but they
will need to look carefully at each sentence to apply the grammar. Final -s/-es is troublesome.
Some of the grammar is probably new to them (e.g., the use of *offspring*).

EXPANSION: This practice can also be used in class discussion to identify the basic structures of the simple sentence.

S + V + O = items 1, 2, 3, 5, 7, 8, 9, 10.
S + V + PrepPhr = item 4.
S + *be* + Noun = items 6 and 10.

ANSWERS: 1. <u>Chicago</u> has busy <u>streets</u> and <u>highways</u>.   2. <u>Boxes</u> have six <u>sides</u>.
3. Big <u>cities</u> have many <u>problems</u>.   4. <u>Bananas</u> grow in hot, humid <u>areas</u>.   5. <u>Insects</u> don't have <u>noses</u>. [Insects' sense of smell is located in their antennae, or "feelers." They do not have noses through which they detect scents.]   6. <u>Lambs</u> are the <u>offspring</u> of <u>sheep</u>.   7. <u>Libraries</u> keep <u>books</u> on <u>shelves</u>.   8. <u>Parents</u> support their <u>children</u>.   9. <u>Indonesia</u> has several active <u>volcanoes</u>.   10. <u>Baboons</u> are big <u>monkeys</u>. They have large <u>heads</u> and sharp **teeth**. They eat <u>leaves</u>, <u>roots</u>, <u>insects</u>, and <u>eggs</u>.

◇ WORKBOOK PRACTICE 2, p. 61. *Plural nouns. (Chart 4-1)*

Transformation. [Selfstudy]

ANSWERS: 1. mouse   2. pockets   3. tooth   4. tomato   5. fish   6. woman
7. branches   8. friends   9. duties   10. highways   11. thief   12. beliefs
13. potatoes   14. radios   15. offspring   16. child   17. seasons   18. customs
19. businesses   20. century   21. occurrences   22. phenomenon   23. sheep
24. loaf

◇ WORKBOOK PRACTICE 3, p. 62. *Plural nouns. (Chart 4-1)*

Pronunciation. [Guided Study]
Explain and model the pronunciation of the examples in the box. To explain voiceless vs. voiced, tell the students to put their hand to their voice box to feel vibrations. A voiceless sound such as /t/ comes from air being pushed through the tongue and teeth; a voiced sound such as /d/ emanates from the voice box. Point out that in voiceless-voiced pairs such as /t/ and /d/, the tongue and teeth are in the same position. The only difference is the addition of the voice box to the /d/ sound. Some other voiceless vs. voiced pairs are /s/ and /z/, /p/ and /b/, /f/ and /v/.

Use the items listed in the exercise to clarify the information in the box. For example, point out that final -*s* is pronounced /s/ in item 1 because /t/ is a voiceless sound and pronounced /z/ in item 2 because /d/ is a voiced sound.

◇ WORKBOOK PRACTICE 4, p. 62. *Plural nouns. (Chart 4-1)*

Pronunciation. [Guided Study]
Tell the students to read the sentence aloud but to cover the line where the pronunciation is given if they want to check themselves. Students could work in groups and listen carefully to each other's pronunciation prior to general class discussion of this practice.

As an extension of this practice, you can ask the students to read the sentences in Practices 1 and 5 aloud, paying special attention to pronunciation of final -*s*/-*es*. The sentences in these two practices contain plural nouns.

EXPANSION: You can make up similar exercises by using any sentences with plural nouns—or singular present tense verbs, for that matter. The pronunciation rules are the same whether the word with final -*s*/-*es* is a noun or a verb.

CHART 4-2: SUBJECTS, VERBS, AND OBJECTS

- This is, of course, a simplified explanation of the simple sentence, but the students need only a basic understanding of subjects, verbs, and objects.

- You may want to delay a discussion of intransitive vs. transitive verbs until Chapter 11, where the distinction is dealt with in connection with the passive form. If you decide to introduce the terminology here, you could point out that most dictionaries label intransitive verbs as v.i. and transitive verbs as v.t.

☐ EXERCISE 4, p. 70. *Subjects, verbs, and objects. (Charts 4-2 and 4-3)*

Structure identification.

The text doesn't include determiners in identifying simple subjects and objects, but you could explain that a noun phrase (e.g., *the carpenter*) functions as a noun *(carpenter)*. The emphasis in this exercise is simply on students focusing in on nouns and verbs and how they are used.

ANSWERS:

3. cows=**S** eat=**V** grass=**O**
4. dog=**S** barked=**V**
5. dog=**S** chased=**V** cat=**O**
6. accidents=**S** happen=**V**
7. roommate=**S** opened=**V** window=**O**
8. birds=**S** build=**V** nests=**O**
9. guests=**S** arrived=**V**

10. Teachers=**S** assign=**V** homework=**O**
11. Steam=**S** rises=**V**
12. Jack=**S** raised=**V** hand=**O**
13. Irene=**S** is watching=**V** children=**O**
[*Sister's* is a possessive noun that functions as an adjective, not as a subject or object.]

CHART 4-3: OBJECTS OF PREPOSITIONS

- What is a preposition? A simplified definition: A preposition is a word that occurs most often in front of nouns (or pronouns) to give information about place, time, and other relationships.

- A definition may not be necessary or desirable. The text approaches recognition of prepositions: (1) by supplying a list and simply telling the students that these words are prepositions; and (2) by demonstrating their grammatical structure and function in the examples and exercises.

☐ EXERCISE 5, p. 71. *Subjects, verbs, objects, and prepositional phrases. (Charts 4-2 and 4-3)*

Structure identification.

Ask the students to analyze (i.e., parse) the sentences prior to class discussion. They can work alone, in pairs, or in groups. It is important in using this textbook that learners be able to identify the basic elements of a simple sentence. (With older or somewhat advanced students, you might ask them to think of how their own language connects the elements that are in these simple sentences. This might help them remember the differences in English.)

ANSWERS:

2. Sara=**S** looked=**V** at=**P** pictures=**O of P**
3. Emily=**S** waited=**V** for=**P** friend=**O of P** at=**P** restaurant=**O of P**
4. sun=**S** rises=**V** in=**P** east=**O of P**

5. Sue=**S**   lost=**V**   ring=**O**   in=**P**   sand=**O of P**   at=**P**   beach=**O of P**
6. moon=**S**   disappears=**V**   from=**P**   view=**O of P**   during=**P**   day=**O of P**
7. Eric=**S**   talked=**V**   to=**P**   friend=**O of P**   on=**P**   phone=**O of P**
   for=**P**   minutes=**O of P**
8. Children=**S**   throughout=**P**   world=**O**   play=**V**   with=**P**   dolls=**O of P**
9. Astronauts=**S**   walked=**V**   on=**P**   moon=**O of P**   in=**P**   1969=**O of P**
10. woman=**S**   in=**P**   suit=**O of P**   sat=**V**   beside=**P**   me=**O of P**   until=**P**
    end=**O of P**   of=**P**   meeting=**O of P**

□ EXERCISE 6, p. 72. *Review: prepositions of place. (Charts 4-2 → 4-3)*

Oral.
Prepositions of place were first discussed in Chapter 1 in Exercise 12, p. 16, of the main text.
See pages 15 and 16 of this *Teacher's Guide* for notes on these prepositions of place.
   Have the students physically demonstrate the spatial relationships.

◇ WORKBOOK PRACTICE 5, p. 63. *Subjects, verbs, objects, and prepositions.(Charts 4-2 and 4-3)*

Identification. [Selfstudy]

ANSWERS:
1. [Bridges=**S**]   [cross=**V**]   [rivers=**O**].
2. [A terrible earthquake=**S**]   [occurred=**V**]   [in Turkey=**PP**].
3. [Airplanes=**S**]   [fly=**V**]   [above the clouds=**PP**].
4. [Trucks=**S**]   [carry=**V**]   [large loads=**O**].
5. [Rivers=**S**]   [flow=**V**]   [toward the sea=**PP**].
6. [Salespeople=**S**]   [treat=**V**]   [customers=**O**]   [with courtesy=**PP**].
7. [Bacteria=**S**]   [can cause=**V**]   [diseases=**O**].
8. [Clouds=**S**]   [are floating=**V**]   [across the sky=**PP**].
9. [The audience=**S**]   [in the theater=**PP**]   [applauded=**V**]   [the performers=**O**]
   [at the end=**PP**]   [of the show=**PP**].
10. [Helmets=**S**]   [protect=**V**]   [bicyclists=**O**]   [from serious injuries=**PP**].

◇ WORKBOOK PRACTICE 6, p. 63. *Nouns and verbs. (Charts 4-1 → 4-3)*

Structure identification. [Selfstudy]
You might want to discuss the sentence structure of some of these items. Ask the students how
they know the italicized word is a noun or a verb.

ANSWERS: **1.** v.   **2.** n.   **3.** n.   **4.** v.   **5.** v.   **6.** n.   **7.** n.   **8.** v.
9. n.   **10.** v   **11.** v.   **12.** n.   **13.** v.   **14.** n.   **15.** v.   **16.** n.   **17.** n.
18. v.   **19.** v.   **20.** n.   **21.** n.   **22.** v.

◇ WORKBOOK PRACTICE 7, p. 64. *Nouns and verbs. (Charts 4-1 → 4-3)*

Written. [Guided Study]
This practice requires a good understanding of the fundamental structure of the simple
sentence and the grammatical functions of nouns and verbs. Students who are unable to
complete it successfully may need special help before they proceed in the chapter. Students
who can't identify nouns and verbs will be at a great disadvantage throughout the rest of the
text.

SAMPLE RESPONSES: **1.** *Noun*: <u>Snow</u> drifts over the roads in winter.   *Verb:* In many
northern countries, it <u>snows</u> heavily during the winter months.   **2.** *Noun:* <u>Paint</u> can be very
expensive.   *Verb:* I <u>will paint</u> the living room this weekend.   **3.** *Noun:* I wore the <u>tie</u> you

bought me.   *Verb:* I <u>tied</u> a string around the package.   **4.** *Noun:* The <u>phone</u> kept ringing last night, but I didn't get out of bed to answer it.   *Verb:* If you <u>don't phone</u> by 11:00 A.M., I'll know you don't plan to meet us for the movie.   **5.** *Noun:* The <u>smoke</u> from her cigarette blew into my face.   *Verb:* She <u>smokes</u> a pack of cigarettes a day.   **6.** *Noun:* His <u>face</u> was familiar, but I couldn't remember his name.   *Verb:* I <u>can't face</u> my boss after the terrible mistake I made at work.   **7.** *Noun:* We couldn't drink the <u>water</u> because the stream was polluted.   *Verb:* I <u>watered</u> the vegetable garden this morning.   **8.** *Noun:* My sister drew a <u>circle</u> around the correct answer.   *Verb:* I <u>will circle</u> the correct answer to that question. **9.** *Noun:* The postal carrier didn't deliver the <u>mail</u> because of the barking dog.   *Verb:* I <u>mailed</u> the letter on my way to work.

CHART 4-4: USING ADJECTIVES TO DESCRIBE NOUNS

- The emphasis in this chart is on the terminology "adjective" and its function and form.

- Some languages inflect adjectives, i.e., change their form for number, gender, or some other category. Be sure to make clear that an adjective in English is neither singular nor plural and has no inflected endings.

☐ EXERCISE 7, p. 72. *Adjectives. (Chart 4-4)*

Structure identification.
This can be done quickly in class or in groups. The goal is to make sure everyone in the class understands what an adjective is. The concept of adjectives will be revisited in the chapters on adjective clauses and comparisons.
    Ask the students to identify the noun each adjective modifies.

ANSWERS: **2.** dry (modifies *deserts*)   **3.** funny (modifies *joke*)   **4.** sensible (modifies *people*) . . . comfortable (modifies *shoes*)   **5.** sharp (modifies *Knives*)   **6.** big (modifies *teeth*)   **7.** dark (modifies *places*) . . . small (modifies *children*)   **8.** soapy (modifies *water*) **9.** local (modifies *police*) . . . stolen (modifies *car*) . . . illegal (modifies *drugs*)   **10.** primitive (modifies *people*) . . . wild (modifies *plants*)

◇ WORKBOOK PRACTICE 8, p. 65. *Adjectives. (Chart 4-4)*

Semi-controlled completion. [Selfstudy]
Answers other than the ones given below are possible. Students may want to check alternative answers with you.

EXPECTED RESPONSES: **1.** old   **2.** old   **3.** hot   **4.** slow   **5.** happy   **6.** bad **7.** dry   **8.** hard   **9.** hard/difficult   **10.** narrow   **11.** dirty   **12.** full   **13.** safe **14.** quiet   **15.** deep   **16.** sour   **17.** expensive   **18.** light   **19.** light **20.** private   **21.** right   **22.** right   **23.** strong   **24.** short

◊ WORKBOOK PRACTICE 9, p. 65. *Adjectives and nouns. (Chart 4-4)*

    Structure identification. [Selfstudy]

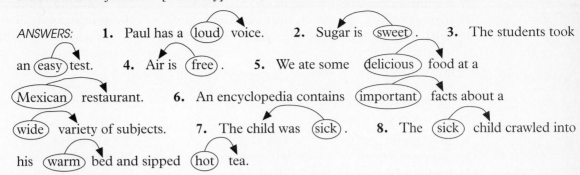

ANSWERS: **1.** Paul has a (loud) voice. **2.** Sugar is (sweet). **3.** The students took an (easy) test. **4.** Air is (free). **5.** We ate some (delicious) food at a (Mexican) restaurant. **6.** An encyclopedia contains (important) facts about a (wide) variety of subjects. **7.** The child was (sick). **8.** The (sick) child crawled into his (warm) bed and sipped (hot) tea.

◊ WORKBOOK PRACTICE 10, p. 65. *Adjectives and nouns. (Chart 4-4)*

    Combination. [Guided Study]
    The emphasis here is on the placement and function of adjectives.

    ANSWERS: **1.** <u>Red</u> roses are <u>beautiful</u> flowers.   **2.** <u>Cold</u> rain fell from the <u>dark</u> clouds.
3. The waiter poured <u>hot</u> coffee into my <u>empty</u> cup.   **4.** The <u>young</u> girl in the <u>blue</u> dress was looking for a telephone.   **5.** Annie sleeps on a <u>soft</u> bed in a <u>quiet</u> room.   **6.** Mrs. Fox gave the <u>hungry</u> children some <u>fresh</u> fruit.   **7.** After we finished our <u>delicious</u> dinner, Frank helped me with the <u>dirty</u> dishes.   **8.** When Tom was getting a haircut, the <u>inexperienced</u> barber accidentally cut Tom's <u>right</u> ear with the scissors.

CHART 4-5: USING NOUNS AS ADJECTIVES

- Nouns in this structure can be called "noun adjuncts" or simply referred to as "nouns that are used as adjectives."

- Common problems that arise with this structure are:
  (1) making the noun adjunct possessive: e.g., INCORRECT: *a flowers' garden;* and
  (2) making the noun adjunct plural: e.g., INCORRECT: *black beans soup.*

- Sometimes a noun describing another noun becomes a single compound noun: *firefighter, doorbell, earphone,* etc. Tell the students to use their dictionaries when in doubt about spelling a noun-noun combination as one word or two. There is no hard-and-fast rule to predict the form. (ERRATUM: The author should have followed that advice in Exercise 8 below. The correct spelling of *flagpole* in item 10 is as one word; the text treated it as though it were spelled as two words. This error is corrected in later printings.)

☐ EXERCISE 8, p. 73. *Nouns as adjectives. (Chart 4-5)*

    Transformation.
    The items are intended to illustrate the grammar in Chart 4-5. The students will have to be able to identify this structure in later exercises in this text and in the *Workbook* when they are asked to decide which nouns need to be plural and which don't.

ANSWERS:
2. **television** program   5. **government** worker   8. **weather** forecaster
3. **mountain** climber   6. **bean** soup   9. **grammar** book
4. **history** lesson   7. **automobile** factory   10. **photograph** album
ERRATUM: Item 10 is changed from **flag**poles to **photograph** album in later printings.

◇ WORKBOOK PRACTICE 11, p. 66. *Nouns as adjectives. (Chart 4-5)*

Transformation. [Selfstudy]

ANSWERS:
1. **newspaper** articles   5. **key** chains   8. **shoulder** pads
2. **page** numbers   6. **city** governments   9. **pocket** knives
3. **paper** money   7. **duck** ponds   10. **traffic** lights
4. **apartment** buildings

□ EXERCISE 9, p. 74. *Review of nouns. (Charts 4-1 → 4-5)*

Error analysis.
Students need time to prepare this exercise ahead of class discussion. It requires careful analysis of mistakes in form that are common for learners of English as a second/foreign language. Also discuss pronunciation of final -s/-es.

ANSWERS: 2. Cats . . . m**ice**   3. mosquit**oes** [also acceptable in some dictionaries: mosquitos] . . . insect**s**   4. eyelash**es**   5. Ge**ese** . . . duck**s**   6. program**s**   7. Forest**s** . . . Forest fir**es** . . . animal**s**   8. kitchen kni**ves** . . . weapon**s**   9. kind**s** . . . people . . . world   10. universit**ies** . . . year   11. Ted . . . university student**s**   12. offspring . . . animal**s** . . . hors**es** . . . zebra**s** . . . deer   13. book**s** . . . magazine article**s** . . . experience**s**   14. device**s** . . . batter**ies** . . . . Flashlight**s** . . . pocket calculator**s** . . . radio**s** . . . tape recorder**s** . . . kind**s** . . . toy**s** . . . batter**ies**

□ EXERCISE 10, p. 75. *Review of nouns. (Charts 4-1 → 4-5)*

Error analysis.
Allow students time to do this as homework. (It might be best to have everyone write the whole exercise on paper.) Class discussion can be in groups as the students compare their analyses. Each student can read a sentence aloud and point out the changes. Pay attention to pronunciation of final -s/-es.

ANSWERS: (1) Whale**s** . . . fish . . . mammal**s** . . . Mi**ce** . . . tiger**s**   (2) being**s** [*Being* = a gerund, i.e., a verb form used as a noun; *human being* = a noun phrase to distinguish people from other existing creatures such as animals.] . . . example**s** . . . mammal**s** . . . Whale**s**   (3) animal**s** . . . dog**s** . . . chimpanzee**s** . . . sea**s** . . . ocean**s**   (4) river**s** . . . whale**s** . . . fish . . . Fish . . . egg**s** . . . offspring   (5) Mammal**s** . . . birth . . . offspring   (6) kind**s** . . . whale**s** . . . . whale**s** . . . creature**s**   (7) whale**s** . . . whale**s** . . . fe**et** . . . meter**s**   (8) length . . . ton**s** . . . kilogram**s** . . . whale**s**   (9) elephant**s** . . . dinosaur**s**   (10) heart . . . whale . . . size . . . car   (11) blood [noun used as adjective] . . . vessel . . . aorta (ey**or**tə) . . . person   (12) being**s** . . . whale**s** . . . times   (13) people . . . whale**s** . . . enem**ies** . . . people   (14) hunting [a gerund] . . . whale**s**

◇ WORKBOOK PRACTICE 12, p. 66. *Nouns. (Charts 4-1 → 4-5)*

Error analysis. [Selfstudy]
You may wish to have the students identify the noun adjuncts (i.e., the nouns used as adjectives).

ANSWERS: 1. bottles . . . caps [*Medicine* a noun adjunct, i.e., a noun used as an adjective.]
2. seats [*Airplane* is a noun adjunct.]   3. students . . . experiments . . . classes [*Laboratory* is a
noun adjunct.]   4. Houseflies . . . pests . . . germs   5. Computers . . . operators
6. kinds . . . flowers   7. reporters . . . jobs [*Newspaper* is a noun adjunct.]   8. manners
[*Telephone* is a noun adjunct.]   9. tickets [*Theatre* and *Thursday* are noun adjuncts.]   10. lives
. . . ways . . . years . . . lamps . . . candles . . . houses . . . chickens . . . fires [*Oil* is a noun adjunct.]

◇ WORKBOOK PRACTICE 13, p. 67. *Nouns.* *(Charts 4-1 → 4-5)*

Error analysis. [Guided Study]
Students have to be very alert to catch all the nouns that need to have a final -*s*/-*es*. They need
time to prepare this practice. They might enjoy putting their heads together and working in
groups.

ANSWERS: 1. kinds . . . birds   2. Birds . . . eggs   3. birds . . . nests . . . weeks . . .
months . . . parents   4. eggs . . . animals . . . eggs   5. Foxes . . . snakes . . . enemies . . .
birds. . . birds . . . eggs   6. birds . . . seeds . . . plants . . . birds . . . insects . . . earthworms
7. Weeds . . . plants . . . crops . . . flowers . . . Birds . . . farmers . . . seeds . . . insects
8. Rats, rabbits . . . mice . . . losses . . . farms . . . crops . . . birds . . . hawks . . . farmers . . .
animals   9. feathers . . . kinds . . . birds . . . pillows . . . mattresses . . . feathers . . . geese . . .
pillows . . . feathers . . . jackets   10. feathers . . . geese . . . pens . . . pens

---

**CHART 4-6: PERSONAL PRONOUNS: SUBJECTS AND
OBJECTS**

• In examples (e) and (f), the use of *I* instead of *me* after *and* as an object pronoun seems to have taken
the English-speaking world by storm. One can hear a lot of sentences like *Ann met Eric and I at the
museum,* even from educated speakers. It's really quite an interesting linguistic phenomenon.   You
might mention to your students that they might hear native speakers misusing subject pronouns in this
way as it is a common occurrence, but it is not yet accepted as standard in speech or writing. Perhaps
someday it will be?

☐ EXERCISE 11, p. 76. *Personal pronouns.* *(Chart 4-6)*

Structure identification.
Again, the intention of this exercise is to clarify the grammar presented in the preceding chart.
Pair work or group work would be fine here, although it should be followed by teacher-led
discussion of the connection between the answers and the information in Chart 4-6.

ANSWERS: 2. me   3. me   4. I   5. I   6. us   7. us   8. me . . . us . . . We
9. them . . . They are   10. it . . . it . . . it . . . it   11. them   12. them . . . They . . . her
. . . it . . . She   13. me . . . him   14. me . . . him   15. me . . . I

◇ WORKBOOK PRACTICE 14, p. 68. *Personal pronouns.* *(Chart 4-6)*

Structure identification. [Selfstudy]
The students are asked to identify each pronoun by putting brackets around it and, in addition,
to describe its grammatical function. The emphasis is on helping the students distinguish
between subject and object forms and uses of personal pronouns.

ANSWERS: **1.** me (O of vb) **2.** I (S) . . . me (O of prep) **3.** He (S) . . . it (O of vb) . . . It (S) . . . him (O of vb) **4.** me (O of prep) . . . We (S) . . . her (O of vb) . . . she (S) . . . us (O of vb) . . . We (S) . . . her (O of prep) **5.** He (S) . . . them (O of vb) . . . them (O of vb) . . . They (S) **6.** I (S) . . . him and me (O of prep) . . . He and I (S)

◇ WORKBOOK PRACTICE 15, p. 68. *Personal pronouns. (Chart 4-6)*

Structure identification. [Selfstudy]
The emphasis here is on identifying antecedents. One component of successful reading comprehension is the ability to recognize antecedents for pronouns.

ANSWERS: **1.** She = *Janet* . . . it = *a green apple* **2.** her = *Betsy* **3.** They = *Nick and Rob* **4.** they = *phone messages* **5.** him = *Louie* . . . He = *Louie* . . . her = *Alice* . . . She = *Alice* **6.** She = *Jane* . . . it = *letter* . . . them = *Mr. and Mrs. Moore* . . . They = *Mr. and Mrs. Moore* . . . her = *Jane*

◇ WORKBOOK PRACTICE 16, p. 68. *Personal pronouns. (Chart 4-6)*

Controlled completion. [Selfstudy]
This gives practice in identifying antecedents and supplying the correct pronoun. To do so, the students must consider function, meaning, and form (subject vs. object, singular vs. plural, and gender).

Even though this is a selfstudy practice, it can be discussed in class. Ask the students why they chose their answers.

ANSWERS: **1.** It **2.** He . . . them **3.** They . . . her **4.** it **5.** it . . . it . . . him . . . he **6.** they . . . them . . . they **7.** them **8.** it **9.** it . . . It **10.** them . . . They . . . They . . . them

◇ WORKBOOK PRACTICE 17, p. 69. *Personal pronouns. (Chart 4-6)*

Controlled completion. [Selfstudy]
If you discuss this practice in class, ask the students how they determined the correct answers. How do they know that the correct completion for item 1 is *me*?

ANSWERS: **1.** me **2.** He **3.** him **4.** he **5.** her **6.** She **7.** me . . . He . . . us **8.** her . . . They **9.** I . . . They . . . us . . . it . . . We . . . them **10.** them **11.** me . . . him **12.** she **13.** I . . . him and me

---

CHART 4-7: POSSESSIVE NOUNS

• Proper placement of apostrophes in possessive nouns can be confusing. (Obviously, this is a problem only in the written language, not in speech.) Use ample examples of your own to explain this chart, writing them on the chalkboard.

• You may wish to point out that the apostrophe has more than one meaning and use. In this chart, it expresses possession (and number). In contractions, it indicates the omission of letters (e.g., *isn't* = *is not*, with the "o" omitted).

☐ EXERCISE 12, p. 78. *Possessive nouns. (Chart 4-7)*

Transformation.
This exercise and Practice 18 in the *Workbook* survey the basic uses of the apostrophe with the possessive forms of regular nouns, irregular nouns, and nouns that end in *-y/-ies*.

ANSWERS: **3.** daughter's **4.** daughters' **5.** man's **6.** woman's **7.** men's
8. women's **9.** people's **10.** person's **11.** earth's **12.** elephant's
13. teachers' **14.** teacher's **15.** enemy's **16.** enemies'

◇ WORKBOOK PRACTICE 18, p. 70. *Possessive nouns. (Chart 4-7)*

Transformation. [Selfstudy]

ANSWERS: **1.** friend's **2.** friends' **3.** son's **4.** sons' **5.** baby's **6.** babies'
7. child's **8.** children's **9.** person's **10.** people's **11.** teacher's
12. teachers' **13.** man's **14.** men's **15.** earth's

◇ WORKBOOK PRACTICE 19, p. 70. *Possessive nouns. (Chart 4-7)*

Error analysis. [Selfstudy]
This practice might be a little difficult for some students. Always invite students to bring questions about selfstudy practices to class, and you can also always initiate discussion of a selfstudy practice by asking questions about certain items.

Point out that there is no difference in pronunciation between *king's* and *kings'*, *babies'* and *baby's*, etc. They are different only in written form, not in spoken form.

ANSWERS: **1.** A king's chair **2.** Kings' chairs **3.** Babies' toys **4.** a baby's toys
5. the caller's words **6.** A receptionist's job . . . callers' names **7.** yesterday's news . . .
today's events **8.** The pilots' seats **9.** the earth's surface **10.** Mosquitoes' wings
11. A mosquito's wings **12.** A cat's heart . . . an elephant's heart **13.** the elephants'
tricks **14.** the animals' bodies **15.** an animal's footprints

◇ WORKBOOK PRACTICE 20, p. 71. *Possessive nouns. (Chart 4-7)*

Error analysis. [Guided Study]
Items 12 through 15 may be difficult due to unfamiliar vocabulary. Part of the intention here is for you to discuss with the class the English names of the planets.
(NOTE: Astronomers report that Neptune is temporarily the farthest planet from the sun and will be until around 1999. The text chooses to stay with the traditional presentation of the planets' positions.)

ANSWERS: Dan's sister **2.** *(no change)* **3.** Jack's roommates **4.** *(no change)*
5. roommate's desk **6.** roommates' desks **7.** *(no change)* **8.** Betty's sister . . .
sister's name **9.** sisters' names **10.** woman's work **11.** women's roles . . . men's
roles **12.** Jupiter's surface **13.** Mercury's atmosphere **14.** Mars' surface OR
Mars's surface . . . earth's surface **15.** earth's twin . . . Venus' surface OR Venus's
surface **16.** planets' English names . . . Jupiter's son . . . Venus' son OR Venus's son

◇ WORKBOOK PRACTICE 21, p. 73. *Review of nouns + -S/-ES. (Charts 4-1 and 4-7)*

Error analysis. [Guided Study]
This practice reviews final *-s* vs. *-es*, irregular noun plurals, and possessive nouns.

ANSWERS: **1.** leaves **2.** mother's **3.** Potatoes **4.** birds **5.** Tom's **6.** thieves
. . . Lee's **7.** Mountains . . . valleys **8.** child's **9.** Children's toys **10.** actors' names
11. Teachers . . . people's ideas **12.** monkeys . . . thumbs . . . hands . . . thumbs . . . hands

CHART 4-8: POSSESSIVE PRONOUNS AND ADJECTIVES

• The term "possessive adjective" can be confusing. *My, your, our,* etc., are pronouns in that they are noun substitutes, but they function as adjectives, i.e., they modify nouns. In this way, they are different from *mine, yours, ours,* etc., which the text labels "possessive pronouns."

☐ **EXERCISE 13, p. 79.** *Possessive pronouns and adjectives. (Chart 4-8)*

Controlled completion.

ANSWERS: **1.** their **2.** A: my . . . yours B: mine . . . Yours . . . your **3.** its . . . its **4.** It's **5.** Hers **6.** her **7.** your . . . It . . . is . . . you **8.** a. They b. Their c. Our . . . theirs d. They're . . . their e. They're . . . there . . . they're . . . their

◇ **WORKBOOK PRACTICE 22, p. 73.** *Possessive pronouns and adjectives. (Chart 4-8)*

Controlled completion. [Selfstudy]
This purpose of this practice is to clarify the difference in usage between possessive pronouns and possessive adjectives.

ANSWERS: **1.** your . . . yours **2.** her . . . . hers **3.** his . . . his **4.** your . . . yours **5.** their . . . our . . . theirs . . . ours

CHART 4-9: *A FRIEND OF* + POSSESSIVE

• *A friend of* is a common expression. This chart presents not a major grammar point, but just a quick explanation of a special expression students sometimes have questions about.

☐ **EXERCISE 14, p. 81.** *A FRIEND OF + possessive. (Chart 4-9)*
Oral (books closed).
This is a quick oral exercise to make the students comfortable with the expression presented in Chart 4-9. It's also a good review of possessive pronouns.
   Use the names of students in your class in the parentheses (. . .).

ANSWERS: **1.** (. . .) wrote a letter to a friend of his/hers in . . . . **2.** I wrote a letter to a friend of mine in . . . . **3.** (. . .) and (. . .) visited friends of theirs in . . . . **4.** I want to introduce you to a good friend of mine. **5.** We ran into a mutual friend of ours at . . . . **6.** I met a good friend of (. . .)'s. **7.** I invited a friend of mine to spend the weekend with my family. **8.** (. . .) and (. . .) usually have dinner with some friends of theirs.

◇ **WORKBOOK PRACTICE 23, p. 74.** *Possessive pronouns vs. possessive adjectives.*
(Charts 4-8 and 4-9)

Controlled completion. [Guided Study]

ANSWERS: **1.** her **2.** hers **3.** Our **4.** Ours **5.** your **6.** mine . . . my . . . yours **7.** their . . . theirs **8.** mine . . . yours **9.** ours

CHART 4-10: REFLEXIVE PRONOUNS

- Explain the form and meaning by using a mirror (just a small pocket mirror will do). Perhaps mention that *reflexive* means "to bounce back or reflect," as light or images are reflected by a mirror.

- Briefly answer questions about the vocabulary listed at the bottom of the chart. Some notes:
  - *feel sorry for yourself* = engage in self-pity
  - *help yourself* = usually used to mean "serve yourself," as at a cafeteria
  - *pinch yourself* = usually used jokingly and figuratively, as in *I couldn't believe my good fortune. I had to pinch myself to make sure it was real.*
  - *work for yourself* = be self-employed

- Remind students that talking to *themselves* is a good way to practice English.

☐ EXERCISE 15, p. 82. *Reflexive pronouns. (Chart 4-10)*

Oral (books closed).
Use the idea of this exercise while talking about Chart 4-10. Vary the leading questions you ask so that you cover all of the pronouns, singular and plural: *myself, ourselves,* etc.

☐ EXERCISE 16, p. 82. *Reflexive pronouns. (Chart 4-10)*

Controlled completion.

ANSWERS: **2.** himself   **3.** yourself (also possible: yourselves) . . . themselves
4. ourselves   **5.** herself   **6.** himself   **7.** yourselves   **8.** yourself   **9.** myself
10. itself   **11.** themselves   **12.** myself

☐ EXERCISE 17, p. 83. *Reflexive pronouns. (Chart 4-10)*

Oral/Written.
Orally, students can invent various sentences about themselves and their classmates. The exercise could also be written. The purpose is to familiarize the students with common expressions in which reflexive pronouns are used.

◇ WORKBOOK PRACTICE 24, p. 74. *Reflexive pronouns. (Chart 4-10)*

Controlled completion. [Selfstudy]
This is a straightfoward check on the form and use of reflexive pronouns.

ANSWERS: **1.** myself   **2.** himself   **3.** ourselves   **4.** yourself   **5.** yourselves
6. herself   **7.** themselves

◇ WORKBOOK PRACTICE 25, p. 74. *Reflexive pronouns. (Chart 4-10)*

Controlled completion. [Selfstudy]
This practice contains some common expressions in which reflexive pronouns are used.

ANSWERS: **1.** blamed myself   **2.** are going to/will cut yourself   **3.** introduced myself
4. was talking to himself   **5.** work for ourselves   **6.** taught themselves   **7.** killed
himself   **8.** wished myself   **9.** is taking care of herself   **10.** believe in ourselves
11. felt sorry for myself   **12.** help themselves

◇ WORKBOOK PRACTICE 26, p. 75. *Pronouns.* *(Charts 4-6 → 4-10)*

Controlled completion. [Selfstudy]
This is a cumulative review practice.

ANSWERS: **1.** me . . . him **2.** yourselves **3.** itself **4.** its . . . its **5.** hers
6. him **7.** yourself . . . your **8.** our . . . our **9.** ours **10.** themselves
11. itself **12.** himself

◇ WORKBOOK PRACTICE 27, p. 76. *Pronoun review.* *(Charts 4-6 → 4-10)*

Controlled completion. [Guided Study]
This is a cumulative review practice.

ANSWERS: **1.** his . . . He . . . himself . . . he . . . him **2.** Her . . . She **3.** Our . . . We
4. her **5.** my . . . I **6.** hers **7.** mine **8.** They . . . themselves . . . them . . . theirs
. . . Their . . . their **9.** hers . . . his **10.** himself . . . him . . . he . . . his . . . He . . . him
11. her . . . she . . . herself . . . she . . . her **12.** your . . . ours

---

CHART 4-11: SINGULAR FORMS OF *OTHER*: *ANOTHER* vs.
**   *THE OTHER***

• The sole focus of this chart is to distinguish between *another* and *the other*. Additional forms of *other* are discussed in the next chart.

• Many learners erroneously put *the* in front of *another*. Point out that *another* is simply two words, *an* (meaning *one*) and *other*, written together. *An* is an article. *The* is an article. You use only one article in front of a noun, never two articles together. You can't say *This is the an apple*. Similarly, you can't put

---

☐ EXERCISE 18, p. 85. *Singular forms of OTHER.* *(Chart 4-11)*

Controlled completion.

ANSWERS: **3.** another **4.** The other **5.** The other **6.** another **7.** another
8. another **9.** the other **10.** the other **11.** The other **12.** Another . . . Another
. . . Another . . . The other

◇ WORKBOOK PRACTICE 28, p. 77. *Singular forms of OTHER.* *(Chart 4-11)*

Controlled completion. [Selfstudy]

ANSWERS: **1.** The other **2.** a. Another b. The other **3.** a. Another
b. Another c. Another d. another **4.** The other **5.** Another **6.** The other
7. a. Another b. the other **8.** a. another b. another c. another d. another
e. another

CHART 4-12: PLURAL FORMS OF *OTHER: OTHER(S)*
               vs. *THE OTHER(S)*

• The key here is to distinguish between the use of *other(s)* as a pronoun and *other* as an adjective. Remind students that adjectives are not inflected: they have no added endings such as *-s/-es*.

• A good way to explain the meaning of forms of *other* is to use your fingers. Example: Hold up your hand and say, "We have five fingers on one hand." Then say, pointing to your thumb, "This is my thumb. There are four *other* fingers on my hand. This one is called the thumb. *The others* have names, too. What is *another (one)* called?" (The common names are index finger, middle finger, ring finger, and little finger.)

    Or you could gather pens or books and discuss them in terms of *other*. Example: *This is one pen, this is another, these are others, these are other pens,* etc.

    Another technique is to use Cuisinaire rods—sticks of wood or plastic of varied colors and lengths. Give each group of students some rods and have them describe the rods to each other using *others, another, the other,* and *the others.* A variation of this is to give identical sets of rods to two groups. One group builds something that the other group can't see. Then the builders must describe it accurately to the second group, who must try to copy the design with their rods. (This also gives practice in the use of prepositions of place, among many other things.)

☐ EXERCISE 19, p. 87. *Plural forms of OTHER.* *(Chart 4-12)*

    Controlled completion.

    ANSWERS: **5.** The others   **6.** The other   **7.** Other . . . others   **8.** The other
    9. The others   **10.** Others   **11.** Other   **12.** Others   **13.** The others   **14.** The other

◇ WORKBOOK PRACTICE 29, p. 78. *Plural forms of OTHER. (Chart 4-12)*

    Controlled completion. [Selfstudy]

    ANSWERS: **1.** The other   **2.** The others   **3.** a. Other   b. Others   c. Others
    d. Other   **4.** a. the other   b. The others   **5.** a. other   b. others   **6.** others
    7. other   **8.** Others   **9.** Other   **10.** a. The other   b. The others

CHART 4-13: SUMMARY OF FORMS OF *OTHER*

• The main point of this chart is to show when *other* has a final *-s.* A common problem is that learners add final *-s* to *other* when it is used as an adjective: e.g., INCORRECT: *I bought some others books.*

• This unit on *other* does not deal with all of its uses. See *Understanding and Using English Grammar,* Chart 5-21, for more information.

☐ EXERCISE 20, p. 88. *Forms of OTHER. (Chart 4-13)*

Controlled completion.

ANSWERS: **2.** the other   **3.** Others   **4.** Other   **5.** The other   **6.** another . . .
other   **7.** another . . . Other   **8.** Others . . . other . . . other   **9.** The other
10. another . . . others   **11.** The others   **12.** The other   **13.** another   **14.** The
other   **15.** Others . . . other

☐ EXERCISE 21, p. 90. *Summary forms of OTHER. (Charts 4-11 → 4-13)*

Oral (books closed).
This is intended to be teacher-led and to provide usage situations as well as the opportunity to
summarize the grammar.
      ERRATUM: The first printings of the text have an error in the example. The second
response should be *another,* not *the other. The other* is a misprint that escaped scrutiny. In other
words, the second of the three pens is *another pen* and the third of the three pens is *the other pen.*

◇ WORKBOOK PRACTICE 30, p. 79. *Summary forms of OTHER. (Charts 4-11 → 4-13)*

Controlled completion. [Selfstudy]

ANSWERS: **1.** A   **2.** C   **3.** D   **4.** B   **5.** E   **6.** C   **7.** A   **8.** D   **9.** B
10. E

◇ WORKBOOK PRACTICE 31, p. 80. *Summary forms of OTHER. (Charts 4-11 → 4-13)*

Open completion. [Guided Study]

SAMPLE RESPONSES: **1.** blue . . . the other is red.   **2.** Others ride the bus.   **3.** one glass
of water . . . he drank another one.   **4.** several . . . Tagalog . . . the others are German and
English.   **5.** like to watch TV . . . others don't.   **6.** two sisters . . . 30 . . . the other is 24.
7. Ms. Gray. The other is Mr. Halprin.   **8.** Juan and Pedro . . . Others are Maria and Luis.
9. Some . . . Japan. Other . . . China, Indonesia, Turkey, and Colombia.   **10.** soccer.
Another . . . baseball. Others are tennis and golf.

CHART 4-14: CAPITALIZATION

• One of the principal ideas for the students to understand from this chart is that nouns are capitalized
when they are part of a name (i.e., a proper noun). The text does not use the term "proper noun." You
may decide to use it if it helps your class.

• This is a reference chart. You might want to proceed directly to the exercises, then refer to the chart as
questions arise.

• Correct capitalization can be a problem in student writing. Some language groups, such as Spanish
speakers, have different rules for capitalizing words; for example, words related to nationality are not
capitalized in Spanish, but are in English. This causes interference in their using correct English
capitalization. Some students from other language groups seem to consider capitalization to be of not
much import. It may be necessary to convey to them that proper capitalization is a value in English
rhetoric, for it signals a writer's competent, educated use of the language.

□ EXERCISES 22 AND 23, p. 92. *Capitalization. (Chart 4-14)*

Error analysis.

EX. 22 ANSWERS: **2. D**o . . . **R**ichard **S**mith . . . **H**e   **3. I** . . . **P**rofessor **S**mith . . . **U**niversity of **A**rizona [Make sure the whole class understands why *professor* and *university* are not capitalized in item 2 but are in item 3.]   **4. T**he **N**ile **R**iver . . . **M**editerranean **S**ea   **5. J**ohn . . . **C**atholic . . . **A**li . . . **M**oslem   **6. A**nna . . . **F**rench . . . **S**he . . . **F**rance   **7. I**'m **8. I**'m . . . **M**odern **E**uropean **H**istory   **9. W**e . . . **V**ancouver, **B**ritish **C**olumbia   **10. V**enezuela . . . **S**panish-speaking   **11. C**anada . . . **N**orth **A**merica   **12. C**anada . . . **U**nited **S**tates   **13. T**he   **14. T**he **M**ississippi **R**iver

EX. 23 ANSWERS: **1. S**aturday   **2. B**iology   **3. E**nglish   **4. B**rookfield **Z**oo . . . **C**hicago   **5. O**live **S**treet   **6. C**anada . . . **M**ontreal . . . **J**uly   **7. V**ietnamese   **8. S**audi **A**rabia . . . **I**slam   **9. X**erox **C**orporation   **10. L**atin **A**merica   **11. S**t. **L**ouis . . . **U**ncle **B**ill   **12. V**alentine's **D**ay [February 14]   **13. W**oodland **P**ark   **14. U**niversity of **O**regon . . . **O**regon **S**tate **U**niversity   **15. O**regon

◇ WORKBOOK PRACTICE 32, p. 80. *Capitalization. (Chart 4-14)*

Error analysis. [Selfstudy]

ANSWERS: **1. R**obert **J**ones   **2.** *(no change)*   **3. U**ncle **J**oe . . . **A**unt **S**ara   **4.** *(no change)*   **5. S**usan **W. M**iller   **6. P**rof. **M**iller's   **7. J**anuary   **8.** *(no change)* **9. M**onday   **10. L**os **A**ngeles   **11. C**alifornia   **12.** *(no change)*   **13. U**nited **S**tates of **A**merica   **14.** *(no change)*   **15. A**tlantic **O**cean   **16.** *(no change)*   **17. M**arket **S**treet . . . **W**ashington **H**igh **S**chool   **18.** *(no change)*   **19. H**ilton **H**otel . . . **B**angkok **20. J**apanese . . . **G**erman

□ EXERCISE 24, p. 93. *Prepositions. (Chapter 4)*

Controlled completion.

ANSWERS: **2.** from   **3.** for   **4.** on   **5.** with   **6.** in   **7.** at   **8.** to   **9.** of **10.** to   **11.** . . . about   **12.** to . . . about

◇ WORKBOOK PRACTICE 33, p. 81. *Prepositions. (Chapter 4)*

Controlled completion. [Selfstudy]

ANSWERS: **1.** for   **2.** A: to . . . about   B: at . . . for   **3.** to   **4.** from   **5.** for **6.** A: on   B: about   **7.** in   **8.** of   **9.** with . . . about/on   **10.** to

◇ WORKBOOK PRACTICE 34, p. 81. *Prepositions. (Chapters 1, 3 and 4)*

Controlled completion. [Selfstudy]
This draws from the prepositions practiced in Chapters 1, 3, and 4.

ANSWERS: **1.** about   **2.** from   **3.** of   **4.** to . . . with   **5.** to   **6.** for **7.** from   **8.** with   **9.** with   **10.** to   **11.** in   **12.** at   **13.** for . . . at   **14.** at **15.** A: with . . . about   C: to   A: to . . . about . . . with

Chapter 5: MODAL AUXILIARIES

ORDER OF CHAPTER	CHARTS	EXERCISES	WORKBOOK
Introduction to form	5-1	Ex. 1	Pr. 1 → 2
Ability: *can* and *could*	5-2	Ex. 2 → 4	Pr. 3 → 5
Possibility: *may* and *might* Permission: *may* and *can*	5-3	Ex. 5 → 6	Pr. 6
Possibility: *could*	5-4	Ex. 7	Pr. 7 → 9
Polite questions	5-5 → 5-6	Ex. 8 → 11	Pr. 10 → 11
Should, ought to, had better	5-7	Ex. 12 → 14	Pr. 12 → 13
Have to, have got to, must	5-8 → 5-9	Ex. 15 → 17	Pr. 14 → 19
Logical conclusions: *must*	5-10	Ex. 18	Pr. 20 → 21
Imperative sentences	5-11	Ex. 19 → 20	Pr. 22 → 23
Cumulative review		Ex. 21	
Let's and *why don't*	5-12	Ex. 22 → 24	Pr. 24 → 25
Stating preferences: *prefer, like . . . better, would rather*	5-13	Ex. 25 → 28	Pr. 26 → 27
Cumulative review			Pr. 28 → 31
Prepositions		Ex. 29	Pr. 32

General Notes on Chapter 5

- OBJECTIVE: Students must control both the forms and the meanings of verb phrases that contain modal auxiliaries because these words communicate small but important differences in the user's attitude and feelings. Misuse of modal auxiliaries can result in confusion and even, at worst, anger among people who are trying to communicate in either speech or writing.

- APPROACH: After one exercise on the form of modal auxiliaries, the chapter is organized on the basis of lexical meanings. Additional structures include imperative sentences, suggestions, and stating preferences. Most exercises are interactive, emphasizing conversational forms.

- TERMINOLOGY: The text uses the term "modal auxiliary" for both single-word and periphrastic modals. The term "helping verb" is mentioned in the first chart as synonymous with "auxiliary."

CHART 5-1: THE FORM OF MODAL AUXILIARIES

• This chart is simply an introduction to terminology and form. Subsequent charts in this chapter deal with meanings and uses of the expressions in detail.

• Discuss the meanings of the example sentences. Mention that there may be other meanings for the same modals. For example, in the sentence "I could meet you for coffee after class," *could* means future possibility, whereas in example (b) in the chart, *could* expresses past ability.

• Point out for (j) and (k) that *study* is the main verb. The word "have" in *have to* and *have got to* is inflected for number and tense (*has to, had* to, etc.). The main verb is never inflected after a modal. This is especially confusing for learners when the main verb is *have*. Examples: *He **ought to have** more patience. She **has to have** a new dress for graduation. Mr. Smith **had to have** an operation.*

☐ EXERCISE 1, p. 94. *TO with modal auxiliaries. (Chart 5-1)*

> *Controlled completion.*
> This is an exercise on form, but discuss meaning as you go along. Paraphrase the sentences for the class as a way of introducing them to the content of this chapter.
>
> ANSWERS: **3.** Ø   **4.** Ø   **5.** to   **6.** Ø   **7.** to   **8.** Ø   **9.** Ø   **10.** Ø
> **11.** Ø   **12.** Ø   **13.** Ø   **14.** to   **15.** Ø   **16.** Ø   **17.** to   **18.** Ø
> **19.** Ø   **20.** Ø . . . Ø   **21.** to . . . Ø

◊ WORKBOOK PRACTICE 1, p. 83. *TO with modal auxiliaries. (Chart 5-1)*

> *Controlled completion.* [Selfstudy]
> Practices 1 and 2 can serve as an overview of the grammar in this chapter. Ostensibly the students are focusing only on form, but both practices lend themselves well to a discussion of the meanings that can be communicated through modal auxiliaries.
>
> ANSWERS: **1.** must Ø   **2.** has <u>to</u>   **3.** should Ø   **4.** ought <u>to</u>   **5.** May I
> Ø   **6.** can Ø   **7.** must Ø   **8.** can't Ø   **9.** have got <u>to</u>   **10.** A: Should I
> Ø   B: have <u>to</u> . . . could Ø   A: ought <u>to</u> . . . might Ø . . . Would Ø
> B: should Ø . . . can Ø . . . will Ø   A: must Ø . . . can't Ø

◊ WORKBOOK PRACTICE 2, p. 83. *TO with modal auxiliaries. (Chart 5-1)*

> *Controlled completion.* [Guided Study]
> Discussion topics: sibling conflicts; chores (assigned tasks) children do at home, etc.
>
> ANSWERS: **1.** has <u>to</u>   **2.** must Ø   **3.** can't Ø . . . may Ø   **6.** couldn't Ø . . .
> had <u>to</u>   **7.** you Ø . . . I'll Ø   **8.** got <u>to</u>   **11.** have <u>to</u>   **12.** better Ø
> **13.** ought <u>to</u>   **14.** has <u>to</u> . . . should Ø   **15.** might Ø   **16.** could Ø . . . ought <u>to</u>
> **17.** must Ø

CHART 5-2: EXPRESSING ABILITY: *CAN* AND *COULD*

- *Can* is presented as expressing ability, but it is richer than that. Usually it expresses a subtle combination of ability and possibility. In this text, however, the term "possibility" is reserved for *may/might/could* (see Charts 5-3 and 5-4).

- It is not easy to define modals. They are not regular vocabulary words. The text seeks principally to give the students a general notion of their meaning and then provide, through the exercises, numerous situations in which they are used so that the students may become familiar with the range of nuances they can express.

- The typical errors in form that learners make are pointed out in Chart 5-1 and the footnote to this chart.

☐ EXERCISE 2, p. 96. *CAN and CAN'T.* (Chart 5-2)

Controlled completion.
Model the pronunciation of *can* and *can't: Can* is reduced to /kn/, spoken with a low tone and no stress. *Can't* is pronounced with a full vowel but not a strong final "t": /kæn/. However, in short answers they both receive full pronunciation and stress: *Yes, I can. No, I can't.*
Try to give the students a feel for the idea that *can* expresses a combination of ability and possibility.

ANSWERS: **2.** can't . . . can **3.** can . . . can't **4.** can . . . can't **5.** can . . . can't
6. can . . . can't **7.** can't . . . can **8.** can . . . can't **9.** can't . . . can **10.** can . . .
can't **11.** can't . . . can **12.** can't . . . can **13.** can . . . can't **14.** can't . . . can

☐ EXERCISE 3, p. 96. *CAN.* (Chart 5-2)

Oral (books closed).
This exercise consists of some ideas you might find useful as you tempt your students to use *can* in a variety of situations.

☐ EXERCISE 4, p. 97. *COULD.* (Chart 5-2)

Oral (books closed).
When *could* expresses past ability, it is usually used in the negative. Other expressions are more commonly used to express affirmative past ability: *managed to, was/were able to,* or a verb that simply says what was accomplished. (Examples: *We managed to find their house. We were able to find their house. We found their house.*) The negative form *(couldn't)* is, however, common when speaking of the past; that usage is emphasized in this exercise.

◇ WORKBOOK PRACTICE 3, p. 84. *Expressing ability.* (Chart 5-2)

Controlled completion. [Selfstudy]
Some of the vocabulary may be difficult in this practice. You might want to take a few minutes to answer questions in class.
As a follow-up activity, conduct an oral (books closed) exercise using some of the information in this practice. Ask leading questions: *What can a giraffe do that a zebra can't? How many mice can a single cat kill in a year? What animals can crush small trees under their huge feet? How long can a camel survive without water?* As an alternative, ask broader questions that the students can answer either from the information in this practice or from their own store of knowledge: *What can a giraffe do? What can a cat do?* Etc.

ANSWERS: **1.** zebra **2.** cat **3.** Elephants **4.** Monkeys **5.** camels **6.** cow **7.** horse **8.** donkey **9.** squirrel **10.** ants

◇ WORKBOOK PRACTICE 4, p. 85. *Expressing ability. (Chart 5-2)*

Oral and written. [Guided Study]

Pair up the students and let them talk to each other. One of the purposes of this practice is to provide relaxed time for directed conversation. The end result should be seven written sentences from each student containing the target structure. Of course, you don't need to follow the directions in the book. You can simply lead a general discussion with your class based on the given items.

Note on item 6: You might want to bring a deck of cards to class in case any of your students can perform card tricks. You might want to initiate a cross-cultural discussion of card-playing and see if there is any interest among your class.

Note on item 8: Students should take a piece of paper and fold it in half as many times as they can. In the author's experience, six is the maximum number with regular paper, while seven folds are possible with very thin tissue paper.

Note on item 9: As a follow-up activity, each student could try to draw a picture of another student, then the rest of the class could try to identify the subject of the portrait. Friendly conclusions may be drawn about who can and can't draw well.

◇ WORKBOOK PRACTICE 5, p. 85. *Expressing past ability. (Chart 5-2)*

Open completion. [Guided Study]

SAMPLE RESPONSES: **1.** couldn't walk **2.** could play with my friends all day long in the summer **3.** could ride a bike **4.** could run a marathon **5.** Last year I couldn't speak English very well

---

CHART 5-3: EXPRESSING POSSIBILITY: *MAY* AND *MIGHT*
EXPRESSING PERMISSION: *MAY* AND *CAN*

- Perhaps compare *may/might* to *will: It will rain tomorrow* = the speaker is as close as possible to being 100% certain. *It may/might rain tomorrow* = the speaker gives it a 50-50 chance.

- The difference between the adverb *maybe* and the verb *may be* should be clarified for the class through several additional examples. Emphasize that the adverb *maybe* usually comes at the beginning of a sentence, while the verb *may be* comes in the main verb position following a subject.

- Make it clear that **two** meanings of *may* are being presented in this chart: possibility and permission. Listeners can ascertain the meaning from the speaking context.

- *Can* is regularly and correctly used to ask for and give permission, and it has been used that way for centuries. Using *may* for permission, however, communicates a certain tone of propriety and formality that may be absent from *can*.

- The negative contractions for *may* and *might* are *mayn't* and *mightn't*. They are rarely used.

□ EXERCISE 5, p. 98. *MAY, MIGHT, MAYBE.* (Chart 5-3)

> *Oral (books closed).*
> Include *will* and *be going to* in the discussion to distinguish between degrees of certainty. For example, compare *I will/am going to go downtown* to *I may/might go downtown.*

□ EXERCISE 6, p. 99. *Expressing possibility.* (Chart 5-3)

> *Oral; open completion.*
> This situational-use exercise can be done in pairs or groups. Tell the students to use their imaginations. Many students are comfortable doing role-playing in hypothetical situations and benefit from this type of practice. Some students, however, may be reluctant to engage in pretending or playacting. Learning styles differ.
> In some of the student responses in this exercise, appropriate use of *could* for possibility (see next chart) might naturally occur and should be encouraged.

◇ WORKBOOK PRACTICE 6, p. 86. *Expressing ability and possibility.* (Charts 5-2 and 5-3)

> *Controlled completion.* [Selfstudy]
>
> ANSWERS: **1.** can . . . can't   **2.** may   **3.** can   **4.** may . . . may not   **5.** may   **6.** may   **7.** can't   **8.** may   **9.** might . . . might not   **10.** can . . . can't   **11.** might   **12.** can . . . might . . . might not   **13.** can't . . . Can . . . might

---

CHART 5-4: USING *COULD* TO EXPRESS POSSIBILITY

• *Could* is a complex modal with several meanings and many nuances. Questions that students may ask about *could* are not as easy to answer as the charts may make it seem. Sometimes *could* is interchangeable with *may/might* for possibility, and sometimes it's not. The text seeks to minimize confusion by presenting *could* separately from *may/might*.

It should be noted that *could* to express possibility is not appropriate in many of the items in Exercises 5 and 6. The use of *could* in many of those situations implies the idea of conditional possibility. Compare: *I may go downtown* = maybe I will and maybe I won't.   *I could go downtown* = an *if*-clause may be implied: *I could go downtown if I wanted to.* In Exercise 7, however, *could* is presented as interchangeable with *may/might*. The text very simply is seeking to make information about *could* manageable for students at this level and provide practice in typical usage situations.

• When *could* is used in the negative to express possibility, it takes on the meaning of "99% impossible." For example: *That could be true.* = Maybe it is true and maybe it isn't.   *That couldn't be true!* = I think it is impossible for that to be true. (Compare: The speaker would say *That isn't true* to express 100% certainty about impossibility.)

The use of *couldn't* to express impossibility is presented not in this text but in *Understanding and Using English Grammar*, Chart 2-14.

□ EXERCISE 7, p. 98. *Expressing possibility.* (Charts 5-3 and 5-4)

> *Oral (books closed).*
> Adapt the entries to your style of speaking and make a game out of this exercise. You could set this up as a team game with points for the greatest number of logical guesses and a bonus for the correct answer. Correct grammar should be required. Give extra clues as necessary so

students can, without too much frustration, figure out what you're thinking about. It is hoped that *could* occurs frequently and naturally to express possibilities.

◇ WORKBOOK PRACTICE 7, p. 87. *Meanings of COULD. (Charts 5-2 → 5-4)*

Controlled completion. [Selfstudy]
The purpose of this exercise is to distinguish between two meanings of *could* by relying on context. It should be noted that a context in which grammar is presented does not need to be long and involved. The dictum to teach "grammar in context" does not necessitate connected discourse in long paragraphs or dialogues. Indeed, clear but brief contexts often enhance students' ability to understand and learn aspects of English by allowing them to focus on particular forms and meanings without distraction. Concentrating on smaller contexts is an efficient language-learning device that leads to increased understanding and usage ability in larger contexts.

ANSWERS: **1.** A   **2.** B   **3.** B [A *mall* is AmE and designates an area where many shops are clustered together.]   **4.** B   **5.** B   **6.** A   **7.** B   **8.** A [The illustration demonstrates the meaning of "to jump rope."]

◇ WORKBOOK PRACTICE 8, p. 87. *Expressing possibility. (Chart 5-4)*

Oral. [Guided Study]
Elicit several responses for each. This exercise could be done in small groups with the leaders reporting their groups' ideas to the rest of the class.
    EXPANSION: Include *should* in the discussion to compare expressing possibilities *(could)* with expressing advice *(should)*. *Should* is introduced in Chart 5-7.

SAMPLE RESPONSES: **1.** Nancy could borrow an umbrella from a friend. She could take the bus home. She could ask someone at school for a ride. She could go shopping in a nearby mall. **2.** Ann and Carmen could clean the snow off the tennis court. They could go to a gym to get their exercise. They could take a long walk. They could make a date to play tennis another day. **3.** Sam could ask a friend who knows Japanese to translate the instructions for him. He could take the camera back to the shop and ask the owner how to operate the camera. He could ask someone who has a similar camera how to operate it. He could return the camera and buy a different one. He could try to operate the camera without any instruction. **4.** Tomorrow, Dennis could go to his country's consulate and ask for advice. He could cable his family or a friend for money. He could ask a stranger for help. He could go to a youth hostel and work for room and board. He could sleep in a park.

◇ WORKBOOK PRACTICE 9, p. 88. *Expressing possibility. (Charts 5-2 → 5-4)*

Open completion. [Guided Study]

SAMPLE RESPONSES: **1.** Tonight I could go to the theater. Or I might go across town to visit my friends. Of course, I may go to a dance with my cousin. But I'll probably stay home and watch TV because I'm tired. **2.** Next year, I might go home and get a job. But I could go to California and surf. I may go to Singapore and live with my cousin. But I'll probably stay here and finish my studies. **3.** My friend Talal may visit me this weekend, but I'm not sure. He might visit his brother. He could also simply decide to stay home. But he'll probably come to visit me. **4.** One hundred years from now, people may have mini-helicopters instead of cars. They may fly rather than drive to work. Cars could be obsolete in a hundred years. But cars will probably still be more common than personal helicopters.

CHART 5-5: ASKING FOR PERMISSION: *MAY I,*
** *COULD I, CAN I***

• Modal auxiliaries allow the speaker to show politeness. Discuss the difference between *Give me your pen* vs. *May I please borrow your pen?*   *Give me your pen* may sound aggressive and could imply that the speaker feels s/he is superior to or has authority over the listener. The use of modals allows the speaker to show respect for the listener.

• Compare the meanings of *could* that the text presents.

>   I **could** *run fast when I was younger.* = past ability (Chart 5-2)
>   **Could** *I help you?* = polite question (Charts 5-5 and 5-6)
>   *It* **could** *start raining any minute.* = possibility (Chart 5-4)

• As in the note in this *Teacher's Guide* for Chart 5-2, the use of *can* to request permission is common and acceptable. The use of *can* instead of *may* does, however, signal a subtle difference in the relationship between the speaker and the listener: *can* may signal familiarity and equality; *may* keeps a polite distance. *Can* is less formal than *may.*

☐ EXERCISE 8, p. 101. *Polite questions. (Chart 5-5)*

> *Semi-controlled completion.*
> You might want to take the role of "A," the person who answers the phone. Then, after discussing the exercise in class, set up additional telephone role-plays. For example: Assign Student A to place a call to Student B but talk to Student C (Student B's roommate). Or tell Student A to call a school office for certain information and have Student B play the role of the school's secretary, who must look up the information and call back later. Etc.
>
> *ANSWERS:*   **1.** May/Could I speak [possibly too informal: Can I talk?]   **2.** May/Could I speak [too informal: Can I speak?]   **3.** Can I talk [also possible: May/Could I talk/speak?]   **4.** May/Could/Can I help   **5.** May/Could/Can I speak . . . May/Could I take   **6.** May/Could/Can I speak . . . May/Could I leave   **7.** May/Could/Can I speak

☐ EXERCISE 9, p. 102. *Polite questions. (Chart 5-5)*

> *Oral (books closed).*
> Pair up students and have them practice asking polite questions, or lead the discussion yourself and encourage a variety of responses.

CHART 5-6: ASKING FOR ASSISTANCE: *WOULD YOU,*
** *COULD YOU, WILL YOU, CAN YOU***

• The use of *may* with this pattern is an occasional problem, as noted in the chart.

• If you want to assign "degrees of politeness," *would* and *could* could be called the politest. *Will* is possibly a little less polite in the sense of less obsequious.   And *can* loses a slight degree of politeness by signaling familiarity rather than respectful distance.   For the students' purposes, however, any of these modals will allow them to show appropriate politeness when making a request as compared to using an imperative such as *Open the door.*

• Even polite modals can be made threatening or angry by the speaker's tone of voice.

☐ EXERCISE 10, p.103. *Polite questions.* (Chart 5-6)

> *Semi-controlled completion.*
> Students could work in pairs or groups to complete the dialogues and then share them with the rest of the class during later discussion.

> *POSSIBLE RESPONSES:*   **2.** A: Would/Could/Will/Can you answer the phone for me?   B: Sure. A: Thanks.   **3.** Would/Could/Will/Can you turn it down?   **4.** Would/Could/Will/Can you please turn the volume up?   **5.** Would/Could/Will/Can you please pick some up? **6.** Would/Could/Will/Can you please get the door for me?   **7.** Would/Could/Will/Can you please say that again?   [*Walabaxitinpundoozit* is intended to represent an incomprehensible utterance.]

☐ EXERCISE 11, p. 104. *Polite questions.* (Charts 5-5 and 5-6)

> *Oral (books closed); pair or group work.*
> In item 3, a noun clause might naturally occur: *Could you please tell me* **what time it is**? Students may have difficulty with the word order (e.g., INCORRECT: *Could you please tell me what time is it?*). Word order in noun clauses is discussed in Chapter 14.

◇ WORKBOOK PRACTICE 10, p. 88. *Polite questions.* (Charts 5-5 and 5-6)

> *Controlled completion.* [Selfstudy]

> *ANSWERS:*   **1.** Can   **2.** may   **3.** Would   **4.** could [*What's up?* = *What's happening?* In this instance, it means "What do you need to talk to me about? What is happening that you want to talk about?"]   **5.** Can   **6.** A: Could   B: May   **7.** A: Can   B: Will   **8.** Could

◇ WORKBOOK PRACTICE 11, p. 89. *Polite questions.* (Charts 5-5 and 5-6)

> *Dialogue construction.* [Guided Study]
> Students could work in pairs. Their written dialogues could be performed for the rest of the class.

CHART 5-7: EXPRESSING ADVICE: *SHOULD,*
        OUGHT TO, HAD BETTER

• When advice is given with these modal expressions, they indicate that results which are usually implied rather than stated will occur if a certain course of action is taken. These results may be good or bad.

• Your students may wonder about distinctions between the three modal expressions in this chart. *Had better* is a little stronger than *should* and *ought to*. In the negative, *had better not* usually communicates a threat of bad results, and the affirmative *had better* may also imply a warning that is not conveyed by *should* and *ought to*. In the exercises, no real distinction is made between the three modal expressions, as *had better* is also frequently used simply to give friendly advice among peers. *Had better* is not used to give advice to a superior, but *should* and *ought to* can maintain a polite enough distance to allow for such. For example, one might say to one's boss, "I think you should consider Mr. Loo for that project." One would not say to one's boss, "I think you'd better consider Mr. Loo for that project."

• *Ought to* is often pronounced /ədə/ or /atə/.

• *Should* can also be used to express expectations. (For example: *Mary left at ten. She should arrive by ten-thirty.*) This usage is not introduced in this text. See *Understanding and Using English Grammar,* Chart 2-16.

☐ EXERCISE 12, p. 105. *Expressing advice: SHOULDN'T. (Chart 5-7)*

Controlled and/or open completion.
Discuss the possible results the speaker is implying by using *shouldn't*. The purpose of this exercise is to discuss the notion of advisability. Encourage open completions too.

ANSWERS: **2.** shouldn't smoke. **3.** shouldn't exceed the speed limit. **4.** shouldn't give too much homework. **5.** shouldn't miss any classes. **6.** shouldn't be cruel to animals. **7.** shouldn't be late for . . . . **8.** shouldn't throw trash out . . . .

☐ EXERCISE 13, p. 106. *Expressing advice. (Chart 5-7)*

Controlled and/or open completion.
Students can work these out in pairs or as homework. In class discussion, encourage original completions in addition to covering the ones suggested in the text.

ANSWERS: **2.** You ought to drink a glass of water. OR You should hold your breath. **3.** He ought to speak English outside of class every day. **4.** You ought to get a job. OR You had better borrow some money. OR You should marry someone who is rich. **5.** You should call the police. **6.** You ought to soak it in cold water. **7.** Tom had better use a dictionary when he writes. **8.** Ann had better take it back to the store. **9.** You should/ought to call the landlord and complain. **10.** You should send her a dozen roses. OR You had better find a new girlfriend. **11.** You ought to go back to the restaurant and . . . . **12.** You ought to put cotton in your ears.

☐ EXERCISE 14, p. 107. *Expressing advice. (Chart 5-7)*

Oral; group work.
Divide the class into groups. Appoint the leaders. Tell each member of a group to present a problem for the others to give advice on. It is hoped that the students will get into meaningful conversations that share actual problems they are having. But if not, they will still get some good conversation practice.

◇ WORKBOOK PRACTICE 12, p. 89. *Expressing advice. (Chart 5-7)*

Controlled completion; multiple choice. [Selfstudy]
This practice is directed almost solely to form. Its purpose is to make the students look closely at the differences in form among modals that have a similar or same meaning.

ANSWERS: **1.** A **2.** C **3.** B **4.** A **5.** B **6.** C **7.** A **8.** C **9.** B **10.** C

◇ WORKBOOK PRACTICE 13, p. 90. *Expressing advice. (Chart 5-7)*

Open completion. [Guided Study]
Lead the discussion yourself and elicit several suggestions for each item. Alternatively, students could work in groups. Ask them to discuss several suggestions for each situation and then decide what would be their "best advice." Leaders could later share this advice with the rest of the class.

CHART 5-8: EXPRESSING NECESSITY: *HAVE TO,*
            HAVE GOT TO, MUST

• *Must* generally carries a forceful meaning, often too forceful to use in everyday conversation about everyday affairs. *Have to* and *have got to* are usually employed to convey the notion of necessity. The text emphasizes the use of *have to* and *have got to* to express necessity.

• Model the usual pronunciation of *have to* and *have got to* and let the students experiment producing it, but don't insist that they use the contracted forms. Contracted speech develops as the students become aware of it and gain experience with English.

☐ EXERCISE 15, p. 108. *Expressing necessity. (Chart 5-8)*

> *Open completion.*
> This is an exercise on form and meaning. The students need to pay attention to form—singular vs. plural and present/future vs. past—and create meaningful completions.
>
> *PARTIAL ANSWERS:*   **2.** I have to   **3.** I had to   **4.** he has to   **5.** I had to   **6.** you have to   **7.** I had to   **8.** she has to   **9.** I have to   **10.** I had to   **11.** you have to   **12.** we had to   **13.** but I had to

☐ EXERCISE 16, p. 109. *Expressing necessity and advice. (Charts 5-7 and 5-8)*

> *Oral (books closed).*
> The intention in this exercise is to give the students some oral practice and provide opportunities for questions and discussion about the target structures.
>   In item 3, a fine distinction does not need to be drawn between *should* and *must*. Sometimes the meanings of *should* and *must* can shade into each other. Either can be used in a given situation depending upon the speaker's depth of conviction. Keep the distinction broad: *should* = it's a good idea; *must* = it's necessary.

◊ WORKBOOK PRACTICE 14, p. 90. *Expressing necessity. (Chart 5-8)*

> *Controlled completion.* [Selfstudy]
> *ANSWERS:*   **1.** C   **2.** A   **3.** D   **4.** C   **5.** B   **6.** A   **7.** D   **8.** C

◊ WORKBOOK PRACTICE 15, p. 91. *Expressing necessity. (Chart 5-8)*

> *Combination.* [Guided Study]
> The emphasis in this practice is on understanding the form and meaning of the target structures by understanding the reasons why a speaker would choose these verbs in the given situations.

CHART 5-9:	EXPRESSING LACK OF NECESSITY: *DO NOT HAVE TO*
	EXPRESSING PROHIBITION: *MUST NOT*

• Use gestures and tone of voice to reinforce the distinction between these two forms. For *do not have to,* shrug your shoulders and look nonchalant. For *must not,* use facial expressions and gestures that show sternness. For example, English speakers often shake their head from side to side or shake their index finger up and down (mostly to small children) to gesture *must not.*

☐ EXERCISE 17, p. 110. *Lack of necessity and prohibition. (Chart 5-9)*

Controlled completion.
This exercise is for clarification of the differences in meaning presented in Chart 5-9. The meaning of each item should be restated in terms of lack of necessity and prohibition. For example, item 1 means "do not eat the soup" as compared to item 2, which means "it's not necessary to eat soup."

ANSWERS:　　**3.** doesn't have to　　**4.** must not　　**5.** doesn't have to　　**6.** must not
7. must not [*Trip* = impede the legs and cause to fall.]　　**8.** don't have to　　**9.** don't have to
10. must not　　**11.** don't have to　　**12.** must not　　**13.** must not　　**14.** don't have to
15. must not　　**16.** must not　　**17.** don't have to　　**18.** must not . . . don't have to . . . must not

◇ WORKBOOK PRACTICE 16, p. 91.　　*Expressing necessity and prohibition. (Charts 5-8 and 5-9)*

Controlled completion. [Selfstudy]

ANSWERS:　　**1.** must not　　**2.** don't have to　　**3.** must not　　**4.** don't have to
5. don't have to　　**6.** must not　　**7.** don't have to　　**8.** must not　　**9.** must not
10. don't have to

◇ WORKBOOK PRACTICE 17, p. 92. *Expressing necessity and prohibition. (Charts 5-8 and 5-9)*

Controlled completion. [Selfstudy]

ANSWERS:　　**1.** have to/must　　**2.** doesn't have to　　**3.** don't have to　　**4.** must not
5. has to/must　　**6.** doesn't have to　　**7.** has to/must　　**8.** must not

◇ WORKBOOK PRACTICE 18, p. 92. *Expressing advice and necessity. (Charts 5-7 → 5-9)*

Oral. [Guided Study]
Students could work in groups.

SAMPLE RESPONSES:　　**1.** Sara shouldn't drive her brother's car. She might get in trouble with the police if she tries to drive. She had better think about the consequences. She might call her friend for a ride. She could walk there if it isn't too far. She ought to call her friend and talk on the phone instead of driving to her house. **2.** Steve had better decide what his priorities are. He could take an art history course now, but he has got to take the required chemistry course sometime. He ought to see if he can find a better chemistry teacher. He should consider changing his major. He might prefer a liberal arts major. **3.** Matt and Amy should wait until they're older to get married. They should get to know each other better. Matt ought to have a job before they marry. They could be making a big mistake getting married now. They had better get an education so that they can find good jobs. They might be happy now, but it won't last if they have a lot of money problems.   **4.** Kate should excuse herself from the meeting and call her friend.   She might reschedule their dinner for another night. She could suggest that they meet later at a restaurant instead of her house.   Kate ought to do her grocery shopping early when she plans to have company for dinner.   Kate had better decide what to do soon.   **5.** Parents should/shouldn't let their children choose their own friends. Frog and Rabbit should continue to be friends/should respect their parents' wishes and end their friendship. Frog and Rabbit should try to talk with their parents about their friendship. They could suggest that the two families meet to get to know one another. Parents shouldn't teach their children to be prejudiced. People shouldn't judge other people by their appearance.

◇ WORKBOOK PRACTICE 19, p. 93. *Expressing advice and necessity. (Charts 5-7 → 5-9)*

    Oral/written. [Guided Study]
    This is a good practice for group discussion. Together, the group could prepare written advice. You might want to ask them to underline the modals they use.

CHART 5-10: MAKING LOGICAL CONCLUSIONS: *MUST*

- Compare: *She must be sleepy* = the speaker is 95%-99% sure.
            She is sleepy = the speaker is 100% sure.

- Point out that this chart has three different meanings of *must:* logical conclusion, necessity, and prohibition.

☐ EXERCISE 18, p. 112. *Making logical conclusions. (Chart 5-10)*

    Controlled completion.
    All the completions include *must.* The students need to decide whether the completions should be negative or affirmative.

    ANSWERS: **3.** must have a cold.   **4.** must not feel well.   **5.** must be hungry.
    6. must be very wise.   **7.** must not have a lot of . . . . must be busy all . . . .   **8.** He must like movies a lot. He must not spend . . . .   **9.** must love books. She must like books . . . .
    10. She must not want to . . . She must be tired. She must not want to . . . .   **11.** must not know the answer. He must be embarrassed.   **12.** must be upset. She must want to be alone. She must not want to talk . . . . She must like . . . .   **13.** must be smart birds.

◇ WORKBOOK PRACTICE 20, p. 94. *Making logical conclusions. (Chart 5-10)*

    Controlled completion. [Selfstudy]

    ANSWERS: **1.** must   **2.** must not   **3.** must   **4.** must   **5.** must not   **6.** must not   **7.** must [*Must be doing* = the progressive form of modal auxiliaries. Progressive modals are not presented in a chart in *Fundamentals of English Grammar.* See *Understanding and Using English Grammar,* Chart 2-17.]

◇ WORKBOOK PRACTICE 21, p. 95. *Making logical conclusions. (Chart 5-10)*

> *Sentence construction.* [Guided Study]
> Students could do this in pairs as seatwork.
>
> *POSSIBLE RESPONSES:* **1.** She must be happy. **2.** He must have a cold. **3.** He must be married. [In many cultures, a gold band or diamond ring on the fourth finger of the left hand signifies marriage.] **4.** He must be cold. **5.** His house/apartment must have mice. **6.** She must have a computer. **7.** He must be hot. **8.** He must dislike doing homework. **9.** She must like to watch movies. **10.** She must be a good student. **11.** He must be very strong.

CHART 5-11: GIVING INSTRUCTIONS:
IMPERATIVE SENTENCES

- Discuss the form of imperative sentences. Explain the concept of the "understood *you*" as the subject of an imperative verb, with *you* being the listener(s). For example, in

   (a): *Open the door! = You,* (i.e., the soldier the speaker is addressing) *open the door!*

- The addition of *please* and a pleasant tone of voice can make an imperative sentence quite polite, as in *Please open the door.* When making a polite request, however, the students can be assured of a high level of politeness if they use *would* or *could* (e.g., *Could you please open the door?*). *Please open the door* in the wrong tone of voice can seem unfriendly or haughty.

- Demonstrate varying tones of voice that can be used with imperative sentences, from barking out an order to requesting politely.

☐ EXERCISE 19, p. 114. *Using imperative sentences. (Chart 5-11)*

> *Open completion.*
> It is assumed that students are familiar with imperative sentences. This exercise allows them to explore what one person might say to another using an imperative sentence and how the second person might respond.
> During class discussion, elicit several possible completions for each item.

☐ EXERCISE 20, p. 115. *Using imperative sentences. (Chart 5-11)*

> *Oral.*
> Even though the students are using imperative sentences, they should not be using an authoritarian tone of voice. The imperative sentences should be said pleasantly, as though the students are giving each other directions in a game.
> This exercise can be done in groups or as a class.

☐ EXERCISE 21, p. 115. *Cumulative review. (Chapter 5)*

> *Written.*
> Any one of these topics could become a full-length composition of 500 words or so. Or you could ask the students to write only a paragraph of 75-100 words. Using one of the topics in item 1, you might write a practice composition on the board, copying down what the students tell you to write. It is hoped that many modal expressions will occur naturally with these topics.

Item 3 is not appropriate for some cultural groups, but young people from other cultures have fun with the topic. You might take this opportunity for a brief cross-cultural discussion of dating and courtship.

◇ WORKBOOK PRACTICE 22, p. 95. *Imperative sentences. (Chart 5-11)*

Structure identification. [Selfstudy]

ANSWERS: **1.** <u>Wait</u>   **2.** <u>Don't wait</u>   **3.** <u>Read</u>   **4.** <u>Don't put</u>   **5.** <u>Come in</u> . . . <u>have</u>   **6.** <u>Don't cross</u>   **7.** <u>Don't</u> . . . <u>stand</u> . . . <u>Do</u>   **8.** <u>Call</u>   **9.** <u>Take</u> . . . <u>Go</u> . . . <u>Walk</u> . . . <u>give</u>   **10.** <u>Capitalize</u> . . . <u>Put</u> . . . <u>use</u>

◇ WORKBOOK PRACTICE 23, p. 96. *Imperative sentences. (Chart 5-11)*

Structure identification. [Guided Study]
Students should be encouraged to solve the number puzzle in item 1. For item 2, you may want to take a little time to talk about stress in the students' lives and how they handle it.

ANSWERS: **1.** <u>Write</u> . . . <u>write</u> . . . <u>Write</u> . . . <u>Double</u> . . . <u>Add</u> . . . <u>Multiply</u> . . . <u>Add</u> . . . <u>Subtract</u> . . . <u>Try</u>   **2.** <u>Get</u> . . . <u>Manage</u> . . . <u>Don't overload</u> . . . <u>Take</u> . . . <u>Learn</u> . . . <u>Read</u>, <u>reflect</u>, <u>listen</u> . . . <u>do</u> . . . <u>Don't waste</u> . . . <u>Recognize</u> . . . <u>accept</u>

CHART 5-12:   MAKING SUGGESTIONS: *LET'S* AND
WHY DON'T

• Relate *let's* and *why don't* to *should*. In (a) and (b), the speaker is saying "We should go to the beach. Going to the beach is a good idea."

• The speaker isn't using *why* to ask for a reason. The listener would not respond to these questions by giving a reason. *Why don't* is an idiomatic use of *why*.

☐ EXERCISE 22, p. 116. *LET'S, WHY DON'T WE. (Chart 5-12)*

Open completion.
Suggestion: Have students work in pairs prior to class discussion. Then for each item, ask several pairs to say their dialogues without looking at their texts.

☐ EXERCISE 23, p. 117. *WHY DON'T YOU. (Chart 5-12)*

Oral.
Elicit a couple of responses for each item during class discussion.

☐ EXERCISE 24, p. 118. *Directions and suggestions with IF-clauses. (Chart 5-12)*

Combination.
This exercise covers suggestions and requests while reviewing the use of the simple present in *if*-clauses.
   ERRATUM: In the original printing, the combined sentence for item 10 doesn't fit with the rest of the grammar in this exercise. It somehow sneaked in despite the author's vigilence. In the completed sentence "If you're hungry, I'd be happy to make a sandwich for you," *would* is used to make a polite offer. It is similar to the use of *would* to make a polite request. Later printings have the following completion for item 10: *If you're hungry, I could make a sandwich for you.*

ANSWERS:
1. If you need . . . , (8) please call me.
2. If the weather is . . . , (10) let's go sailing.
3. If you have a . . . , (2) you should . . . .
4. If I'm not at . . . , (4) wait for me . . . .
5. If Matt wants to . . . , (7) he should . . . .
6. If you are tired, (3) why don't . . . .
7. If Sara doesn't get . . . , (9) she should . . . .
8. If you don't know . . . , (1) guess.
9. If Alice calls . . . , (5) please take . . . .
10. If you're hungry, (6) I'd be happy to . . . [Later printings: I could make . . . .]

◇ WORKBOOK PRACTICE 24, p. 96. *LET'S and WHY DON'T.* *(Chart 5-12)*

Semi-controlled completion. [Selfstudy]

ANSWERS: **1.** A: go . . . fly B: see **2.** B: get A: take **3.** A: go B: play
4. A: take B: take . . . save **5.** A: stop . . . fill up B: pick up/get **6.** A: go
A: call . . . see

◇ WORKBOOK PRACTICE 25, p. 97. *WHY DON'T YOU.* *(Chart 5-12)*

Oral. [Guided Study]
This practice is suitable for group work.

SAMPLE RESPONSES: **1.** Why don't you invite (Ali and Pedro) over for dinner? Why don't you go to the new jazz club? **2.** Why don't you join a fitness club? Why don't you take a long walk every day? Why don't you ride your bike more often? **3.** Why don't you wear a belt? Why don't you wear suspenders? [BrE: braces] Why don't you buy smaller pants? Why don't you tie a rope around your waist? **4.** Why don't you ask Professor Black if you can turn it in tomorrow? Why don't you cut class? **5.** Why don't you call the apartment manager and ask him/her to let you in? Why don't you go to dinner and a movie until your roommate gets home? Why don't you spend the evening with a friend? **6.** Why don't you call your friend and discuss the problem? Why don't you write your friend a letter to explain how you feel? **7.** Why don't you join an amateur sports team? Why don't you take a short vacation? Why don't you join a hiking club? **8.** Why don't you spend time outside the classroom with English-speaking friends? Why don't you go to English-speaking movies? Why don't you try reading newspapers and magazines written in English?

• The forms of these patterns need special attention when the chart is presented in class. Elicit additional examples from the class and write them on the chalkboard, pointing out the characteristics of each pattern.

• *Would rather* may be new to some students. Perhaps do a chain exercise to introduce the pattern orally:

TEACHER:	*What would you rather do than study?*
STUDENT A:	*I'd rather watch TV than study.*
TEACHER:	*What would you rather do than watch TV?*
STUDENT B:	*I'd rather read a book than watch TV.*
TEACHER:	*What would you rather do than read a book?*
STUDENT C:	*Etc.*

• The "-ING VERB" referred to in the explanation in this chart is a gerund. It is also possible to use an infinitive after *like;* the text chose to present only the gerund pattern here. Using an infinitive with *like . . . better than* can lead to awkward sentences that a native speaker would be likely to avoid.

☐ EXERCISE 25, p. 119. *Stating preferences: THAN vs. TO. (Chart 5-13)*

Controlled completion.
This is an exercise on the form of the expressions introduced in Chart 5-13.

ANSWERS: **4.** to **5.** than **6.** than **7.** to **8.** than **9.** than **10.** than **11.** to **12.** than **13.** than **14.** than **15.** to **16.** to **17.** than **18.** than

☐ EXERCISE 26, p. 120. *Stating preferences. (Chart 5-13)*

Oral (books closed), teacher-led, group work or pair work.

☐ EXERCISE 27, p. 121. *WOULD RATHER . . . THAN.*

Oral (books closed), teacher-led, group work or pair work.

☐ EXERCISE 28, p. 122. *Stating preferences. (Chart 5-13)*

Open completion.
Suggestion: Have students do seatwork in pairs prior to class discussion. Then for each item, ask several pairs to present their dialogues. Ask them not to read them but to speak after only a quick glance at the text.

◊ WORKBOOK PRACTICE 26, p. 98. *Stating preferences. (Chart 5-13)*

Controlled completion. [Selfstudy]

ANSWERS: **1.** prefer **2.** like **3.** would rather **4.** prefer **5.** would rather **6.** A: prefer B: likes B: would rather **7.** would rather **8.** would rather **9.** B: prefer A: like **10.** prefer

◊ WORKBOOK PRACTICE 27, p. 98. *Stating preferences.* *(Chart 5-13)*

Transformation. [Guided Study]

ANSWERS: **1.** Kim prefers salad to dessert.   **2.** In general, Nicole likes coffee better than tea.   **3.** Bill would rather teach history than work as a business executive.   **4.** When considering a pet, Sam likes dogs better than cats.   **5.** On a long trip, Susie prefers driving to riding in the back seat.   **6.** I would rather study in a noisy room than (study) in a completely quiet room.   **7.** Alex would rather sing in a choir than play soccer.

◊ WORKBOOK PRACTICE 28, p. 99. *Cumulative review.* *(Charts 5-1 → 5-13)*

Controlled completion. [Selfstudy]

ANSWERS: **1.** A   **2.** C   **3.** A   **4.** A   ["What's up with Ken?" = "What's going on with Ken? What is happening in regard to Ken?" The speaker is asking for information about Ken.]   **5.** B   **6.** C [AmE = driver's license; BrE = driving licence.]   **7.** B   **8.** C   [*Iffy* = an adjective in informal usage meaning "full of doubts or questions."]   **9.** B   **10.** A   **11.** C [*Denim* = the fabric blue jeans are made from.]   **12.** A   **13.** B   **14.** C   **15.** B

◊ WORKBOOK PRACTICE 29, p. 100. *Cumulative review.* *(Charts 5-1 → 5-13)*

Controlled completion. [Guided Study]

ANSWERS: **1.** A   **2.** B   **3.** C   **4.** A   **5.** C   **6.** B   **7.** A   **8.** A   **9.** A   **10.** C   **11.** B   **12.** A   **13.** C   **14.** C   **15.** A

◊ WORKBOOK PRACTICE 30, p. 101. *Review of auxiliary verbs.* *(Chapters 1 → 5)*

Semi-controlled completion. [Guided Study]
This practice covers the auxiliary verbs presented from the beginning of the text through this chapter.

ANSWERS: **1.** May (Could/Can)   **2.** don't   **3.** Would   **4.** Is   **5.** Did   **6.** A: May/Could/Can   B: Would/Could/Can/Will   **7.** Would/Could/Can/Will . . . was   **8.** should/had better/ought to   **9.** A: are   B: am [The speaker would probably stress *am* in this sentence.]   **10.** had better/must/has to/has got to   **11.** Don't   **12.** A: are . . . Do   B: Would/Could/Can/Will   **13.** B: May/Could/Can   A: must   **14.** shouldn't/must not/can't   **15.** A: should/must/has to/ought to/had better/has got to   B: will not/cannot [also possible: may not/might not]

◊ WORKBOOK PRACTICE 31, p. 103. *Cumulative review.* *(Chapter 5)*

Controlled completion. [Guided Study]
Students should prepare this practice outside of class prior to discussion.   It was designed so that students do not have to make subtle distinctions between two choices, but the students must understand the context well to make the correct choices.

ANSWERS: **(1)** may . . . is . . . can . . . can   **(2)** should . . . can . . . should . . . should not . . . is . . . Will   **(3)** do not have to . . . do not have to . . . can   **(4)** have to . . . cannot . . . must . . . do . . . is . . . can . . . should   **(5)** ought to . . . prepare   **(6)** are . . . might . . . may . . . Maybe . . . could . . . is . . . are . . . should   **(7)** should . . . will . . . can change . . . should . . . should   **(8)** is . . . should

□ EXERCISE 29, p. 122. *Prepositions.* *(Chapter 5; Appendix 1)*

Controlled completion.

ANSWERS: **2.** to   **3.** for   **4.** for   **5.** of   **6.** for . . . for   **7.** for   **8.** to . . . from   **9.** to   **10.** about . . . in [*To be crazy about* = informal English meaning "to like very, very much."]   **11.** of   **12.** of

◊ WORKBOOK PRACTICE 32, p. 104. *Prepositions.* *(Chapter 5; Appendix 1)*

Controlled completion. [Selfstudy]

ANSWERS: **1.** A: with/to   B: about   **2.** for   **3.** to   **4.** of   **5.** A: in   B: for   **6.** to   **7.** of   **8.** for   **9.** of/about   **10.** for   **11.** of   **12.** for   **13.** from

Chapter 6: ASKING QUESTIONS

ORDER OF CHAPTER	CHARTS	EXERCISES	WORKBOOK
Yes/no and information questions (*where, when, what time, why*)	6-1 → 6-2	Ex. 1 → 7	Pr. 1 → 9
Who, who(m), and *what*	6-3	Ex. 8	Pr. 10 → 11
Cumulative review		Ex. 9 → 10	
What + a form of *do*	6-4	Ex. 11 → 12	Pr. 12 → 14
What kind of	6-5	Ex. 13 → 14	Pr. 15
Which	6-6	Ex. 15	Pr. 16
Whose	6-7	Ex. 16 → 18	Pr. 17
Cumulative review		Ex. 19	Pr. 18
How	6-8 → 6-12	Ex. 20 → 25	Pr. 19 → 21
Cumulative review		Ex. 26 → 27	
How continued	6-13	Ex. 28 → 30	Pr. 22
Cumulative review		Ex. 31	Pr. 23 → 26
How about and *what about*	6-14	Ex. 32 → 34	Pr. 27
Tag questions	6-15	Ex. 35 → 37	Pr. 28 → 30
Cumulative review			Pr. 31
Prepositions		Ex. 38	Pr. 32

General Notes on Chapter 6

• OBJECTIVE: Although questions were introduced in earlier chapters, this chapter summarizes those patterns, adds other types, and provides exercises to help students gain control of question words and forms.

• APPROACH: The chapter begins with a review of yes/no questions and short answers in various tenses. After a chart presents contrasts between yes/no questions and information questions, most of the chapter practices the latter type. Exercises on tag questions complete this chapter. Parts of this chapter could well be included or reviewed with other sections of the textbook; the teacher can decide if an alternative sequence is more useful for the learners.

• TERMINOLOGY: Information questions are also called WH-questions because they use the words *who, which, when, where,* and *how.* This chapter generally uses the term "helping verb" for an auxiliary, to distinguish it from the "main verb" in a sentence or clause.

CHART 6-1: YES/NO QUESTIONS AND SHORT ANSWERS

- Remind the students of the names of the tenses for the first three examples: (a) simple present [discuss the use of *does* also], (b) simple past, and (c) present progressive. This chart, like the rest of this chapter, contains only the tenses and modals presented through Chapter 5.

- The forms of yes/no questions and short answers were presented in earlier chapters. This is a summary review chart.

- Model the spoken form of the short answers. The emphasis on the auxiliary verb *(Yes, I **do**)* except in the negative answer in (c), where the emphasis is on *not (No, I'm **not**)*. If a negative contraction is not used in a short answer, the emphasis is placed on *not* rather than the verb *(No, I do **not**)*.

- "Uh huh" is meant to represent the voiced but unspoken sound that signals *yes*, and "huh uh" is meant to represent the sound for *no*.

- The presentation pattern in this chart of *question + short answer + (long answer)* is used in the exercises on form in this chapter.

☐ EXERCISE 1, p. 125. *Yes/no questions and short answers. (Chart 6-1)*

Transformation.
This is an exercise on the form of yes/no questions and short answers. It can be done as seatwork or in pairs.

ANSWERS: **2.** A: Does Jane eat lunch at the cafeteria every day? B: she does.
3. A: Does this/that pen belong to you? B: it doesn't. **4.** A: Do the students in this class speak English well? B: they do. **5.** A: Did you sleep well last night? B: I did.
6. A: Did Ann and Jim come to class yesterday? B: they didn't. **7.** A: Are you studying your grammar book? B: I am. **8.** A: Are the children watching TV?
B: they aren't/they're not. **9.** A: Is Tim Wilson in your astronomy class? B: he is.
10. A: Was it foggy yesterday? B: it wasn't. **11.** A: Will you be home tonight?
B: I won't. **12.** A: Is Jason going to be at work tomorrow? B: he isn't/he's not.
13. A: Will Karen finish her work before she goes to bed? B: she will. **14.** A: Can you play the piano? B: I can't. **15.** A: Can some birds swim under water? B: they can.
16. A: Should I make an appointment to see the doctor? B: you should.
17. A: Do I need to make ... B: you do. **18.** A: Do you have a bicycle? [also possible: Have you a bicycle?] B: I do. **19.** A: Does Greg have a roommate? [also possible: Has Greg a roommate?] B: he doesn't. **20.** A: Do you have to study tonight? B: I do.

☐ EXERCISE 2, p. 126. *Yes/no questions and short answers. (Chart 6-1)*

Oral (books closed).
Students can handle this exercise by themselves in small groups if time is available. Otherwise, it can be a quick teacher-led review of the forms of the target structures. Students should give truthful answers.
   Note on item 19: Giraffes are vegetarians.

☐ EXERCISE 3, p. 127. *Yes/no questions and short answers. (Chart 6-1)*

> *Oral (books closed), pair work.*
> Students can practice yes/no questions and short answers in pairs. They can alternate being questioner and responder or switch roles after the first 10 items.
> > Item 17: *Indexes* is the more common plural of *index* rather than the equally correct *indices*.

CHART 6-2: YES/NO QUESTIONS AND INFORMATION QUESTIONS

- One purpose of this chart is to relate the form of yes/no questions to the form of information questions so that the students can see the overall pattern in English. Make sure the students understand that the inverted subject-verb form is the same in both kinds of questions—with the exception of examples (k) and (l), where the question word is the subject of the question.

- Write on the board the basic question pattern so students will have it as a reminder and reference throughout the discussion of this chapter:

(QUESTION WORD) + HELPING VERB + SUBJECT + MAIN VERB

☐ EXERCISE 4, p. 128. *Form of yes/no and information questions. (Chart 6-2)*

> *Boardwork.*
> Draw a chart on the chalkboard with the question pattern headings:

(QUESTION WORD) + HELPING VERB + SUBJECT + MAIN VERB + (REST OF SENTENCE)

1. (a)
   (b)

2. (a)
   (b)

3. (a)
   (b)

etc.

> Ask the students to fill in the chart by writing on the board. Have the students name the tenses or identify modals.
> > Alternatively, draw a chart on paper, copy it, and pass it out; have the students fill it in as seatwork. No students should go any further in this chapter until they thoroughly grasp the basic question patterns in Chart 6-2 [with the exception of the pattern in examples (k) and (l), which is dealt with in more depth in Chart 6-3].

ANSWERS: **1.** (a) Does she live there?   (b) Where does she live?   [simple present]
2. (a) Do the students live there?   (b) Where do the students live?   [simple present]
3. (a) Did Bob live?   (b) Where did Bob live?   [simple past]   **4.** (a) Are you living there?   (b) Where are you living?   [present progressive]   **5.** (a) Is Mary living there?
(b) Where is Mary living?   [present progressive]   **6.** (a) Were you living there?
(b) Where were you living?   [past progressive]   **7.** (a) Was he living there?
(b) Where was he living?   [past progressive]   **8.** (a) Are they going to live there?
(b) Where are they going to live?   [future: *be going to*]   **9.** (a) Will John live there?
(b) Where will John live?   [simple future; modal *will*]   **10.** (a) Can the students live there?
(b) Where can the students live?   [modal *can*]   **11.** (a) Should Alice live there?
(b) Where should   Alice live?   **12.** (a) Does Tom have to live there?   (b) Where does
Tom have to live?   [Note on the periphrastic modal *have to*: There were so many points to cover related to *have to* in Chapter 5 that question form was delayed until this chapter. The footnote presents this grammar for the first time in the text. The question form for *have to* may need some special attention in class. It will be presented more clearly in the next edition of the text.]

□ EXERCISE 5, p. 129. *Information questions. (Chart 6-2)*

Transformation.
The students have to look at the sentence in parentheses in order to know what question to ask.
Essentially they are transforming a statement to a question, but the dialogue form allows for a more natural-sounding sequence of *question + short answer + long answer.*
    Model normal contracted speech.

ANSWERS: **2.** Where did you /<u>wɛr</u>(d)ǰə/ eat lunch today?   **3.** What time did you
/<u>wətaym</u>(d)ǰə/   ["d+y" becomes one sound] / When did you /<u>wɛn</u>(d)ǰə/ eat lunch?   **4.** Why
do you /<u>wayd</u>əyə/ eat lunch at the cafeteria?   **5.** Where do your aunt /<u>wɛrd</u>əyərant/ and
uncle live?   **6.** When are you going to /<u>wɛn</u>əryəgənə/ visit your . . . ?   **7.** What time will
you /<u>wətaym</u>əlyə/ / When will you /<u>wɛn</u>əlyə/ get home tonight?   **8.** Where is George going to
/<u>wɛrz</u> ǰɔrǰ gənə/ study tonight?   **9.** Why does George /<u>wayd</u>əz ǰɔrǰ/ study . . . ?
10. Where can I /<u>wɛrk</u>ənay/ catch a bus?   **11.** What time / When do you have to leave?
/<u>wɛn</u>dəyə hæftr <u>liv</u>/   **12.** Where were you living /<u>wɛr</u>wəryə <u>lɪvɪŋ</u>/ in 1988?   **13.** Why are
/<u>way</u>ər/ the students writing in their books?   **14.** What time/When should I /<u>wɛn</u>šuday/ call
you?   **15.** Why is Yoko /<u>way</u>zyoko/ absent?

□ EXERCISE 6, p. 130. *Information questions. (Chart 6-2)*

Transformation.
Only after the students have a clear and thorough understanding of all the items in Exercise 5 should they go on to this exercise.
    Again model normal contracted speech.

ANSWERS: **1.** When are you going to go /<u>wɛn</u>əryəgənə<u>gow</u>/ downtown?   **2.** Why did you
stay /<u>way(d)</u>ǰəstey/ ["d+y" becomes one sound] home yesterday?   **3.** Where did you go
/<u>wɛr(d)</u>ǰəgow/ last night?   [If the students want to say "What did you go to last night?" tell them that that question is not idiomatic, i.e., is not the way in which a native speaker of English would normally ask a question to get the information "to a movie."]   **4.** Where can I /<u>wɛrk</u>ənay/ /Where can you buy
/<u>wɛrk</u>ənyɛ<u>bay</u>/ a hammer?   [If *you* is used in the question, it is an impersonal pronoun meaning "any person or all people."   See *Understanding and Using English Grammar*, Chart 5-20.]   **5.** What time
does /<u>wətaym</u>dəz/ / When does /<u>wɛn</u>dəz/ class begin?   **6.** Why do you need to go
/<u>wayd</u>əyənitəgow/ ["d+t" becomes one sound] to the post office?   **7.** When will your /<u>wɛn</u>əlyr/
daughter graduate . . . ?   **8.** Where do your /<u>wɛr</u>dəyr/ children go to school?   **9.** When
did you /<u>wɛn</u>(d)ǰə/ ["d+y" becomes one sound] meet the Smiths?   **10.** What does /<u>wə</u>dəz/

["t+d" becomes one sound] "attempt" mean?   **11.** What is a /wɑtsə/ frog?
12. What is an /wɑtsən/ amphibian?   **13.** What do /wədə/ ["t+d" becomes one sound] frogs
eat?   **14.** What does /wəts/ or /wədəz/ "occupation" mean?   **15.** Why are you /wayəryə/
studying English?

☐ EXERCISE 7, p. 131. *Information questions: WHY.* *(Chart 6-2)*

Oral.
Incorrect question word order with *why* is a common problem. (For example: *Why you are tired
today?*)   This exercise seeks to give a little extra practice on a structure that may cause some
difficulty for some students.

ANSWERS: *Questions only.*   **1.** Why were you . . . ?   **2.** Why are you going to . . . ?
3. Why did you go . . . ?   **4.** Why did you take . . . ?   **5.** Why do you need . . . ?
6. Why are you going to buy . . . ?   **7.** A: Why didn't you do . . . ?   **8.** Why aren't you
coming . . . ?   **9.** Why can't you come . . . ?   **10.** Why didn't you eat . . . ?   **11.** Why
won't you be . . . ?   **12.** Why don't you like . . . ? [If the question arises, it may be necessary to
compare this use of *why don't* with the *why don't* in Chart 5-12, where *why don't* is used idiomatically to
make a suggestion. Here *why don't* is used to seek information.]

◇ WORKBOOK PRACTICE 1, p. 106. *Asking interview questions.* *(Charts 6-1 → 6-13)*

Semi-controlled completion. [Selfstudy]
Students can work in pairs or groups prior to class discussion.
    EXPANSION: Have students interview each other. Another possibility: Have two students
role-play the interview in front of the class, glancing at their texts only briefly.

POSSIBLE RESPONSES:
  1. *(Student supplies own name.)*
  2. What is (What's) your name?
  3. Is that your first name? / Is Anna your first name?
  4. What's your last name?
  5. How do you spell that? /   How do you spell your last name?
  6. Where are you from? / What country are you from? / What country do you come from?
  7. What city? (What city are you from?) / Where in Poland? (Where do you come from in
       Poland?) / What's your hometown?
  8. When did you come to *(name of this city/country/school)*? / When did you arrive here?
  9. Why did you come here?
  10. What is your major? / What are you going to study? / What are you studying? / What field
       are you in? /   What's your field?
  11. How long are you going to stay here? / How long do you plan to stay?
  12. Where are you living?
  13. Do you live far from/a long way from school? / Is their house far from school?
  14. How far is it? / How far is their house from school? / How far away are you?
  15. How do you get to school every day?
  16. How do you like going to school here? / Do you like it here, too?

◇ WORKBOOK PRACTICE 2, p. 107. *Yes/no questions and short answers.* *(Charts 6-1 and 6-2)*

Controlled completion. [Selfstudy]
This is a review of present time auxiliary verbs and main verb *be*.

ANSWERS: **1.** A: Do   B: I don't   **2.** A: Is   B: it is   **3.** A: Do   B: they don't
4. A: Are   B: I am   **5.** A: Does   B: it does   **6.** A: Are   B: they aren't

7. A: Do   B: they do   **8.** A: Are   B: I am   **9.** A: Is   B: it isn't
10. A: Do   B: they do   **11.** A: Does   B: it does

◇ WORKBOOK PRACTICE 3, p. 108. *Yes/no questions. (Chapters 1, 2, 3, 5, and Chart 6-1)*

Controlled completion. [Selfstudy]
This is a review of question forms of the main verb structures presented thus far in the text.

ANSWERS:

	helping verb	subject	main verb	rest of sentence
1.	Do	you	like	coffee?
2.	Does	Tom	like	coffee?
3.	Is	Ann	watching	TV?
4.	Are	you	having	lunch with Rob?
5.	Did	Sara	walk	to school?
6.	Was	Ann	taking	a nap?
7.	Will	Ted	come	to the meeting?
8.	Can	Rita	ride	a bicycle?

	form of *be*	subject		rest of sentence
9.	Is	Ann		a good artist?
10.	Were	you		at the wedding?

◇ WORKBOOK PRACTICE 4, p. 109. *Yes/no questions. (Charts 6-1 and 6-2)*

Dialogue construction. [Guided Study]

SAMPLE RESPONSES: **1.** A: Did Roberto buy the coat?   B: No, he didn't. It was too expensive.   **2.** A: Did Nasser get home from his trip?   B: Yes, he did. Yesterday.
3. A: Did you give Mr. Kwan my message? B: No, I didn't. I forgot.   **4.** A: Did you taste the dessert Fatima brought to the party? B: Yes, we did. It was delicious.   **5.** A: Will Natasha and Ming get here in time for dinner? B: Yes, they will. Don't worry.   **6.** A: Can you swim?   B: No, I can't.   I never learned how to.   **7.** A: Are you warm enough? B: Yes, I am. What about you?   **8.** A: Would you like to go to the rock concert with us Saturday?   B: Maybe. Let me think about it.   **9.** A: Will Marsha be coming to the football game Saturday?   B: Probably. She usually does.   **10.** A: Should we ask Sam if we can use his boat to go fishing?   B: Sure. Sounds like a good idea to me.

◇ WORKBOOK PRACTICE 5, p. 109. *Yes/no and information questions. (Charts 6-1 and 6-2)*

Transformation. [Selfstudy]
The intention of this practice is to underscore the similarity of form between yes/no and information questions. Some students seem to need special and deliberate work on figuring out question word order in English. Other students will find a practice like this too easy to bother with.

ANSWERS:

	(question word)	helping verb	subject	main verb	rest of sentence
1.	Ø	Did	you	hear	the news yesterday?
2.	When	did	you	hear	the news?
3.	Ø	Is	Eric	reading	today's paper?
4.	What	is	Eric	reading	Ø?
5.	Ø	Did	you	find	your wallet?
6.	Where	did	you	find	your wallet?
7.	Why	does	Mr. Li	walk	to work?

8. Ø	Does	Mr. Li	walk	to work?
9. Ø	Will	Ms. Cook	return	to her office at one o'clock?
10. When	will	Ms. Cook	return	to her office?

(question word)	form of *be*	subject	rest of sentence
11. Ø	Is	the orange juice	in the refrigerator?
12. Where	is	the orange juice	Ø?

◊ WORKBOOK PRACTICE 6, p. 110. *Information questions. (Charts 6-1 and 6-2)*

Transformation. [Selfstudy]

ANSWERS: **1.** What time/When do the fireworks start **2.** Why are you waiting **3.** When does Rachel start **4.** What time/When do you usually leave **5.** Why didn't you get **6.** Where can I/you buy [If you is used in the question, it is an impersonal pronoun meaning "any person or all people." See *Understanding and Using English Grammar*, Chart 5-20.] **7.** What time/When are you leaving **8.** Where did you study . . . Why did you study . . . Why didn't you go **9.** When do you expect **10.** Where will the spaceship go [also possible: What/Which planet will the spaceship go to? To what/which planet will the spaceship go?]

◊ WORKBOOK PRACTICE 7, p. 111. *Yes/no and information questions. (Charts 6-1 and 6-2)*

Dialogue construction. [Guided Study]
This practice can be written. Ask the students to write the entire dialogue, including the answer given in the text. Another possibility would be to have the students write the twelve questions in random order. Then these questions could be given to Student B, who would write in the appropriate responses from the text and the long answer. Student B could also be asked to correct Student A's question forms.

SAMPLE DIALOGUES: **1.** A: When was your math final? B: The day before yesterday. My math final was the day before yesterday. **2.** A: Do you own a brown and white cat? B: Yes, I do. I own a brown and white cat. **3.** A: Why did you borrow money from the bank? B: Because I had to. I borrowed money from the bank because I had to. [The grammar here may be a little difficult for some students. Adverb clauses introduced by *because* are presented in Chart 9-6. Uncompleted infinitives are presented in Chart 10-6.] **4.** A: What time does your math class begin each morning? B: At 8:30. My math class begins at 8:30 each morning. **5.** A: Is Jacob your brother? B: Yes, he is. Jacob is my brother. **6.** A: Where can I/you [impersonal *you*] find a ripe melon? B: In a supermarket. You can find a ripe melon in a supermarket. **7.** A: When are you and Gisela going shopping at the new mall? [This sample uses the present progressive with a future meaning. Any verb with a future meaning is possible.] B: Tomorrow afternoon. Gisela and I are going shopping at the new mall tomorrow afternoon. **8.** A: What did you buy at the bookstore? B: A notebook. I bought a notebook at the bookstore. **9.** A: Can you come with me to Sally's party tonight? B: No, I can't. I can't come with you to Sally's party tonight. **10.** A: Why are you interested in Japan? B: Because I hope to visit there someday. I'm interested in Japan because I hope to visit there someday. **11.** A: Would you take my nephew to the zoo this afternoon while I study for my history test? B: Yeah, sure. Why not. Yeah, sure I'll take your nephew to the zoo this afternoon. Why not? **12.** A: Do you think Ali would like to go to the concert with us? B: I don't know. Maybe. I don't know if Ali would like to go to the concert with us. Maybe. [This item requires a noun clause introduced by *if* in the long answer. Some students may not be ready for this. Tell them they'll study it later and refer them to Chart 14-4.]

◇ WORKBOOK PRACTICE 8, p. 111. *Asking for the meaning of a word. (Charts 6-2 and 6-3)*

Oral. [Guided Study]

This practice is not as easy as it may look. It is directed at a common problem in learners' production: the correct question form in asking the meaning of a word. A question beginning with *What means . . . ?* is a typical error. The practice presents only two common ways for asking for meaning. Note that in Part II, main verb *be* is often used in asking for the meaning of a noun rather than *mean*. Other common ways of asking for meaning that are not presented here are *What is the meaning of . . . ?* and *Could you please tell me what . . . means?* Students might spontaneously come up with these variations even though the text tries to direct them toward specific patterns that it is trying to teach.

You might note that either the simple (e.g., *explore*) or inflected (e.g., *explored)* form can be used in the question about meaning.

How to answer a question about meaning also adds difficulty, for the form of the word to be defined and the definition should be parallel. For example, *"Explored" means "going to new places"* or *"Explore" means "people go to new and different places"* are both grammatically incorrect because they are not parallel. You'll need to decide if it's worth the time to concentrate on the form of not only the question but also the answer. You might also want to teach your students how to write definitions of words. The suggested approach is to keep the focus solely on the question form.

Another factor in the difficulty of this exercise is the likelihood that the vocabulary is unfamiliar to some or many of the students. They should be encouraged to use their dictionaries.

This practice can be done in pairs or small groups.

POSSIBLE QUESTIONS:

PART I: **1.** A: What does "explored" mean? B: "Explored" means "went to a new place and found out about it." **2.** A: What does "mad" mean? B: "Mad" can mean "crazy" or "angry." **3.** A: What does "essential" mean? B: "Essential" means "necessary." **4.** A: What does "float" mean? B: "Float" means "to move gently on the surface of a liquid." **5.** A: What does "evaporate" mean? B: "Evaporate" means "to change from a liquid into air." **6.** A: What does "perhaps" mean? "Perhaps" means "maybe." **7.** A: What does "bury" mean? B: "Bury" means "to put in the ground and cover with earth." **8.** A: What does "beneath" mean? B: "Beneath" means "below." **9.** What does "grab" mean? B: "Grab" means "to seize suddenly, eagerly, or roughly." **10.** A: What does "blink" mean? B: "Blink" means "to open and close your eyes rapidly."

PART II: **11.** A: What is an orchard? B: An orchard is a place where fruit trees grow. **12.** A: What are nightmares? B: Nightmares are very bad dreams. **13.** A: What are photographs? B: Photographs are pictures you take with a camera. **14.** A: What is a bug? B: A bug is an insect. **15.** A: What are pearls? B: Pearls are small, smooth, round balls that come from oysters and are used to make jewelry. **16.** A: What is an archaeologist? B: An archaeologist is a person who digs in the earth to learn about ancient civilizations. **17.** A: What are fables? B: Fables are short stories used to teach a moral. **18.** A: What is a honeymoon? B: A honeymoon is a trip that a newly married couple takes. **19.** A: What are margins? B: Margins are the borders of space around printed material on a page. **20.** A: What is small talk? B: Small talk is light, conversational talk. **21.** A: What is a keyboard? B: A keyboard is a piece of equipment that has letters and numbers. **22.** A: What are hedges? B: Hedges are bushes planted close together in rows.

◇ WORKBOOK PRACTICE 9, p. 112. *Questions with WHY. (Chart 6-2)*

Transformation, open completion. [Guided Study]
Mention that in normal conversation a person would probably not ask the full *why*-question. The students understand that they are producing the full question in order to practice a grammar pattern here. Tell Student A to be alert to the proper form in Student B's *why*-question. The form of *why*-questions is troublesome for many students at this level. Reinforce the idea that *Because I have to study for a test* is a short answer to a question, not a complete sentence that can stand by itself in written discourse.

SAMPLE RESPONSES: **1.** B: Why?   Why did you eat two breakfasts this morning?
A: Because I was very hungry.   **2.** B: Why not? Why don't you like to ride on airplanes?
A: Because I'm afraid they'll crash.   **3.** B: Why?   Why are you going to sell your guitar?
A: Because I don't play it anymore and I need the money.   **4.** B: Why?   Why didn't you go to bed last night?   A: Because I was studying for an exam.   **5.** B: Why?   Why are you happy today?   A: Because I got a raise at work.   **6.** B: Why? Why did you have to call the police last night?   A: Because someone broke into my car.   **7.** B: Why? Why can't you explain it to me?   A: Because I don't have enough time.   **8.** B: Why not? Why aren't you speaking to your cousin?   A: Because she was rude to my wife. [*To be not speaking to someone* is an idiom meaning to be so angry at someone that you won't talk to her/him.]

CHART 6-3: USING *WHO, WHO(M)*, AND *WHAT*

• This grammar will be difficult unless students clearly understand subjects and objects. Refer to Chart 4-2 (Subjects, Verbs, Objects) if necessary.

• *Whom* is rarely used in everyday discourse. Native speakers prefer *who: Who did you see at the party? Who did you talk to?   Who does Bob remind you of?   Etc.*

☐ EXERCISE 8, p. 132. *Information questions: WHO, WHO(M), WHAT. (Chart 6-3)*

Transformation.
Students should be asked to identify subjects and objects throughout. You might want to parse some of these items, pointing out the elements and patterns of the simple sentence in statements and questions.

ANSWERS: **2.** What did Mary see?   **3.** Who saw an accident?   **4.** Who(m) did Mary see?   **5.** Who saw John?   **6.** What happened?   **7.** What did Alice buy?   **8.** Who bought a new coat?   **9.** What are you looking at?   **10.** Who(m) are you looking at?
11. Who(m) did you talk to?   **12.** What did Tom talk about?   **13.** What did the teacher look at?   **14.** Who looked at the board?   **15.** Who(m) did the teacher look at?

◇ WORKBOOK PRACTICE 10, p. 113. *Questions with WHO, WHO(M), and WHAT. (Chart 6-3)*

Transformation. [Selfstudy]
Help the students make the connection between subjects and objects in statements and in questions by showing that the answer *(someone/something)* parallels the grammatical function of the question word. The question word can be substituted for *someone/something*. If it is a subject, no change is made in word order. If it is an object, the word order is inverted. The purpose of this practice is to help the students figure out if the word order is or is not inverted when the question word is *who* or *what*.

ANSWERS:
S
1. Who knows?
O
2. Who(m) did you ask?
S
3. Who knocked on the door?
O
4. Who(m) did Sara meet?
S
5. Who will help us?
O
6. Who(m) will you ask?
O
7. Who(m) is Eric talking to on the phone? OR To whom is Eric talking on the phone.
S
8. Who is knocking on the door?
S
9. What surprised them?
O
10. What did Mike learn?
S
11. What will change Ann's mind?
O
12. What can Tina talk about? OR About what can Tina talk?

◇ WORKBOOK PRACTICE 11, p. 113. *WHO, WHO(M), and WHAT. (Chart 6-3)*

Transformation. [Selfstudy]

ANSWERS: **1.** Who taught you to play chess? **2.** What did Robert see? **3.** Who got a good look at the bank robber? **4.** Who(m) are you making the toy for? OR For whom are you making the toy? **5.** Who(m) does the calculator belong to? OR To whom does the calculator belong? **6.** What do you have in your pocket? [also possible, especially in BrE: What have you (got) in your pocket?] **7.** What did the cat kill? **8.** What killed the cat? **9.** Who(m) did you get a letter from? OR From whom did you get a letter? **10.** Who wrote a note on the envelope? **11.** What makes an apple fall to the ground from a tree?

☐ EXERCISE 9, p. 134. *Question words: spoken contractions. (Chart 6-3)*

Oral.
The quotation marks below indicate that the contraction is usually spoken but rarely, if ever, written.

ANSWERS: **1.** Where's **2.** What's **3.** Why's **4.** Who's **5.** Who're **6.** Where're **7.** What're **8.** Where'd **9.** What'd **10.** Why'd **11.** Who'd **12.** Where'll **13.** When'll **14.** Who'll

☐ EXERCISE 10, p. 134. *Information questions. (Chart 6-3)*

Open completion.
Students should create written questions. Perhaps they can correct each other's questions prior to class discussion. Alternatively, they can hand the dialogues in if you ask them to use a separate sheet of paper and write both the question and the answer.

EXPANSION: Give the students this list of question words: *where, why, when, what time, who, what.* Tell them to make up an exercise for a classmate in which these words need to be used (and only these question words at this point). The format of the exercise they make up can be like Exercise 10 (or Exercise 8). Outline exactly what you have in mind when you make the assignment. Asking the students to make up exercises for their classmates is a good technique for many areas of grammar. It puts the student in the role of the teacher and enhances his/her learning.

CHART 6-4: USING *WHAT* + A FORM OF *DO*

• Use your students' lives and activities to demonstrate *what + do* questions. For example, *What is Miguel doing? What was Yoko doing before she sat down? What did you do yesterday? What is Keh Kooi going to do after class today?* Show the relationship between the verb form in the answer and the form of *do* in the question.

☐ EXERCISE 11, p. 135. *WHAT + a form of DO. (Chart 6-4)*

Transformation.
This is an exercise on the form of the verbs in questions in which *what + do* is used to ask about activities.

ANSWERS: **2.** What did you do   **3.** What are you going to do   **4.** What do you want to do   **5.** What do you need to do   **6.** What would you like to do   **7.** What are you planning to do   **8.** What do you do   **9.** What do you do   **10.** What will you do [*Book (a flight)* = make a reservation.]   **11.** What should I do   **12.** What did Steve do   **13.** What did Jane do   **14.** What did he do   **15.** What is Yoko doing?   **16.** What does a bear do   **17.** What should I do?   [*Hiccups* can also be spelled *hiccoughs*.]   **18.** What should he do?   **19.** What does your husband do?   **20.** What does your wife do?

☐ EXERCISE 12, p. 137. *WHAT + a form of DO. (Chart 6-4)*

Oral (books closed).
If done in small groups, this exercise could profitably lead to short, informal conversations. Have the leader of the group, book open, give a cue to an individual student; that student then decides to whom in the group s/he would like to address the question.

◇ WORKBOOK PRACTICE 12, p. 114. *WHAT + a form of DO. (Chart 6-4)*

Transformation. [Selfstudy]
In addition to providing practice with a useful question pattern, this and the next practice are essentially verb form exercises.

ANSWERS: **1.** What is Alex doing?   **2.** What should I do if someone calls while you're out?   **3.** What do astronauts do?   **4.** What should I do?   **5.** What are you going to do Saturday morning?   **6.** What do you do when you get sick?   **7.** What can I do to help you?   **8.** What did Sara do when she heard the good news?

◇ WORKBOOK PRACTICE 13, p. 115. *WHAT + a form of DO. (Chart 6-4)*

Transformation. [Guided Study]

ANSWERS: **1.** What is Emily going to do after she graduates?   **2.** What can I do to help you get ready for the meeting?   **3.** What did you do when the fire alarm sounded?   **4.** What would you like to do after school today?   **5.** What are you trying to do?   **6.** What does Kevin need to do if he wants to pass advanced algebra?   **7.** What does Nick do for a living?   **8.** What did he do when you bumped into him? . . . What did you do? . . . Then what did he do?

◇ WORKBOOK PRACTICE 14, p. 115. *WHAT + a form of DO. (Chart 6-4)*

Dialogue construction. [Guided Study]
This practice requires relatively sophisticated understanding and usage ability of verb forms.
Congratulate your students.

SAMPLE DIALOGUES: **1.** A: What do you plan to do tonight? B: Watch TV.
2. A: What was Ben doing when you stopped by his house? B: Washing his dog.
3. A: What did you do after your big weekend in New York? B: Went home and slept.
4. A: What are you doing? B: Writing dialogues. **5.** A: What would you like to do
tonight? B: Go to a movie. **6.** A: What would you like to do after you graduate?
B: Get a job on a cruise ship.

CHART 6-5: USING *WHAT KIND OF*

• You might want to introduce the expression *what sort of* as well. It has the same meaning as *what kind of.*

• Use objects in the classroom to demonstrate what information can be elicited when *what kind of* is used. Ask students what kind of shoes they're wearing, what kind of watches they have, etc.

☐ EXERCISE 13, p. 138. *WHAT KIND OF. (Chart 6-5)*

Semi-controlled completion.
This exercise is intended to give a basic survey of the information that can be elicited by asking
what kind of. Emphasize the idea of specific kinds within a category. The question asks about a
category. The answer supplies a specific kind.

ANSWERS:
   3. A: music B: classical, country, jazz, folk, etc.
   4. A: car/automobile B: a Buick, a Honda, a van, a four-door sedan, etc.
   5. A: books B: historical novels, biographies, mysteries, etc.
   6. A: candy, sweets B: caramels, jelly beans, fudge, Snickers bars, etc.
   7. A: computer B: an Apple II, an IBM, a Macintosh, etc.
   8. A: possessions B: watch, pen, TV, camera, dog, dictionary, notebook, bicycle, etc.

☐ EXERCISE 14, p. 138. *WHAT KIND OF. (Chart 6-5)*

Oral (books closed).
Other possible questions: (Note that *what kind of* can elicit a physical description.)
   What kind of earrings is Wai-Leng wearing? (Gold. Gold hoops.)
   What kind of book is this? (A grammar book. An English book.)
   What kind of notebook is that? [A spiral notebook. A (brand name) notebook.]
   What kind of lights are those? (Fluorescent. Ceiling lights. General Electric 100-watt bulbs.)
   What kind of shirt is Julio wearing? (Cotton. Turtleneck. Sport shirt. Pullover.)

◇ WORKBOOK PRACTICE 15, p. 116. *WHAT KIND OF. (Chart 6-5)*

Oral/written. [Guided Study]
Have the students walk around and interview each other then write a report of the information
they learned.

CHART 6-6: USING *WHICH*

- *Which* in questions essentially means "what one(s) out of this/that particular group?" The questioner is asking the listener to choose from a given group of possibilities.

- In the text, the examples and exercises deal only with *which* as an object of a verb or preposition, but *which* can also be used as the subject or part of the subject of a question. Example: *Which book has the best information?* Perhaps pose to your students this philosophical question that is familiar to most English speakers: *Which came first, the chicken or the egg?*

- The text focuses only on the use of *which* with "things"; however, *which* can refer to people as well as things. Example: *Which player scored the winning goal?*

- *Which* is also used in adjective clauses. *(The book, which no one liked, was required reading.)* See Chapter 12. You may or may not wish to mention this dual usage at this point.

☐ EXERCISE 15, p. 139. *WHICH vs. WHAT.* *(Chart 6-6)*

Transformation.

Distinguish between *which* and *what:* Questions with *which* ask the listener to choose from a specific known group. Questions with *what* ask for a choice from an unknown or unlimited group of possibilities.

For example: Put two books on a student's desk. Focus the attention of the class on the group of two books. Pick up one and ask "Which one did I pick up, the grammar book or the dictionary?" For contrast, walk to another student's desk and pick up a pen or piece of paper, asking "What did I pick up?" Explain that *which* is used when the speaker and listener(s) are thinking about the same known group (e.g., the books on Ahmad's desk), and that *what* is used when there is no known group. The answer to *what* can be anything that exists in the universe. The answer to *which* can only be something that is part of a limited and specific group.

ANSWERS: **3.** Which (pen/one) would you like? **4.** What did Chris borrow from you? **5.** Which (tie/one) are you going to buy? **6.** What did Tony get when he went shopping? **7.** Which (shoes, ones) should I buy? **8.** Which (flight/one) are you going to take? **9.** What does "huge" mean? **10.** What is the meaning of "rapid"? **11.** Which (knife/one) would you like? **12.** Which class [also possible: What class] are you in? **13.** What countries [also possible: Which countries] did you visit? . . . Which (country/one) did you like best?

◇ WORKBOOK PRACTICE 16, p. 116. *WHICH vs. WHAT* *(Chart 6-6)*

Controlled completion. [Selfstudy]

ANSWERS: **1.** Which [*Gray* is spelled *grey* in BrE and variantly in AmE. Either spelling is correct.] **2.** What **3.** Which **4.** What **5.** What . . . Which **6.** What **7.** Which **8.** which

CHART 6-7: USING *WHOSE*

- The two principal ways of asking questions about possession are to use *whose* or *belong to: Whose (book) is this?* vs. *Who(m) does this (book) belong to?*

- *Whose* is also used in adjective clauses. (Example: *That's the man whose house burned down.*) See Chart 12-7.

- *Whose* and *who's* have the same pronunciation. [NOTE: the text says that *who's = who is*. *Who's* can also be a contraction for *who has* when *has* is used as the auxiliary in the present perfect. (Example: *Who's been to Disneyland?*) This contraction is not mentioned in this chart because the present perfect isn't covered until the next chapter. You may or may not wish to mention this meaning of *who's*.]

☐ EXERCISE 16, p. 141. *WHOSE vs. WHO'S. (Chart 6-7)*

Transformation.
The focus of this exercise is on distinguishing between *whose* and *who's*. Oral practice with *whose* alone follows in Exercises 17 and 18.

ANSWERS: **3.** Whose notebook is that? **4.** Whose tapes are these? **5.** Who's (Who is) that? **6.** Whose clothes are those? **7.** Whose coat is that? **8.** Who's (Who is) in a gym? **9.** Who's (Who is) sitting down? **10.** Whose hair is longer? **11.** Whose umbrella did you borrow? **12.** Whose book did you use? **13.** Whose book is on the table? **14.** Who's (Who is) on the phone? **15.** Whose house is that? **16.** Who's (Who is) living in that house? **17.** Who's (Who is) that? **18.** Whose is that?

☐ EXERCISE 17, p. 142. *Questions with WHOSE. (Chart 6-7)*

Oral.
Students shouldn't have any difficulty with this exercise. A few questions are all that are needed to make sure the class understands how to ask questions with *whose + be*. Be sure learners are aware of singular vs. plural forms: *Whose **is** this?* vs. *Whose **are** those?*

☐ EXERCISE 18, p. 143. *Questions about possession. (Chart 6-7)*

Oral.
This is an exercise on possessive nouns and pronouns (see Charts 14-7 and 14-8) as well as questions with *whose*.

Notice the two patterns for asking yes/no questions about possession using *be* and possessive nouns or pronouns. (Examples: *Are these Yoko's pens?* and *Are these pens Yoko's?*) Students should use whichever pattern they are comfortable with.

In discussing the examples in the text, point out that Student B's first response should be negative. In other words, Student A asks a question to which s/he knows that the answer is *no*.

◇ WORKBOOK PRACTICE 17, p. 117. *WHO vs. WHOSE. (Chart 6-7)*

Controlled completion. [Selfstudy]

ANSWERS: **1.** Who **2.** Whose **3.** Whose **4.** Who **5.** Who **6.** Whose **7.** Whose **8.** Who [Note on the grammar in B's response: Formal, prescriptive grammar says a subject pronoun should follow main verb *be: It wasn't I,* not *It wasn't me.* In actual usage, the object pronoun is far more common and preferred by native speakers. In the text in general, possibly substandard usages that are common and accepted across the social and educational spectrum are modeled for the students, but usages such as *it don't* that might bring negative judgments are not modeled.]

☐ EXERCISE 19, p. 143. *Question words. (Chart 6-7)*

> *Written.*
> This is a general review of question words and forms covered so far in this chapter.

◇ WORKBOOK PRACTICE 18, p. 117. *Asking questions. (Charts 6-1 → 6-7)*

> *Oral/Written.* [Guided Study]
> You might have to clarify the directions as this is a one-of-a-kind exercise; the students aren't familiar with the format. Emphasize that Student A should choose an answer at random and then make up a question that will produce that answer.

CHART 6-8: USING *HOW*

- In general, *how* asks about manner, means, condition, degree, extent. It doesn't lend itself to a quick definition. Starting with this chart, the text introduces common uses of *how* in six separate charts so that students may slowly build their understanding of its meanings and uses.

☐ EXERCISE 20, p. 144. *Questions with HOW. (Chart 6-8)*

> *Transformation.*
> This exercise consists of further examples for discussion of Chart 6-8.
>
> ANSWERS: **2.** How important is education?   **3.** How do you get to school?   **4.** How deep is the ocean?   **5.** How heavy is your suitcase?   **6.** How are you going to get to Denver?   **7.** How well does Roberto speak English?   **8.** How high is Mount Everest?   **9.** How hungry are you?   **10.** How did you get to school today?   **11.** How should I send that letter?   **12.** How safe is that neighborhood at night?   **13.** How difficult was the test?   **14.** How tall is Mary?   **15.** How fast do you drive?

◇ WORKBOOK PRACTICE 19, p. 118. *Using HOW. (Chart 6-8)*

> *Controlled completion.* [Selfstudy]
>
> ANSWERS: **1.** hot . . . hot   **2.** soon   **3.** expensive   **4.** busy . . . busy   **5.** serious . . . serious   **6.** well . . . well   **7.** fresh . . . fresh. . . fresh   **8.** safe

---

CHART 6-9: USING *HOW OFTEN*

- COMPARE: *How often* is the common way to ask for general information about frequency, as in (a). The listener can respond in many different ways. *How many times* is used to elicit more specific information about repetitions within a given length of time (e.g., a day, a month) and limits the way in which the listener can respond, as in (b).

□ EXERCISE 21, p. 145. *HOW OFTEN/HOW MANY TIMES.* *(Chart 6-9)*

> *Oral.*
> This exercise focuses not only on questions with *how often* but, just as important, common ways to answer such questions. Even though these frequency expressions are not presented in a separate chart, some of your teaching should focus on them.

CHART 6-10: USING *HOW FAR*

• This chart teaches expletive *it* for expressing distances as well as how to ask questions about distance. Elicit further examples of the grammar patterns in (b) by using local places your class is familiar with.

□ EXERCISE 22, p. 147. *Questions with HOW FAR.* *(Chart 6-10)*

> *Transformation.*
> ANSWERS: **1.** How far (How many miles) is it from . . . ?   **2.** How far (How many kilometers) is it from . . . ?   **3.** How far (How many miles) is it to . . . ?   **4.** How far (How many blocks) is it to . . . ?   **5.** How far (How many blocks) is it to . . . ?   **6.** How far (How many miles) do you live from . . . ?   **7.** How far (How many miles) does Karen jog . . . ?   **8.** How far did you get before . . . ?

□ EXERCISE 23, p. 147. *HOW FAR.* *(Chart 6-10)*

> *Oral.*
> This exercise in intended for small group discussion of regional geography. The purposes are to familiarize the students with the geography of the surrounding area, make sure they know how to read a map in English and decipher a mileage chart, practice the target structures, and engage in directed conversation with their classmates.
>   Supply one road map to each small group. (Perhaps some of the students have road maps and can bring them to class. If not, it might require a small investment from a visual-aids budget.)   Students can ask *how far* questions using place names on the map, make guesses about distance, and then figure out exact distances. Another possibility is for you to supply several pairs of place names (e.g., the names of this city and that city) and see which groups can figure out the correct distances from their maps. You could make it a game with prizes.

CHART 6-11: EXPRESSING LENGTH OF TIME: *IT + TAKE*

• In this chart, the text is pausing a moment to teach expletive *it* + *take* for expressing length of time before teaching how to ask questions about length of time using *how long* (the next chart).

• Ask spontaneous *how long* questions about your students' lives to elicit *it* + *take* answers. Possible topics: get dressed in the morning, eat lunch, walk from here to somewhere, fly from somewhere to here, etc.

☐ EXERCISE 24, p. 148. *IT + TAKE to express length of time.* (Chart 6-11)

Transformation.
This exercise supplies further examples for discussion of the grammar in Chart 6-11.

ANSWERS: **2.** It takes me twenty minutes to walk to class. **3.** It took George an hour and a half to finish the test. **4.** It will take us forty-five minutes to drive to the airport. **5.** It took Ann six hours to make a dress. **6.** It took Alan two weeks to hitchhike to Alaska. **7.** It took Jennifer five minutes to put on her makeup. **8.** It takes me two hours to wash my clothes at the laundromat. [Sometimes students enjoy sharing their difficulties keeping their clothes clean as students living away from home. For some, it is the first time in their lives they've been responsible for such, and they find laundromats or a college dorm laundry room a challenge. Some cultural attitudes may find a discussion of cleaning clothes unsuitable.]

CHART 6-12: USING *HOW LONG*

• *How long* is a special expression used to ask about length of time. *How long* can also ask literal questions about the physical length of something: *How long is that board of wood?* In this question, *long* is an adjective used with *how*, just like the adjectives in Chart 6-8. Questions about this usage may or may not arise; how much information you want to supply to your class depends upon the level of the class as well as their interest and ability to understand somewhat subtle differences in the language.

☐ EXERCISE 25, p. 149. *Questions with HOW LONG.* (Chart 6-12)

Transformation.
You may wish to model normal contracted speech, as represented below in the brackets for items 2 through 5.

ANSWERS: **2.** How long does it ["how long'uzit"] take you to walk to class? **3.** How long did it ["how long'dit"] take Mike to finish his composition? **4.** How long will ["how long'll"] it take us/you to drive to the stadium? **5.** How long is ["how long's"] Mr. McNally going to be in the hospital? **6.** How long will you be at the University of Maryland? **7.** How long does it take to bake a cake? . . . How long does it take to bake cookies? [Note: *how about* is discussed in Chart 6-14. Prepare the class by pointing out its use here and in the next three items in this exercise.] **8.** How long were you out of town? . . . How long was she out of town? **9.** How long does it take you to change a flat tire? . . . How long does it take you to change the oil? **10.** How long does it take to learn a second language? [Reassure your students that learning a second language takes time, persistence, and a lot of practice and experience. They should not be discouraged if they've been working intensively on their English for only a few weeks or months. Share your language learning experiences with your class.] . . . How long does it take to learn a computer language?

◊ WORKBOOK PRACTICE 20, p. 119. *Using HOW FAR and HOW LONG.* (Charts 6-10 and 6-12)

Controlled completion. [Selfstudy]

ANSWERS: **1.** far **2.** long **3.** far **4.** far **5.** long **6.** far **7.** long **8.** long **9.** far **10.** long

◇ WORKBOOK PRACTICE 21, p. 119. *Using HOW. (Charts 6-8 → 6-12)*

Controlled completion. [Selfstudy]

ANSWERS: **1.** often **2.** long **3.** many **4.** far **5.** many **6.** many
7. long **8.** many **9.** often **10.** many **11.** long **12.** often **13.** far
14. many **15.** often **16.** far **17.** long

☐ EXERCISE 26, p. 150. *Review of information questions. (Chart 6-12)*

Transformation.

If there is any interest in baseball among your students, you might discuss a little baseball vocabulary as shown in the illustration: the outfield (left fielder, center fielder, right fielder), infield, first base, second base, two men on base. The net is protection for the spectators immediately behind home plate so they don't get hit by a foul ball.

ANSWERS: **2.** Which (one/game) are you going to go to? **3.** Did you go to the game yesterday? **4.** Who went to the game yesterday? **5.** How often do you go to a baseball game? **6.** Who(m) are you going to go to the game with? [very formal: With whom are you going to go to the game?] **7.** Where is the stadium? **8.** How far is it to the stadium from here? **9.** How long does it take to get there? **10.** What time/When does the game start? **11.** Why do you like to go to baseball games? **12.** What do you do when you go to a baseball game?

☐ EXERCISE 27, p. 151. *Question words. (Chart 6-12)*

Oral (books closed).

This exercise reviews the grammar to this point in the chapter. It can be done quickly if teacher-led, or more leisurely if student-led in small groups. Pair work would also be appropriate.

In many items, more than one question is possible. Encourage contractions with question words.

EXPECTED OR POSSIBLE ANSWERS: **1.** What did you do last night? **2.** Where did you study? **3.** How long did you study at the library last night? **4.** What are you going to do tonight? **5.** Where are you going to study? **6.** Who(m) are you going to study with? **7.** Why are you going to study together? **8.** Who(m) did you see yesterday? **9.** Who called you last night? **10.** Who(m) did you talk to last night? **11.** How often do you go to the library? **12.** How far is the library from here? **13.** Where do you live? OR What city do you live in? **14.** Where were you born? **15.** Where did you grow up? **16.** Why did you stay home yesterday? **17.** What are you looking at? **18.** Who(m) are you looking at? **19.** Whose pen is that? **20.** Which pen do you want? **21.** What kind of shoes is (. . .) wearing? **22.** What are you going to wear tomorrow? **23.** Who(m) are you going to write a letter to? **24.** Who wrote you a letter? **25.** How far is it to (name of a city) from here? **26.** What kind of car do you have? **27.** How long does it take to drive . . . ? **28.** How often do you drive to . . . ? **29.** What does "glad" mean? **30.** Where and when was the first oil well in history drilled?

CHARTS 6-13: MORE QUESTIONS WITH *HOW*

- This chart consists of some miscellaneous common questions with *how*.

- In (d) through (f), the answer *so-so* means not bad but not good. It means things are okay but one might wish they were better.

- In the answers in (g), students might be interested in the derivation of *lousy*. It means *very bad*, but the word itself comes from the noun *louse*, the plural of which is *lice*. Lice are international pests that infect humans. The literal meaning of *lousy* is "full of lice," but in everyday conversation native speakers don't connect the word with the pest. They use it simply to mean *very bad* or *miserable*.

- Example (h) needs a little discussion and perhaps role-playing. Ask Student A to introduce B to C. Ask B and C to use *How do you do?* Have them shake hands at the same time.

☐ EXERCISE 28, p. 152. *HOW. (Chart 6-13)*

> *Oral (books closed).*
> This exercise can be a spelling game in small groups. Many of the words on this list are frequently misspelled by second-language students—and native speakers as well.
> Item 1: a mnemonic device for this oft-misspelled word is to remember it consists of three individual words: *to + get + her.*
> Items 4, 5, 9, 13, and 15: Remind the class of the spelling rules they learned in Chart 2-5.
> Item 6: The old spelling rule is: "i" before "e" except after "c" or when pronounced /ey/ as in *neighbor* and *weigh.* That rule accounts for the spelling of *receive* and *neighbor;* it does not, however, account for the spelling of *foreign* in item 8. Tell your students you sympathize with them in any difficulties they have spelling English words. Remind them they can always look words up in their dictionaries.

☐ EXERCISE 29, p. 153. *HOW. (Chart 6-13)*

> *Oral.*
> Expand the exercise to include other words or phrases students may be interested in knowing in one another's languages.
> In some languages there is no direct translation for *thank you.* Surveying the language groups in your class, discuss various ways of expressing thanks.
> Some classes like to list all the ways to say "I love you" in as many languages as they can. Some students assiduously copy down each one.

☐ EXERCISE 30, p. 153. *HOW. (Chart 6-13)*

> *Oral.*
> This is intended as a fun, change-of-pace exercise. Prepare the class for doing the exercise as shown in the example by pronouncing all the words in Group A first. Have them repeat. Then pronounce one word and have the class tell you the number of the word you said. Open the discussion of the pronunciations. At least some students should spontaneously produce correct *how*-questions.

Following are the phonetic transcriptions for the exercise items:

GROUP A:
(1) beat = /biyt/   (6) bat = /bæt/
(2) bit = /bɪt/   (7) but = /bət/
(3) bet = /bɛt/   (8) boot = /buwt/
(4) bite = /bayt/   (9) boat = /bowt/
(5) bait = /beyt/   (10) bought = /bɔt/ or /bat/

GROUP B:
(1) zoos = /zuwz/   (6) chose = /čowz/
(2) Sue's = /suws/   (7) those = /ðowz/
(3) shoes = /šuwz/   (8) toes = /towz/
(4) chews = /čuwz/ or /čɪuz/   (9) doze = /dowz/
(5) choose = /čuwz/   (10) dose = /dows/

NOTE: In Group B, items (4) and (5) have the same pronunciation.

◇ WORKBOOK PRACTICE 22, p. 120. *Using HOW.* *(Charts 6-8 → 6-13)*

Dialogue construction. [Guided Study]
If you assign this as written homework, ask the students to write both the question and the answer.

SAMPLE QUESTIONS: **1.** How expensive was the watch?   **2.** How did you get to the train station last night?   **3.** How long did the exam last?   **4.** How old is your brother Ivan?   **5.** When will dinner be ready?   **6.** How did you cut the melon open?   **7.** How often do you speak with your mother?   **8.** How far is the supermarket from your house?   **9.** How is your sister doing after her operation?   **10.** How do you spell "written?"   **11.** How cold does it get in Siberia?   **12.** How are Talal's grades this quarter?

☐ EXERCISE 31, p. 153. *Question words.* *(Chart 6-13)*

Written; dialogue construction.
This is a summary review exercise of Chapter 6.

◇ WORKBOOK PRACTICE 23, p. 121. *Cumulative review.* *(Charts 6-1 → 6-13)*

Transformation. [Selfstudy]

ANSWERS: **1.** When are you going to buy a new bicycle?   **2.** How are you going to pay for it?   **3.** How long (How many years) did you have your old bike?   **4.** How often/How many times a week do you ride your bike?   **5.** How do you (usually) get to work?   **6.** Are you going to ride your bike to work tomorrow?   **7.** Why didn't you ride your bike to work today?   **8.** When did Jason get his new bike?   **9.** Who broke Jason's new bike?   **10.** What (Whose bike) did Billy break?   **11.** What (Whose bike) is broken?   **12.** How did Billy break Jason's bike?   **13.** Does your bike have a comfortable seat?   [also possible: Has your bike (got) a comfortable seat?]   **14.** What kind of bicycle do you have?   [also possible: What kind of bike have you (got)?]   **15.** Which bicycle is yours, the red one or the blue one?   **16.** Where do you keep your bicycle at night?   **17.** Who(m) does that bike belong to?   OR To whom does that bike belong?   **18.** Whose bike did you borrow?   **19.** Where is Rita?   **20.** What is she doing?   **21.** How far did Rita ride her bike yesterday?   **22.** How do you spell "bicycle"?

◇ WORKBOOK PRACTICE 24, p. 122. *Cumulative review. (Charts 6-1 → 6-13)*

Transformation. [Guided Study]

ANSWERS: **1.** How soon will the clean clothes be dry?   **2.** What did you do last Saturday afternoon?   **3.** Which dictionary did you buy?   **4.** How long did it take you to clean your apartment before your parents came to visit?   **5.** How can I/you reach the top shelf?
6. What kind of bread do you like best?   **7.** Why didn't you answer the phone when it rang?
8. Who(m) are going to the show with?/With whom are you going to the show?   **9.** Who repaired the radio?   **10.** How cold does it get/How's the weather in your hometown in the winter?   **11.** What is Jack doing?   **12.** Who(m) is he playing tennis with?/With whom is he playing tennis?   **13.** What is Anna doing?   **14.** What is she throwing in the air?
15. What are they holding?   **16.** What is between them?   **17.** Where are they?
18. How long have they been playing?   **19.** Who is winning right now?   **20.** Who won the last game?

◇ WORKBOOK PRACTICE 25, p. 124. *Cumulative review. (Charts 6-1 → 6-13)*

Dialogue construction. [Guided Study]

SAMPLE DIALOGUES: **1.** A: When should I meet you?   B: How about 3:00?
2. A: What kind of fruit do you like best?   B: Strawberries.   **3.** A: What country is south of the United States?   B: Mexico.   **4.** A: How many times a week do you go grocery shopping?   B: Three or four.   **5.** A: What do you plan to do tomorrow?   B: Tomorrow my friends and I are going to the horse races.   **6.** A: How far is it from your house to school?
B: Eight blocks.   **7.** A: Who killed Alex's brother?   B: A drunk driver.   **8.** A: Why are you breathing hard?   B: I just ran five miles.   **9.** A: What do you do for a living?
B: I'm a dental assistant.   **10.** A: How do you spell "happened"?   B: With two "p's" but only one "n."   **11.** A: How long does it take to get to our hotel from the airport?   B: About twenty minutes.   **12.** A: Why didn't you call me when Uncle Don arrived?   B: Because I didn't want to wake you up.

EXPANSION: Students can extemporaneously create dialogues. Give each student a strip of paper on which is written a sentence about something that hypothetically happened last night. Write the following format outline on the chalkboard:
A: *I had a . . . experience yesterday.* (The ellipsis represents an adjective Student A needs to
   supply; possibly suggest that *an interesting* would be a possible completion for almost all
   situations.)
B: *Oh?/Really?   What happened?*
A: *(read from strip)*
B: *(question)*
A: *(answer)*
B: *(question)*
A: *(answer)*
B: *Etc.*

Example: The strip says   *I was in an accident.*
A: *I had (a really awful) experience yesterday.*
B: *Oh?   What happened?*
A: *I was in an accident.*
B: *What kind of accident?*
A: *A car accident.*
B: *How did it happen?*
A: *My friend wasn't paying attention to the traffic. He rear-ended the car in front of us.*

B: *Was anyone hurt?*

A: *Etc.*

Possible strip sentences:

> *A tree fell on my (place of residence).*
> *A being from outer space visited me.*
> *I was interviewed on television.*
> *I got stuck in an elevator.*
> *There was a fire in my (place of residence).*
> *A bird flew into my (place of residence).*
> *I got lost.*
> *I had to take my (roommate, friend, spouse) to the emergency room at (name of a local hospital).*
> *Etc.*

SUGGESTION: Make up strip sentences that engage the students' creativity in various imaginary untoward events. For some reason, untoward events seem to activate students' imaginations and zany senses of humor. You can also try more gentle situations such as *I saw a black and gold butterfly* or *I made a new friend.*

NOTE: The author thanks teacher, friend, and colleague Irene Juzkiw (University of Missouri) for the inspiration for this suggested expansion on the text. I'd love to hear from any of you who have similar suggestions for the *Teacher's Guide* or the texts that you would like to share with other in-the-trenches colleagues. My address is in the *Preface.*

◊ WORKBOOK PRACTICE 26, p. 124. *Cumulative review. (Charts 6-1 → 6-13)*

Oral/written. [Guided Study]

Perhaps make this a game. Consider the topics one at a time. The task of each group is to see how many meaningful and correct questions they can come up with in a given time. The group with the most wins. As another possibility, give a prize for the most interesting question. Perhaps the class could vote on which question was the most interesting.

You could, of course, simply break the class into groups and let them talk to each other, with one student as the recorder of the questions the group comes up with. Then the whole class can share questions and attempt answers.

Another possibility is to have groups exchange lists of questions, with one group answering the other's questions, if possible. If the questions are challenging and insightful, you could even send the groups to the library to find the answers.

For item 1, you might want to limit (or even prohibit) questions with *where.* Discuss what the term *geography* encompasses: climate, population, elevation, vegetation, surface water, land use, animal life, natural resources, principal products.

CHART 6-14: USING *HOW ABOUT* AND *WHAT ABOUT*

- *How about* and *what about* invite the listener to respond with how s/he feels about the idea the questioner suggests. The questioner is saying: "I think this is a possible idea for us/you to consider. What do you think?"

- The *-ing* form in examples (c) and (d) is a gerund. Gerunds are introduced in Chapter 10.

- In examples (e) and (f), *how about* and *what about* are "conversation continuers." They are used to promote the sharing of information in polite conversation. In some situations, if someone asks you if you are hungry, it is polite to ask him/her if s/he is hungry, as in (f). Students will practice this use in Exercise 34.

☐ EXERCISE 32, p. 154. *HOW ABOUT and WHAT ABOUT.* (Chart 6-14)

> *Oral (books closed).*
> The idea of this exercise is to make the students comfortable with the use of *how about* and *what about* in informal conversation. Present the cues informally, in your own style. Don't read them verbatim. Through tone of voice and facial expression, invite friendly suggestions with *how about* and *what about.*

☐ EXERCISE 33, p. 154. *HOW ABOUT YOU and WHAT ABOUT YOU.* (Chart 6-14)

> *Open completion.*
> Students could work in pairs and then role-play one or some of their dialogues for the rest of the class.

☐ EXERCISE 34, p. 155. *HOW ABOUT YOU and WHAT ABOUT YOU.* (Chart 6-14)

> *Oral.*
> The directions to Student A say to look "directly into eyes of Student B." In some cultures, looking another person directly in the eye is not polite or has hierarchical implications. In much of the English-speaking world, people look each other straight in the eye. There is no need for international students of English to adopt English-speakers' cultural mannerisms, but it's good for them to be made aware of these mannerisms. And in the environment of the classroom, they may want to experiment with cultural mannerisms different from their own.

◇ WORKBOOK PRACTICE 27, p. 124. *WHAT ABOUT and HOW ABOUT.* (Chart 6-14)

> *Open completion.* [Guided Study]
>
> *POSSIBLE RESPONSES:*   **1.** When will you be ready to leave for town? . . . 8:30   **2.** Would you like to come with me Tuesday to visit my sister? . . . Wednesday   **3.** A: James . . . the movies   B: James . . . he has to babysit   A: Robert   B: Why don't you ask him?
> **4.** B: you   A: you   B: steak

CHART 6-15: TAG QUESTIONS

• It's important for the students to understand that a question with a tag indicates the speaker's belief about the validity of the idea being expressed. The speaker believes to be true what is expressed in the statement before the tag.

• Students are already familiar with the idea of a rising intonation at the end of a question. In the examples and exercises on tags, a rising intonation would be appropriate throughout. You may wish to introduce only that intonation and keep the focus on the form and meaning of tag questions. Although it is not essential, you may wish to explain and demonstrate falling intonation.

If the speaker is truly seeking information, his/her voice rises: *This is your hat, isn't it?* If the speaker is expressing his/her opinion, the voice falls at the end: *This is a good class, isn't it.* (The period instead of a question mark here helps show a falling rather than rising intonation.) In this case, the speaker is simply making a comment and inviting conversation. S/he is not asking if this is a good class, whereas in the previous example the speaker is asking if the hat belongs to the listener.

• Other possible informal tags that turn statements into questions follow:
It's really cold today, **eh**?
This food is delicious, **huh**?
You borrowed my dictionary yesterday, **no**?

☐ EXERCISE 35, p. 156. *Tag questions.* *(Chart 6-15)*

Controlled completion.

ANSWERS:

2. doesn't she? . . . Yes, she does.
3. do you? . . . No, I don't.
4. didn't he? . . . Yes, he did.
5. won't she? . . . Yes, she will.
6. isn't he? . . . Yes, he is.
7. did s/he? . . . No, s/he didn't.
8. can't you? . . . Yes, I can.
9. can they? . . . No, they can't.
10. shouldn't you? . . . Yes, I should.

11. doesn't it? . . . Yes, it does.
12. were you? . . . No, I wasn't.
13. isn't it? . . . Yes, it is.
14. isn't it? . . . Yes, it is.
15. aren't they? . . . Yes, they are.
16. aren't they? . . . Yes, they are.
17. is it? . . . No, it isn't.
18. wasn't it? . . . Yes, it was.

☐ EXERCISE 36, p. 158. *Tag questions.* *(Chart 6-15)*

Oral (books closed).

EXPANSION: Make statements about your students, the classroom, your school and city, current world affairs, and anything else of interest. At the end of your statement, keep your intonation up and nod at a student to add a tag question. If you have taught only rising intonation, avoid statements such as *Maria is very nice* that do not seek information but express opinions. If you do teach falling intonation, make up a series of suitable statements: *Yoko's English is very good,* . . . *This is an old building,* . . . *Mr. Chu never says a bad word about anyone,* . . . *He's a very kind person,* . . .

ANSWERS:

1. doesn't s/he?
2. does s/he?
3. doesn't s/he?
4. does s/he?
5. wasn't s/he?

6. was s/he?
7. didn't s/he?
8. did s/he?
9. isn't s/he?
10. is s/he?

11. can't s/he?
12. isn't s/he?
13. can s/he?
14. is s/he?
15. doesn't s/he?

16. won't s/he?
17. can't s/he?
18. doesn't s/he?
19. didn't s/he?
20. doesn't s/he
    [BrE: hasn't s/he?]

☐ EXERCISE 37, p. 158. *Tag questions.* *(Chart 6-15)*

Oral.

Demonstrate the format of the exercise until the students understand what they're supposed to do, then break them into groups of three. Tell the three to rotate being Students A, B, and C, with one person being Student A for items 1 through 4, another for 5 through 8, and the other 9 through 12. Alternatively, groups of three could be assigned only one item, which they will prepare and perform before the class.

◇ WORKBOOK PRACTICE 28, p. 125. *Tag questions.* *(Chart 6-15)*

Controlled completion. [Selfstudy]
This is an exercise on auxiliary verbs.

ANSWERS:
1. a. don't   b. doesn't   c. don't   d. doesn't   e. isn't   f. aren't   g. does
h. is   2. a. didn't   b. did   c. were   d. wasn't   3. a. aren't   b. is   c. is
d. weren't   e. was   4. a. can't   b. will   c. shouldn't   d. wouldn't   e. do
f. didn't

◊ WORKBOOK PRACTICE 29, p. 126. *Tag questions. (Chart 6-15)*

Controlled completion. [Selfstudy]
This is an exercise on auxiliary verbs and pronouns.

ANSWERS: **1.** wasn't he **2.** can't they **3.** don't they **4.** is he **5.** wouldn't you **6.** aren't they **7.** isn't it **8.** can it **9.** shouldn't you **10.** won't she **11.** doesn't he **12.** did you **13.** is it **14.** do I **15.** is it **16.** weren't they **17.** will she **18.** doesn't it

◊ WORKBOOK PRACTICE 30, p. 125. *Tag questions. Chart 6-15)*

Oral. [Guided Study]
This is an exercise on the meaning and use of tag questions.

POSSIBLE RESPONSES: **1.** Athens isn't the capital of Italy, is it? **2.** Athens is the capital of Greece, isn't it? **3.** Plants can grow in deserts, can't they? **4.** Deserts aren't complete wastelands, are they? **5.** Cactuses thrive in deserts, don't they? **6.** Dinosaurs weighed more than elephants, didn't they? **7.** Blue whales are larger than dinosaurs, aren't they? **8.** Whales don't lay eggs, do they? **9.** Turtles lay eggs, don't they? **10.** Abraham Lincoln wasn't the first president of the United States, was he? **11.** We will have a test on Chapter 6, won't we? **12.** Free response. [Encourage the students to make statements of belief or opinion, and then have them transform their ideas into tag questions that check the validity of these thoughts. You might suggest topics: I think that *(name of a person, city, country, restaurant, street, animal, bird, etc.)* . . . .

◊ WORKBOOK PRACTICE 31, p. 127. *Asking questions. (Chapter 6)*

Dialogue construction. [Guided Study]
Assign one dialogue per pair. Have some or all of the pairs role-play their dialogues in front of the class or small groups.

☐ EXERCISE 38, p. 159. *Prepositions. (Chapter 6; Appendix 1)*

Controlled completion.

ANSWERS: **1.** with **2.** to **3.** from **4.** about **5.** to **6.** about **7.** at **8.** for **9.** for **10.** for **11.** about **12.** to

◊ WORKBOOK PRACTICE 32, p. 127. *Prepositions. (Chapter 6; Appendix 1)*

Controlled completion. [Selfstudy]

ANSWERS: **1.** about **2.** with **3.** to **4.** at **5.** to **6.** to . . . for **7.** of/about **8.** for **9.** about . . . about **10.** from

Chapter 7: THE PRESENT PERFECT AND THE PAST PERFECT

ORDER OF CHAPTER	CHARTS	EXERCISES	WORKBOOK
The past participle	7-1	Ex. 1	
Form and meaning of the present perfect	7-2 → 7-3	Ex. 2 → 4	Pr. 1 → 2
The simple past vs. the present perfect	7-4	Ex. 5 → 7	Pr. 3
Irregular verbs	(2-4)	Ex. 8 → 15	Pr. 4 → 5
Since and *for*	7-5	Ex. 16 → 18	Pr. 6 → 8
Cumulative review		Ex. 20 → 21	Pr. 9
The present perfect progressive	7-6 → 7-7	Ex. 22 → 24	Pr. 10 → 11
Cumulative review		Ex. 25	Pr. 12 → 14
Midsentence adverbs	7-8	Ex. 26 → 29	Pr. 15 → 16
Already, yet, still, anymore	7-9	Ex. 30 → 33	Pr. 17 → 18
Cumulative review		Ex. 34	
The past perfect	7-10	Ex. 35 → 37	Pr. 19 → 22
Cumulative review			Pr. 23 → 24
Prepositions		Ex. 38	Pr. 25

General Notes on Chapter 7

• OBJECTIVE: The perfective aspect of verb tenses is not unique to English, but it is not easy for learners to control. It is one of the most useful features of the language because it relates two or more periods of time to each other. This chapter includes the adverbs that most frequently accompany the present perfect and the past perfect.

• APPROACH: The chapter begins with a short list of verb forms to review, with special emphasis on past participles. Then the present perfect is introduced, practiced, and contrasted with the simple past. Time expressions with *since* and *for* are shown to accompany the present perfect frequently. The progressive form of the present perfect is presented, followed by numerous exercises with adverbs used with several verb tenses. The chapter concludes with a brief presentation of the past perfect and exercises that force choices among various verb forms.

• TERMINOLOGY: The terms "aspect" and "tense" are not used here, only "present perfect" and "past perfect."

CHART 7-1: THE PAST PARTICIPLE

- Chapter 7 is the first time in the text that the students are asked to use the past participle. The principal purpose of this chart is to define the term "past participle."

☐ EXERCISE 1, p. 160. *Past participles. (Chart 7-1)*

Controlled completion.
The verbs in this list are the ones used in the initial form-and-meaning exercises in this chapter. Beginning with Exercise 8, other irregular verbs are introduced.

ANSWERS: **3.** gone   **4.** had   **5.** met   **6.** called   **7.** fallen   **8.** done **9.** known   **10.** flown   **11.** come   **12.** studied   **13.** stayed   **14.** begun   **15.** started **16.** written   **17.** eaten   **18.** cut   **19.** read   **20.** been

CHART 7-2: FORMS OF THE PRESENT PERFECT

- This is the first juncture in the text where the students deal with *have* as an auxiliary in a verb tense. Point out that the past participle is the main verb. Use the illustration of Jim and Ann to discuss the present perfect: question form, short answer, affirmative, negative. For example: *Has Jim (already) eaten lunch? Yes, he has. He's eaten lunch. Has Ann eaten lunch? No, she hasn't. She hasn't eaten lunch.* Try to convey the meaning of "before now," i.e., "at an unspecified time in the past."

- In (e), compare the two possible meanings of the contractions *she's* and *he's:*
  COMPARE: *She's/He's (She is/He is) eating lunch.* vs. *She's/He's (She has/He has) eaten lunch.*

  In (f), compare the two meanings of *it's:*
  COMPARE: *It's (It is) cold today.* vs. *It's (It has) been cold for the last three days.*

◇ WORKBOOK PRACTICE 1, p. 128. *Forms of the present perfect. (Charts 7-1 → 7-3)*

Controlled completion. [Selfstudy]

ANSWERS:
1. A: Have you ever eaten   B: have . . . have eaten   OR   haven't . . . have never eaten
2. A: Have you ever talked   B: have . . . have talked   OR   haven't . . . have never talked
3. A: Has Erica ever rented   B: has . . . has rented   OR   hasn't . . . has never rented
4. A: Have you ever seen   B: have . . . have seen   OR   haven't . . . have never seen
5. A: Has Joe ever caught   B: has . . . has caught   OR   hasn't . . . has never caught
6. A: Have you ever had   B: have . . . have had   OR   haven't . . . have never had

CHART 7-3 MEANINGS OF THE PRESENT PERFECT

• The present perfect relates past events to present time; it basically communicates the information that something occurred before the present time.

• The present perfect is a difficult tense for many students. The text attempts to move slowly. Students need time to digest its meanings and uses. They also need practice with the past participles of irregular verbs.

☐ EXERCISE 2, p. 162. *Present perfect: form and meaning. (Chart 7-3)*

Fill-in-the-blanks.
This exercise presents further examples for discussion of the grammar in Charts 7-2 and 7-3. There's nothing challenging or difficult for the students here. They need to make sure they grasp the forms and understand the meaning of each item. Students might find it helpful if you draw or point to a tense diagram for each item, showing them which diagram applies to which item. For example, item 1 can be represented by the top left diagram in Chart 7-3.

ANSWERS: **2.** I've (I have) finished [top diagram, expressing "before now"] **3.** She's (She has) flown [middle diagram, expressing repeated action in the past "before now"] **4.** They've (They have) known [bottom diagram, expressing duration from past to present] **5.** It's (It has) been [bottom diagram, expressing duration from past to present] **6.** You've (You have) learned [bottom diagram, expressing duration from past to present] **7.** We've (We have) been [bottom diagram, meaning duration from past to present] **8.** He's (He has) finished [top diagram, expressing "before now"] **9.** He's (He has) been [bottom diagram, expressing duration from past to present] **10.** She's (She has) been [middle diagram, expressing repeated action in the past "before now"] [Discuss *lately,* meaning "recently, in the last few days or weeks."]

☐ EXERCISE 3, p. 163. *Spoken contractions with HAVE and HAS. (Chart 7-3)*

Pronunciation.
Discuss the meaning of the sentences as well as the usual spoken contractions.

ANSWERS: **2.** "Jane's been" **3.** "The weather's been" **4.** "My parents've been" **5.** "Mike's already" **6.** "My friends've moved" **7.** "My roommate's been" **8.** "My aunt and uncle've lived"

☐ EXERCISE 4, p. 163. *Present perfect: negative forms. (Chart 7-3)*

Fill-in-the-blanks.
All of these items express situations or activities that have <u>not</u> occurred before the present time. Point out and discuss the meaning of *yet;* it is commonly used in negative present perfect sentences. Students will study it in Chart 7-9.

ANSWERS: **3.** he hasn't finished **4.** I've never met **5.** Ron has never been **6.** Linda hasn't been **7.** They haven't come **8.** We haven't finished **9.** Alice has never gone **10.** I haven't called

◇ WORKBOOK PRACTICE 2, p. 129. *The present perfect. (Charts 7-1 → 7-3)*

Controlled completion. [Selfstudy]
These items can be used in class for further discussion of the meaning of the present perfect. Point out the time expressions used with the present perfect: *for centuries, never, so far this year, all evening, for two days, since the beginning of the term, etc.* Also point out, as in item 2, the absence of any time expression, in which case only the tense itself conveys time information, i.e., before now at an unspecified time in the past.

ANSWERS: **1.** have used   **2.** has risen [*to be over = to be finished*]   **3.** have never played   **4.** have won   **5.** hasn't spoken   **6.** hasn't eaten [Note: A feminine or masculine pronoun is used in the singular with animals such as pets whose sex is known. Otherwise, the pronoun *it* is used.]   **7.** has given   **8.** haven't saved   **9.** Have you ever slept   **10.** have never worn   **11.** has improved   **12.** have looked

---

CHART 7-4: USING THE SIMPLE PAST vs. THE PRESENT PERFECT

• The problem for the teacher in presenting this chart is the fact that the simple past and present perfect are sometimes interchangeable in informal spoken English, especially in sentences containing *already,* as in example sentence (b). The use of the simple past in a sentence such as "I already finished my work" is common and acceptable, especially in American English. The text's intent is to draw clear distinctions between the two tenses for teaching purposes; students can blur and blend the two later as they gain experience with the language. Trying to explain to the students the ways in which the simple past and the present perfect can express the same meaning is more confusing than enlightening at this point, at least in the author's experience. Note that the simple past and present perfect are not interchangeable in examples (a), (c), and (d).

☐ EXERCISE 5, p. 164. *Present perfect vs. simple past. (Chart 7-4)*

Fill-in-the-blanks.
Compare and discuss the two tenses in each item.

ANSWERS: **2.** have . . . have eaten . . . ate   **3.** have . . . have talked . . . talked   **4.** A: have you visited   B: have visited . . . visited . . . was   **5.** A: Has Bob ever had   B: has . . . has had . . . had

☐ EXERCISE 6, p. 165. *Present perfect vs. simple past. (Chart 7-4)*

Fill-in-the-blanks.
This exercise isolates situations in which the simple past and the present perfect might be interchangeable in sentences with *already.* You may or may not choose to discuss this interchangeability. A passing mention will probably suffice.
    NOTE: The use of the simple past with *already* is principally AmE. In BrE, the present perfect is preferred.

ANSWERS: **2.** has already eaten . . . ate   **3.** have already seen . . . saw   **4.** have already written . . . wrote   **5.** has already called . . . called   **6.** have already read . . . read

☐ EXERCISE 7, p. 166. *Present perfect. (Chart 7-4)*

Oral.

The grammar emphasis here is on adverbial expressions frequently used with the present perfect in both questions and statements. This exercise can be done in pairs or groups.

ANSWERS: **1-4.** have you ever been **5-8.** have you ever eaten **9-12.** have you ever ridden **13-16.** have you ever been in **17-20.** have you ever played **21.** have you ever walked to **22.** have you ever stayed up **23.** have you ever gone to **24.** have you ever used

☐ EXERCISE 8, p. 167. *Irregular verbs. (Chart 7-4)*

Controlled completion.

Exercises 8 through 15 come in pairs. First the students produce (from memory, by guess, or by looking at Chart 2-4) the forms of the irregular verbs, and second they practice these verbs in questions and answers. These exercises can be done in pairs or groups. Not all of them need to be done on the same day; you might spread them over two to four days, conducting frequent oral reviews and quizzes as you go along. The text anticipates that the students will memorize the irregular verbs, which are grouped more or less according to similarity of form as a possible aid to memorization.

ANSWERS: **2.** ate, eaten **3.** gave, given **4.** fell, fallen **5.** took, taken **6.** shook, shaken **7.** drove, driven **8.** rode, ridden **9.** wrote, written **10.** bit, bitten [Note: In AmE, but not BrE, *bit* is a possible variation of the past participle *bitten*.] **11.** hid, hidden [Note: In AmE, but not BrE, *hid* is a possible variation of the past participle *hidden*.]

☐ EXERCISE 9, p. 167. *Present perfect: irregular verbs. (Chart 7-4)*

Oral.

ANSWERS: **1.** Have you ever ridden **2.** Have you ever taken **3.** Have you ever written **4.** Have you ever given **5.** Have you ever shaken **6.** Have you ever bitten **7.** Have you ever driven **8.** Have you ever eaten **9.** Have you ever hidden **10.** Have you ever fallen **11.** Have you ever seen

☐ EXERCISE 10, p. 168. *Irregular verbs. (Chart 7-4)*

Controlled completion.

ANSWERS: **1.** broke, broken **2.** spoke, spoken **3.** stole, stolen **4.** got, gotten [Note: *gotten* = AmE. The past participle in BrE is *got*.] **5.** wore, worn **6.** drew, drawn **7.** grew, grown **8.** threw, thrown **9.** blew, blown **10.** flew, flown **11.** drank, drunk **12.** sang, sung **13.** swam, swum **14.** went, gone

☐ EXERCISE 11, p. 168. *Present perfect: irregular verbs. (Chart 7-4)*

Oral.

ANSWERS: **1.** flown **2.** broken **3.** drawn **4.** swum **5.** spoken **6.** gone **7.** worn **8.** gotten (got) **9.** stolen **10.** grown **11.** sung **12.** drunk **13.** thrown **14.** blown

☐ EXERCISE 12, p. 169. *Irregular verbs. (Chart 7-4)*

Controlled completion.

ANSWERS: **1.** had, had **2.** made, made **3.** built, built **4.** lent, lent **5.** sent, sent **6.** spent, spent **7.** left, left **8.** lost, lost **9.** slept, slept **10.** felt, felt **11.** met, met **12.** sat, sat **13.** won, won **14.** hung, hung

☐ EXERCISE 13, p. 169. *Present perfect: irregular verbs. (Chart 7-4)*

Oral.

ANSWERS: **1.** lost **2.** met **3.** had **4.** felt **5.** sent **6.** sat **7.** left **8.** spent **9.** lent **10.** slept **11.** made **12.** built **13.** won **14.** hung

☐ EXERCISE 14, p. 170. *Irregular verbs. (Chart 7-4)*

Controlled completion.

ANSWERS: **1.** sold, sold **2.** told, told **3.** heard, heard **4.** held, held **5.** fed, fed **6.** read, read **7.** found, found **8.** bought, bought **9.** thought, thought **10.** taught, taught **11.** caught, caught **12.** cut, cut **13.** hit, hit **14.** quit, quit **15.** put, put

☐ EXERCISE 15, p. 170. *Present perfect: irregular verbs. (Chart 7-4)*

Oral.

ANSWERS: **1.** taught **2.** held **3.** found **4.** cut **5.** thought **6.** heard **7.** read **8.** fed **9.** told **10.** quit [BrE: quitted] **11.** bought **12.** sold **13.** hit **14.** put **15.** caught

◇ WORKBOOK PRACTICE 3, p. 129. *The present perfect vs. the simple past. (Chart 7-4)*

Fill-in-the-blanks. [Selfstudy]
The text expects the students to use the present perfect with *already* as a way of distinguishing between the meanings of the present perfect and the simple past.

ANSWERS: **1.** have already called . . . called **2.** have already begun . . . began **3.** have already eaten . . . ate **4.** have already bought . . . bought **5.** has already left . . . left **6.** have already locked . . . locked

◇ WORKBOOK PRACTICE 4, p. 130. *Irregular verbs. (Charts 2-3, 2-4, and 7-4)*

Fill-in-the-blanks. [Selfstudy]
One of the purposes of this and the next practice is to compare the simple past and the present perfect. While the students are practicing the forms of the irregular verbs, the text seeks also to give them an understanding of the situations in which the two tenses are used.

ANSWERS: **1.** began . . . have begun **2.** bent . . . have bent **3.** broadcast . . . has broadcast **4.** caught . . . have caught **5.** came . . . have come **6.** cut . . . have cut **7.** dug . . . have dug **8.** drew . . . has drawn **9.** fed . . . have fed **10.** fought . . . have fought **11.** forgot . . . have forgotten **12.** hid . . . have hidden **13.** hit . . . has hit [*A homerun* = a ball that is hit out of the playing field boundaries, thus allowing the hitter to run around first, second, and third bases to arrive at home base and score one point.] **14.** held . . . has held **15.** kept . . . have kept **16.** led . . . has led **17.** lost . . . has lost **18.** met . . . have

met   **19.** rode . . . have ridden   **20.** rang . . . has rung   **21.** saw . . . have seen
22. stole . . . has stolen   **23.** stuck . . . have stuck   **24.** swept . . . have swept   **25.** took
. . . have taken   **26.** upset . . . have upset   **27.** withdrew . . . have withdrawn   **28.** wrote
. . . have written

◇ WORKBOOK PRACTICE 5, p. 132. *Irregular verbs. (Charts 2-3, 2-4, and 7-4)*

> *Fill-in-the-blanks.* [Guided Study]
>
> ANSWERS: **1.** a. have gone   b. went   **2.** a. gave   b. Has she ever given
> **3.** a. have fallen   b. fell   **4.** a. Have you ever broken   b. broke   **5.** a. have never
> shaken   b. shook   **6.** a. heard   b. have heard   **7.** a. flew   b. has flown
> **8.** a. has worn   b. wore   **9.** a. Have you ever built   b. built   **10.** a. has taught
> b. taught   **11.** a. have you ever found   b. found   **12.** a. drove   b. have never driven
> **13.** a. sang   b. have sung   **14.** a. have never run   b. ran   **15.** a. told   b. has told
> **16.** a. stood   b. have stood   **17.** a. spent   b. have already spent   **18.** a. have made
> b. made   **19.** a. has risen   b. rose   **20.** a. felt   b. have felt

---

CHART 7-5: USING *SINCE* AND *FOR*

- Understanding the meaning and use of *since* helps students to understand the meaning and use of the present perfect.

- *Ever* is frequently used as an intensifier in front of *since*. The use of *ever* has little, if any, effect on the meaning of *since*. *I've lived here **ever since** May.*

- In example (a), *since* is used as a preposition, and in examples (f) and (g) as a subordinating conjunction. Subordinating conjunctions are generally called "time clause words" in this text, or "words that introduce adverb clauses." *Since*-clauses can be related to the "time clauses" presented in Chart 2-8; a *since*-clause is an adverb clause of time.

- *Since* has another use not mentioned in the chart. It is also an adverb: *He got a job at the factory in 1975 and has worked there ever since.* The question may or may not arise.

- *Since* has another meaning: *because*. In this case, any tense can be used in the main clause. *Since* meaning *because* is presented not in this text but in *Understanding and Using English Grammar*, Chart 8-6. Example: *Bob's last name is Black.* **Since** *it's a common name, he never has to spell it for people. My last name is Bryzewski.* **Since** *it's an unusual name, I often have to spell it out for people.*

- Try to keep the focus on the use of the present perfect with sentences containing *since*. It is true, however, that sometimes the simple present is used in the main clause rather than the present perfect. In this case, the simple present is usually used to express a general truth. For example, *Fewer people travel by train since the development of the automobile and airplane.* The text chooses not to teach this, as the instances in which the simple present is used are relatively few. The past perfect can also be used in sentences with *since: I hadn't seen George since we were children.* It is possible that your more alert students may find and ask about such sentences. Explain, if necessary, that their grammar book is a guide to useful information about English for second language learners, not a compendium of all there is to know about English grammar. They truly don't want to know all there is to know about English grammar.

☐ EXERCISE 16, p. 172. *SINCE vs. FOR. (Chart 7-5)*

Controlled completion.

ANSWERS: **3.** since   **4.** since   **5.** for   **6.** since   **7.** since   **8.** for   **9.** since
10. for   **11.** since   **12.** since   **13.** for   **14.** for   **15.** since   **16.** for

☐ EXERCISE 17, p. 172. *SINCE vs. FOR. (Chart 7-5)*

Controlled completion.
Students should complete the sentences with accurate information about themselves. Ask them to give accurate answers for item 1 also.

☐ EXERCISE 18, p. 172. *SINCE vs. FOR. (Chart 7-5)*

Oral (books closed).
This exercise could be teacher-led or done in groups with a leader playing the teacher's role. Make it clear that Student A is to use *since* and that Student B is to use *for* to paraphrase Student A's response.

☐ EXERCISE 19, p. 173. *Tag questions: review. (Chart 7-5)*

Controlled completion.
This exercise uses tag questions to review auxiliary verbs and to emphasize the role *have* and *has* play in the present perfect tense. This exercise is an opportunity to compare the form and meaning of the present perfect with other tenses.

ANSWERS:
4. hasn't she? . . . Yes, she has.
5. didn't he? . . . Yes, he did.
6. haven't you? . . . Yes, I have.
7. did you? . . . No, I didn't.
8. don't you? . . . Yes, I do.
9. haven't they? . . . Yes, they have.
10. hasn't she? . . . Yes, she has.

11. doesn't she? [BrE: hasn't she?] Yes, she does. [BrE: Yes, she has.]
12. don't we . . . Yes, we do.
13. does he? . . . No, he doesn't
14. didn't you? . . . Yes, I did.
15. didn't you? . . . Yes, I did.
16. have you? . . . No, I haven't.

☐ EXERCISE 20, p. 174. *Present perfect vs. simple past. (Chart 7-5)*

Fill-in-the-blanks.
Items 1 through 7 are intended to emphasize that the simple past is used in the *since*-clause and the present perfect in the main clause.
    EXPANSION: Ask students to write a paragraph about themselves modeled on item 8.

ANSWERS: **1.** have known . . . was [A first-year student is called a *freshman;* a second year student is a *sophomore;* a third year student is a *junior;* and a fourth year student is a *senior.*]   **2.** has had . . . came   **3.** haven't had . . . came   **4.** began . . . have had   **5.** has been . . . was
6. hasn't been . . . graduated   **7.** started . . . have completed   **8.** have been . . . arrived
. . . began . . . came . . . have done . . . have met . . . have gone . . . went . . . met . . . spoke . . .
didn't practice . . . were . . . came . . . have met . . . have met

☐ EXERCISE 21, p. 175. *Present perfect vs. simple past.* *(Chart 7-5)*

> *Oral (books closed).*
> Ask a question that elicits the present perfect, then follow up with one that elicits the simple past as shown in the example. Pursue interesting responses; encourage spontaneous conversation.

◇ WORKBOOK PRACTICE 6, p. 134. *SINCE vs. FOR.* *(Chart 7-5)*

> *Controlled completion.* [Selfstudy]
>
> ANSWERS: **1.** since **2.** for **3.** since **4.** for **5.** for **6.** since **7.** since **8.** for **9.** since **10.** for **11.** since **12.** for **13.** since **14.** for

◇ WORKBOOK PRACTICE 7, p. 135. *Sentences with SINCE-clauses.* *(Chart 7-5)*

> *Fill-in-the-blanks.* [Selfstudy]
>
> ANSWERS: **1.** have known . . . were **2.** has changed . . . started **3.** was . . . have been **4.** haven't slept . . . left **5.** met . . . hasn't been **6.** has had . . . bought **7.** A: have you eaten . . . got up B: have eaten **8.** had . . . was . . . left . . . have taken . . . have had . . . have learned

◇ WORKBOOK PRACTICE 8, p. 135. *SINCE vs. FOR.* *(Chart 7-5)*

> *Sentence construction.* [Guided Study]
> This practice could also be done orally, teacher-led, books closed.

◇ WORKBOOK PRACTICE 9, p. 136. *Verb tense review.* *(Chapters 1, 2, 3, and 7)*

> *Fill-in-the-blanks.* [Guided Study]
> The students should feel quite proud of themselves if they understand the use of all the tenses in this exercise. If this exercise is easy for them, the teacher, text, and student have all done their jobs well.
>
> ANSWERS: **(1)** need **(2)** Have you ever had **(3)** have . . . have worked . . . started **(4)** had **(5)** did you work **(6)** Did you enjoy **(7)** didn't . . . was **(8)** are you working **(9)** don't have **(10)** Do you want **(11)** plan/am planning **(12)** am going/am going to go . . . is looking **(13)** will do . . . have never looked **(14)** don't know . . . will find . . . go

CHART 7-6: THE PRESENT PERFECT PROGRESSIVE

• A diagram for the present perfect progressive would look exactly the same as the diagram in the bottom box of Chart 7-3:

The present perfect and the present perfect progressive have exactly the same meaning when they express the <u>duration</u> of a situation from the past to the present time. The difference is that the present perfect progressive expresses the duration of "activities" and uses a fairly wide range of verbs, while the present perfect uses only stative verbs with *since* and *for* and expresses duration of "states" rather than "activities." This information may be more confusing than enlightening for the students. Keep the focus on the information presented in the text.

• A use of the present perfect progressive not presented in this text is to express the idea of "recently." For example, *We've been having a lot of rain (recently).* OR: *Mary is tired because she's been working too hard.* See *Understanding and Using English Grammar,* Chart 1-15, for more information.

☐ EXERCISE 22, p. 176. *Present perfect progressive vs. present progressive. (Chart 7-6)*

Fill-in-the-blanks.
The comparison with the present progressive is intended to help clarify the meaning of the present perfect progressive by emphasizing the idea of "in progress." The present progressive expresses what is in progress right now, and the present perfect progressive expresses how long it has been in progress.

ANSWERS: **1.** is watching . . . has been watching   **2.** is waiting . . . has been waiting   **3.** are doing . . . have been doing   **4.** are talking . . . have been talking   **5.** am sitting . . . have been sitting   **6.** A: are you doing   B: am working   A: have you been working   B: have been working

☐ EXERCISE 23, p. 177. *SINCE and FOR with the present progressive. (Chart 7-6)*

Oral (books closed).
The questions are intended to spur the teacher's mind to come up with ways to elicit the present perfect progressive in teacher-student conversation. The questions do not need to be read verbatim. For example, in item 1 set up the situation verbally to lead up to the present perfect progressive questions: "What time is it now? What time did you get to class this morning? Does it seem like you've been here for a long time? How long *have* you *been sitting* here?"

CHART 7-7: THE PRESENT PERFECT vs. THE PRESENT PERFECT PROGRESSIVE

• The text seeks to make the distinction between these two tenses by comparing repeated action to duration.

• With certain verbs, most notably *live, work* and *teach,* there is little or no difference in meaning between the present perfect and the present perfect progressive. *Erica has lived in this city since 1990* and *Erica has been living in this city since 1990* communicate essentially identical information.

☐ EXERCISE 24, p. 178. *Present perfect progressive vs. present perfect. (Chart 7-7)*

Fill-in-the-blanks.

ANSWERS: **1.** have walked   **2.** have been walking   **3.** has worked/has been working
4. have read   **5.** have been reading   **6.** has taught/has been teaching   **7.** has been
writing   **8.** have written

☐ EXERCISE 25, p. 178. *Review of verb tenses. (Chapters 1, 2, 3, and 7)*

Fill-in-the-blanks.
Students need time to work through this exercise. They could do it as seatwork in pairs prior to
class discussion or simply as homework.

ANSWERS: **2.** B: is studying   A: will she get/is she going to get/is she getting   A: has
she been studying   A: Does she study   **3.** A: is talking   B: is she talking   A: have been
talking   **4.** A: Do you know   B: have . . . get . . . will call . . . (will) give   [*Off the top of my
head* means "without thinking or looking it up." To know or say something *off the top of one's head*
means to know or say something without having to think about it.]   **5.** A: has been . . . . Has
anyone seen   B: saw . . . has been . . . will probably be/is probably going to be
6. A: have you had to   B: was   A: Are you   [*Nearsighted* means "able to see things close but not in
the distance." *Farsighted* means "able to see things far away but not close."]   **7.** A: Do you like
B: have never eaten   B: love   A: is . . . have gone   B: have never been . . . will be/is going to
be . . . get   [*hot = spicy*]   **8.** A: Do you smoke   A: have you been smoking/have you
smoked   B: I have been smoking/have smoked . . . was . . . have been smoking/have smoked
A: did you start   B: was   A: Do you want   B: plan/am planning . . . have decided . . . will
smoke/am going to smoke   A: will feel/are going to feel . . . stop   B: Have you ever smoked
A: have never had . . . was . . . smoked . . . sneaked [Some AmE dictionaries now list *snuck* as a
standard variation of *sneaked*.   *Snuck* seems to be gaining currency, even among educated speakers.] . . .
went . . . got . . . have not had

◇ WORKBOOK PRACTICE 10, p. 136. *The present perfect progressive. (Charts 7-6 and 7-7)*

Controlled completion; transformation. [Selfstudy]
This practice combines practice with the form and meaning of the present perfect progressive
with the use of *since* and *for*.

ANSWERS: **1.** A: has Eric been studying   B: has been studying . . . two hours   **2.** A: has
Kathy been working at the computer   B: has been working . . . two o'clock   **3.** A: has it
been raining   B: has been raining . . . two days   **4.** A: has Liz been reading   B: has been
reading . . . half an hour/thirty minutes   **5.** A: has Boris been studying English   B: has
been studying English . . . 1990.   **6.** A: has Nicole been working at the Silk Road Clothing
Store   B: has been working at the Silk Road Clothing Store . . . three months.   **7.** A: has Ms.
Rice been teaching at this school   B: has been teaching at this school . . . September 1992
8. A: has Mr. Fisher been driving a Chevy   B: has been driving a Chevy . . . twelve years
[*Chevy* = a nickname for a Chevrolet, a make of car.]   **9.** A: has Mrs. Taylor been waiting to see
her doctor   B: has been waiting to see her doctor . . . an hour and a half   **10.** A: have Ted
and Erica been playing tennis   B: have been playing tennis . . . two o'clock

◇ WORKBOOK PRACTICE 11, p. 137. *The present perfect progressive. (Charts 7-6 and 7-7)*

Controlled completion. [Selfstudy]

ANSWERS: **1.** B **2.** B **3.** A **4.** B **5.** A **6.** A **7.** B **8.** A

◇ WORKBOOK PRACTICE 12, p. 138. *Verb tenses. (Charts 7-2 → 7-7)*

Sentence construction. [Guided Study]
This practice tries to get the students to focus on the relation between time expressions and verb tenses. They need to understand that verb tenses express time relationships.

◇ WORKBOOK PRACTICE 13, p. 138. *Verb forms. (Chapters 1, 2, 3, and 7)*

Fill-in-the-blanks. [Guided Study]
This is a cumulative review of the verb tenses presented to this point in the text.

ANSWERS: **(1)** haven't written **(3)** haven't been **(4)** haven't heard **(5)** have been **(6)** have been working . . . (have been) going **(7)** wrote **(8)** was going **(9)** (was) studying **(10)** have happened **(11)** were **(12)** lost **(13)** messed . . . got **(14)** showed . . . refused **(15)** felt **(16)** told **(17)** started **(18)** isn't . . . isn't **(19)** fetch **(21)** have met . . . started **(22)** came **(23)** wanted . . . brought **(24)** put . . . was walking [also possible: walked] **(25)** pulled **(26)** started . . . looked **(27)** said . . . Do you like **(28)** twitched **(29)** said . . . turned **(30)** said **(31)** are **(32)** know . . . enter **(33)** come . . . point **(34)** tell . . . try **(35)** buy **(36)** don't agonize **(37)** have learned **(38)** don't want **(39)** need . . . prepares/will prepare/is going to prepare **(41)** have decided [also possible: decided] **(43)** have always wanted **(44)** am . . . have **(45)** lost **(46)** made . . . have been **(47)** are **(48)** am really enjoying **(49)** will continue/am going to continue **(50)** will study/am going to study **(51)** am pursuing/will pursue/am going to pursue **(53)** have told **(54)** have grown **(55)** understand **(56)** has made/made **(57)** feel . . . have finally taken/am finally taking

◇ WORKBOOK PRACTICE 14, p. 140. *Verb forms. (Charts 7-4 and 7-5)*

Written. [Guided Study]
Encourage the students to think of an old friend with whom they have not corresponded for a long time. Almost everyone owes a letter to someone. This topic should encourage use of a variety of verb tenses and is intended, with any luck, to elicit the present perfect and present perfect progressive in at least some of the sentences. Perhaps you could ask the students to underline these tenses.

CHART 7-8: MIDSENTENCE ADVERBS

• Placement of midsentence adverbs can be troublesome. It's difficult for the students to grasp all the information in this chart. Do whatever you can on the board or with other aids to survey the information about where midsentence adverbs go in statements, questions, and negative sentences. Keep the focus on midsentence placement despite the fact that quite a few of these adverbs can be found at the beginning or end of a sentence.

• See the notes on page 7 of this *Teacher's Guide* for Chapter 1, Exercise 4, where the idea of assigning percentage figures to frequency adverbs is discussed (e.g., *always* = 100%, *almost always* = 98%, etc.).

• Emphasize that "negative adverbs" are not used with negative verbs.

☐ EXERCISE 26, p. 182. *Midsentence adverbs. (Chart 7-8)*

Controlled completion.
In each item, discuss the placement of the adverb in relation to the verb. The students have to look at the verb in order to place the adverb. This exercise covers all the placement information in Chart 7-8. It does not include negative adverbs.

ANSWERS: **2.** is always at **3.** can always find **4.** mail usually comes **5.** is usually here **6.** will probably be **7.** Ann often stays **8.** is often at **9.** will probably stay **10.** Jack finally wrote **11.** is finally over **12.** have finally finished **13.** Tom always study **14.** Tom always at **15.** you always find **16.** you usually study **17.** teacher ever absent **18.** you just say **19.** you usually go **20.** you generally eat **21.** son occasionally stays **22.** We frequently have **23.** you sometimes feel **24.** have already read **25.** is already here

☐ EXERCISE 27, p. 182. *Midsentence adverbs. (Chart 7-8)*

Oral; controlled completion.
If you've done the preceding exercise with the whole class, you might want to break the students into groups for this exercise and let them try to puzzle this grammar out together prior to class discussion or prior to handing out a sheet with the correct answers on it. Exercises 26 through 28 deal almost solely with manipulation of form.

ANSWERS:
1. c. Jack frequently doesn't shave
   d. Jack generally doesn't shave
   e. Jack sometimes doesn't shave
   f. Jack occasionally doesn't shave
   g. Jack doesn't always shave
   h. Jack doesn't ever shave
   i. Jack never shaves
   j. Jack hardly ever shaves
   k. Jack rarely shaves
   l. Jack seldom shaves

2. a. I generally don't eat
   b. I don't always eat
   c. I seldom eat
   d. I usually don't eat
   e. I never eat
   f. I don't ever eat
   g. I occasionally don't eat
   h. I rarely eat
   i. I hardly ever eat

3.
  a. Jane never comes
  b. Jane usually doesn't come
  c. Jane seldom comes
  d. Jane occasionally doesn't come
  e. Jane doesn't always come
  f. Jane hardly ever comes
  g. Jane doesn't ever come

4.
  a. roommate usually isn't home
  b. roommate generally isn't home
  c. roommate isn't always home
  d. roommate isn't ever home
  e. roommate is never home
  f. roommate is seldom home
  g. roommate frequently isn't home
  h. roommate is hardly ever home

☐ EXERCISE 28, p. 183. *Midsentence adverbs. (Chart 7-8)*

Controlled completion.
This is a summary of what the students have learned in the preceding two exercises.

ANSWERS: **1.** Brian probably knows   **2.** Pat usually at   **3.** have finally finished
4. Jack seldom writes   **5.** I generally don't . . . I generally go   **6.** Susan probably
won't/will probably stay   **7.** should never allow   **8.** is hardly ever at   **9.** lecturer
frequently came   **10.** temperature seldom drops   **11.** Rita always rides   **12.** don't
always ride   **13.** Tom usually doesn't   **14.** Paul never rides   **15.** is often too

☐ EXERCISE 29, p. 184. *Midsentence adverbs. (Chart 7-8)*

Oral (books closed).
Here is an exercise that focuses on meaning. It is hoped that students will communicate
meaningful sentences with the adverb in the right place.

◇ WORKBOOK PRACTICE 15, p. 140. *Midsentence adverbs. (Chart 7-8)*

Controlled completion. [Selfstudy]
The visual format of this exercise is intended to help the students clarify their understanding of
the grammar and allow them to make certain deductions.

ANSWERS:
PART I:

1.	Ø	*is*	always
2.	always	*finishes*	Ø
3.	always	*finished*	Ø
4.	Ø	*will*	always
5.	Ø	*has*	always
6.	always	*helped*	Ø
7.	Ø	*are*	always
8.	always	*help*	Ø
9.	Ø	*have*	always
10.	Ø	*can*	always
11.	Ø	*are*	usually
12.	usually	*help*	Ø
13.	Ø	*have*	usually
14.	Ø	*can*	usually

PART II:

15.	*Do*	Ø	you	usually
16.	*Is*	Ø	Mike	usually
17.	*Did*	Ø	your mom	usually
18.	*Were*	Ø	you	usually
19.	*Can*	Ø	students	usually
20.	*Do*	Ø	you	ever
21.	*Is*	Ø	Mike	ever
22.	*Did*	Ø	your mom	ever
23.	*Were*	Ø	you	ever
24.	*Can*	Ø	students	ever

PART III:

25.	probably	*won't*	Ø
26.	probably	*isn't*	Ø
27.	probably	*doesn't*	Ø
28.	probably	*hasn't*	Ø
29.	Ø	*won't*	ever
30.	Ø	*isn't*	ever
31.	Ø	*doesn't*	always
32.	Ø	*hasn't*	always

◊ WORKBOOK PRACTICE 16, p. 141. *Frequency adverbs. (Chart 7-8)*

Controlled completion. [Guided Study]
The previous practice is solely on form. This practice is on form and meaning. For some of the items, you'll need to relate the meanings of adverbial expressions in the given sentences with the meanings of the frequency adverbs. For example, in item 1 *without exception* parallels the meaning of *always*. The difficulty in this practice lies in the students' understanding the time expressions in the given sentences. Those time expressions need to be taught and discussed. Don't assume that the students understand the meaning of the given sentences; the adverbial expressions may well be more difficult for them than the frequency adverbs that are ostensibly the focus of the practice.

ANSWERS: **1.** always drives   **2.** is always   **3.** rarely goes   **4.** ever met   **5.** is never   **6.** is sometimes   **7.** is frequently   **8.** is generally   **9.** seldom come   **10.** generally hunt   **11.** rarely kill   **12.** frequently kill   **13.** seldom live

---

CHART 7-9: USING *ALREADY, YET, STILL,* AND *ANYMORE*

• These adverbs are most commonly used to discuss present rather than past events or situations. The text keeps the emphasis on present time even though it is possible to use these words with past verbs.

• These words are hard to explain. In broad terms, *already* talks about events or situations that have occurred "before now" and may imply that they occurred sooner than expected. *Yet* also conveys the idea of "before now or up to now" and talks about events or situations that are expected to happen: *He hasn't come yet* indicates that the speaker expects him to come. *Still* indicates that an event or situation hasn't changed status; it continues to occur. *Anymore* indicates that an event or situation has changed status; it ceases to occur.

• The adverb *anymore* can also be spelled as two words: *any more.* For example, *He doesn't live there any more.* [NOTE: *Any more* is always spelled as two words when *any* is a pronoun or determiner. *Don't give me those books. I can't carry any more (books).* It is also spelled as two words in BrE.]

☐ EXERCISE 30, p. 185. *ALREADY, YET, STILL, ANYMORE. (Chart 7-9)*

Controlled completion.
Discuss the meanings of the sentences.

ANSWERS: **2.** already   **3.** still   **4.** anymore   **5.** still   **6.** anymore   **7.** still
8. already   **9.** yet   **10.** still

☐ EXERCISE 31, p. 185. *YET and STILL. (Chart 7-9)*

Controlled completion.

ANSWERS: **1.** yet   **2.** still   **3.** yet   **4.** yet   **5.** still   **6.** yet   **7.** still
8. still   **9.** yet

☐ EXERCISE 32, p. 186. *ALREADY, YET, STILL, ANYMORE. (Chart 7-9)*

Controlled completion.

ANSWERS: **1.** A: yet B: still   **2.** already   **3.** A: still   B: anymore   **4.** A: yet
B: still   **5.** yet . . . still   **6.** already   **7.** still   **8.** anymore   **9.** still   **10.** already
11. yet . . . still

☐ EXERCISE 33, p. 187. *ALREADY, YET, STILL, ANYMORE. (Chart 7-9)*

Transformation.

ANSWERS: **3.** In other words, he isn't home yet/he still isn't home.   **4.** In other words, I'm
still hungry.   **5.** In other words, she doesn't work there anymore.   **6.** In other words, she
is still working at the bookstore.   **7.** . . . the movie has already started.   **8.** . . . he still
smokes. He still hasn't quit/hasn't quit yet.   **9.** . . . we've already studied Chapter 6. We
haven't studied Chapter 8 yet. [also possible: We still haven't studied Chapter 8.]   **10.** . . . I don't
read comic books anymore.   **11.** . . . we still haven't finished it/haven't finished it yet. We are
still doing this exercise.   **12.** . . . I can't speak French anymore. My sister, however, can still
speak French because . . . .

☐ EXERCISE 34, p. 188. *Cumulative review. (Chapters 1 → 7)*

Written.
These topics are intended to elicit a variety of verb tenses—including, it is hoped, correct and
appropriate use of the present perfect.
   Discuss paragraphing: form and purpose. A paragraph is indented from the left text
margin. It contains one principal idea. When the writer moves on to a new idea, s/he begins a
new paragraph. If your students are more advanced in their understanding of English rhetoric
than these basics would assume, you could use these topics to assign a traditional five-part
essay: introduction, three body paragraphs, conclusion.

◇ WORKBOOK PRACTICE 17, p. 142. *ALREADY, STILL, YET, ANYMORE. (Chart 7-9)*

Controlled completion, multiple choice. [Selfstudy]

ANSWERS: **1.** B   **2.** D   **3.** A   **4.** D   **5.** C   **6.** A   **7.** C   **8.** D   **9.** B
10. C

◇ WORKBOOK PRACTICE 18, p. 143. *Adverb placement. (Charts 7-8 and 7-9)*

> *Open completion.* [Guided Study]
>
> POSSIBLE RESPONSES: **1.** talk in my sleep . . . I don't **2.** take the test . . . studied **3.** you . . . living in town **4.** Don't water the flowers . . . watered them **5.** call you . . . returned from her trip **6.** need to make a dental appointment . . . I haven't done it **7.** want any more food . . . eaten **8.** drive . . . passed my driver's test **9.** became president of the corporation five years . . . holds that position **10.** play golf . . . my sister . . . plays every week

---

CHART 7-10: USING THE PAST PERFECT

- Both the present perfect and the past perfect relate two points of time. The present perfect relates an event in the past to the present. The past perfect relates an event in the past to another event in the past that occurred at a different time.

- The past perfect is not an especially common and useful tense for language students at this level. The text's intention is a quick introduction to its form and meaning. Usage mastery is not expected. The students will use some of what they learn here in Chapter 16, where they use the past perfect in conditional sentences and in noun clauses after *wish*.

☐ EXERCISE 35, p. 190. *Past perfect vs. present perfect. (Chart 7-10)*

> *Fill-in-the-blanks.*
>
> ANSWERS: **3.** have already finished **4.** had already finished **5.** had already finished **6.** had already started **7.** has already started **8.** had already left

☐ EXERCISE 36, p. 190. *Past perfect vs. past progressive. (Chart 7-10)*

> *Fill-in-the-blanks.*
>
> ANSWERS: **3.** was studying **4.** had finished **5.** was washing **6.** had already washed . . . (had already) put

☐ EXERCISE 37, p. 191. *Review of verb tenses. (Chapters 1, 2, and 7)*

> *Fill-in-the-blanks.*
> The emphasis in this exercise is on the past perfect.
>
> ANSWERS: **2.** A: Did you see B: was . . . had not seen **3.** A: haven't seen B: is . . . haven't seen **4.** A: Did you get B: got . . . had already begun **5.** A: Did you go B: got . . . had already made A: was B: had . . . were eating . . . stopped . . . invited . . . had already eaten . . . wasn't A: did you do B: had already seen . . . went . . . was

◇ WORKBOOK PRACTICE 19, p. 143. *The past perfect. (Chart 7-10)*

Discussion of meaning. [Selfstudy]

This is a good practice for in-class pair work, with the students then able to look up the answers themselves.

    NOTE: Many selfstudy practices can be assigned as seatwork by pairs. The students do, of course, have to resist the temptation to look up the answers prematurely if they feel frustrated or lazy.

ANSWERS: **1.** a. 1st   b. 2nd   **2.** a. 2nd   b. 1st   **3.** a. 1st   b. 2nd
4. a. 2nd   b. 1st   **5.** a. 1st   b. 2nd   **6.** a. 2nd   b. 1st   **7.** a. 1st b. 2nd
8. a. 2nd   b. 1st

◇ WORKBOOK PRACTICE 20, p. 145. *The present perfect vs. the past perfect. (Chart 7-10)*

Fill-in-the-blanks. [Selfstudy]

If you discuss this practice in class, use tense diagrams on the chalkboard to demonstrate the similar time relationships expressed by these two tenses: one communicates "before now" and the other communicates "before then."

ANSWERS: **1.** has already left   **2.** had already left   **3.** have already slept   **4.** had already slept   **5.** have already met   **6.** had already met   **7.** have already seen
8. had already seen   **9.** have made   **10.** had made

◇ WORKBOOK PRACTICE 21, p. 145. *The past progressive vs. the past perfect. (Chart 7-10)*

Controlled completion. [Selfstudy]

ANSWERS: **1.** B   **2.** A   **3.** A   **4.** B   **5.** B   **6.** A   **7.** B   **8.** B

◇ WORKBOOK PRACTICE 22, p. 146. *The present perfect, past progressive and past perfect. (Chart 7-10)*

Fill-in-the-blanks. [Selfstudy]

ANSWERS:

1. was sleeping   **2.** have never been   **3.** had already heard   **4.** was still snowing
5. had passed   **6.** were making   **7.** Hasn't he come   **8.** had never been   **9.** was wearing . . . had never worn . . . hasn't worn

◇ WORKBOOK PRACTICE 23, p. 147. *Verb tense review. (Chapters 1, 2, 3, and 7)*

Controlled completion. [Selfstudy]

ANSWERS: **1.** A   **2.** C   **3.** B   **4.** D   **5.** A   **6.** B   **7.** D   **8.** C   **9.** D
10. B

◇ WORKBOOK PRACTICE 24, p. 147. *Verb tense review. (Chapters 1, 2, 3, and 7)*

Controlled completion. [Guided Study]

ANSWERS: **1.** B   **2.** C   **3.** A   **4.** C   **5.** B   **6.** D   **7.** A   **8.** D   **9.** D
10. B

☐ EXERCISE 38, p. 192. *Prepositions. (Chapter 7; Appendix 1)*

    Controlled completion.

    ANSWERS: **1.** to . . . for   **2.** for   **3.** of   **4.** for   **5.** on   **6.** for   **7.** (up)on
    8. to/with   **9.** from   **10.** (up)on   **11.** of   **12.** to

◇ WORKBOOK PRACTICE 25, p. 148. *Prepositions. (Chapter 7; Appendix 1)*

    Controlled completion. [Selfstudy]

    ANSWERS: **1.** (up)on   **2.** from   **3.** of   **4.** (up)on   **5.** to   **6.** to . . . for . . . for
    . . . (up)on   **7.** for   **8.** to/with   **9.** of   **10.** for

Chapter 8: COUNT/NONCOUNT NOUNS AND ARTICLES

ORDER OF CHAPTER	CHARTS	EXERCISES	WORKBOOK
Count and noncount nouns	8-1 → 8-5	Ex. 1 → 9	Pr. 1 → 21
Article usage	8-6	Ex. 10 → 14	Pr. 22 → 27
Cumulative review		Ex. 15	Pr. 28 → 29
Quantifiers as pronouns	8-7 → 8-8	Ex. 16 → 17	Pr. 30 → 33
Cumulative review		Ex. 18 → 19	
Prepositions		Ex. 20	Pr. 34 → 35

General Notes on Chapter 8

• OBJECTIVE: The concept of count and noncount nouns, although not unique to English, is basic to using this language for clear communication. Related to countability is the use of articles and expressions of quantity. Learners will not be able to master these forms at this stage, but they must begin to develop understanding and control of them.

• APPROACH: Because the countability of a noun is somewhat unpredictable, groups of nouns are presented and practiced throughout this chapter in various contexts. Nouns are presented with one or more useful expressions of quantity, always in the context of a complete sentence. As a natural accompaniment to this information, some basic guidelines for using articles are presented.

• TERMINOLOGY: "Count" and "noncount" may also appear as "countable" and "uncountable" in some texts. A noncount noun is sometimes called a "mass" noun.

CHART 8-1: COUNT AND NONCOUNT NOUNS

- The concept of count vs. noncount nouns is often quite difficult for students to understand. Some students find it illogical. Many find it a confusing nuisance. However, just as students need to gain understanding and usage ability of verb forms, they need to understand and be able to use noun forms if they seek to communicate competently and correctly in English.

- In addition, article usage in English cannot make sense unless the students understand the distinction between count and noncount nouns. In many ways, the first half of the chapter seeks to lay the groundwork for the presentation of the bare bones basics of article use in Chart 8-6.

- To make the initial distinction between count and noncount, concentrate on the examples in Chart 8-1 (*chair* vs. *furniture*) and in Exercise 1 (*apple* vs. *fruit; letter* vs. *mail;* and *car* vs. *traffic*). Point out which ones can take a final *-s* and which "count or amount" words (i.e., quantifiers or expressions of quantity) can be used. Try to get across the concept that noncount nouns represent "masses" or "whole categories." (See Chart 8-2.)

- Typical mistakes involve using final *-s* on noncount nouns and using improper expressions of quantity (e.g., *too many homeworks*).

- Most nouns are used as count nouns. Some nouns are used only as noncount nouns. Many nouns have both count and noncount uses (see Chart 8-4). *Fruit* is an example of a noun that can be used as either, but for pedagogical purposes it is presented as a noncount noun throughout this chapter. (When some nouns that are used predominantly or typically as noncount are used as count nouns, they may refer to "different kinds of." For example: *Apples, bananas, and pears are fruits, not vegetables.* Other examples would be different kinds of *breads, foods, teas, soups, world Englishes.*) It is the text's view that students at this level of language study would find these subtleties confusing and disruptive rather than beneficial.

- A good ESL/EFL dictionary will indicate a noun's count and/or noncount status and usages.

☐ EXERCISE 1, p. 193. *Expressions of quantity. (Chart 8-1)*

Controlled completion.
The emphasis in this exercise is on distinguishing which expressions of quantity are used with which kinds of nouns. If a word in the list cannot be used to fill in the blank space, students should cross the word out. Use item 2 to explain the format of the exercise. Give the students time to work out items 3 through 6 as seatwork, alone or in pairs, prior to class discussion.

ANSWERS:

2. a. some
    b. several
    c. ~~a little~~
    d. a few
    e. too many
    f. ~~too much~~
    g. a lot of
    h. two

3. a. a lot of
    b. some
    c. a little
    d. ~~a few~~
    e. too much
    f. ~~too many~~

    g. ~~several~~
    h. ~~three mail~~

4. a. a lot of
    b. some
    c. ~~a little~~
    d. a few
    e. ~~too much~~
    f. too many
    g. several
    h. three

5. a. ~~several~~
    b. some
    c. ~~too many~~
    d. a little

    e. a lot of
    f. ~~a few~~
    g. too much
    h. ~~five~~

6. a. several
    b. some
    c. too many
    d. ~~a little~~
    e. a lot of
    f. a few
    g. ~~too much~~
    h. five

CHART 8-2: NONCOUNT NOUNS

- It is important for students to understand the <u>concept</u> of a noncount noun. That is the purpose of this chart. Discuss the concept in relation to some of the words listed on page 195 of the main text, all of which are "wholes."

- In addition to understanding the concept of a noncount noun, it helps if students simply become aware of some of the common nouns that are usually noncount. That is the purpose of the list on page 195.

- To avoid confusion, it is suggested that you not discuss possible count usages of any of the words in this chart at this point (e.g., **works** *of art, the* **literatures** *of France and England, green* **peppers***, the* **sands** *of time*). Chart 8-4 deals with that usage area briefly in a way appropriate to the students' level.

☐ EXERCISES 2 and 3, pp. 195–196. *Noncount vs. count nouns. (Chart 8-2)*

Controlled completion.
The purpose of these exercises is to clarify Chart 8-2 by comparing "individual parts" to "wholes." At the same time, the students are focusing on the troublesome final -*s*/-*es*.

Usual problems in the usage of nouns are that the learners don't use final -*s*/-*es* with count nouns when they should and do use it with noncount nouns when they shouldn't. Tell your students you sympathize with them. It's not easy.

EX. 2 ANSWERS: **5.** clothing **6.** dresses **7.** is . . . information **8.** are . . . facts
9. grammar **10.** vocabulary **11.** words **12.** slang [*Slang* = very informal speech. Often it refers to language invented by younger generations. Introduce some current slang your students might encounter. If you can't think of any, listen to a native-speaker teenager for five minutes. At this writing, some current slang for *wonderful* is *Rad! Awesome!* Older slang would be *Cool! Out of sight!*]
13. idioms [*Idiom* = A group of words that together has a special meaning; e.g., Mr. Moore *kicked the bucket* = Mr. Moore died. The meaning is not apparent from the individual vocabulary items. Note: That *slang* is noncount and *idiom* count is not necessarily logical.] **14.** is . . . traffic **15.** are . . . cars
16. literature **17.** novels **18.** poems **19.** poetry **20.** mail **21.** letters
22. sand **23.** is . . . dust **24.** homework **25.** assignments **26.** pennies
27. money **28.** coins **29.** change [*Change* = money returned in a different form, e.g., coins instead of paper money, or returned because it is in excess of the cost of an item. The word *change*, of course, has other meanings. Students should be aware that many words have more than one meaning.]
30. is . . . garbage

EX. 3 ANSWERS: **1.** machinery **2.** are . . . machines **3.** is . . . equipment **4.** are . . . tools **5.** hardware **6.** rings . . . bracelets **7.** jewelry **8.** jewels **9.** suggestions
10. advice [There is no especially logical explanation for *suggestion* being count and *advice* being noncount. It's just something the students need to learn in order to use these words appropriately.]
11. information **12.** isn't . . . news **13.** lakes . . . mountains **14.** scenery
15. plants **16.** grass **17.** rice **18.** English **19.** songs **20.** music **21.** things are these **22.** stuff is this [*Stuff* = used informally to mean "personal belongings, property."]
23. corn **24.** peas **25.** makeup **26.** bread **27.** sandwiches **28.** toast

◇ WORKBOOK PRACTICE 1, p. 149. *Count and noncount nouns.* *(Charts 8-1 and 8-2)*

Controlled completion, structure indentification. [Selfstudy]
Workbook Practices 1 through 7 repeat the same nouns. First the students learn which ones are count and which noncount. Once this information is known, they then (in the following practices) decide which expressions of quantity they can use with these nouns. The purpose of these seven practices is to clarify the use of indefinite articles, final-*s*/-*es*, and expressions of quantity with two different kinds of nouns.

ANSWERS: **1.** _/_ furniture—noncount **2.** _one_ table—count **3.** _one_ ring—count **4.** _/_ jewelry—noncount **5.** _/_ homework—noncount **6.** _one_ assignment—count **7.** _one_ job—count **8.** _/_ work—noncount **9.** _one_ question—count **10.** _/_ information—noncount **11.** _one_ new word—count **12.** _/_ new vocabulary—noncount

◇ WORKBOOK PRACTICE 2, p. 149. *A/AN and SOME.* *(Charts 8-1 and 8-2)*

Controlled completion. [Selfstudy]
ANSWERS: **1.** _some_ furniture **2.** _a_ table **3.** _a_ ring **4.** _some_ jewelry **5.** _some_ homework **6.** _an_ assignment **7.** _a_ job **8.** _some_ work **9.** _a_ question **10.** _some_ information **11.** _a_ new word **12.** _some_ new vocabulary

◇ WORKBOOK PRACTICE 3, p. 150. *Adding -S.* *(Charts 8-1 and 8-2)*

Controlled completion. [Selfstudy]
ANSWERS: **1.** furniture_/_ **2.** table_s_ **3.** ring_s_ **4.** jewelry_/_ **5.** homework_/_ **6.** assignment_s_ **7.** job_s_ **8.** work_/_ **9.** question_s_ **10.** information_/_ **11.** word_s_ **12.** vocabulary_/_

◇ WORKBOOK PRACTICE 4, p. 150. *Using TWO.* *(Charts 8-1 and 8-2)*

Transformation. [Selfstudy]
ANSWERS: **1.** *(no change)* **2.** two tables **3.** two rings **4.** *(no change)* **5.** *(no change)* **6.** two assignments **7.** two jobs **8.** *(no change)* **9.** two questions **10.** *(no change)* **11.** two new words **12.** *(no change)*

◇ WORKBOOK PRACTICE 5, p. 151. *Using A LOT OF.* *(Charts 8-1 and 8-2)*

Transformation. [Selfstudy]
ANSWERS: **1.** a lot of furniture **2.** a lot of tables **3.** a lot of rings **4.** a lot of jewelry **5.** a lot of homework **6.** a lot of assignments **7.** a lot of jobs **8.** a lot of work **9.** a lot of questions **10.** a lot of information **11.** a lot of new words **12.** a lot of new vocabulary

◇ WORKBOOK PRACTICE 6, p. 151. *TOO MANY and TOO MUCH.* *(Charts 8-1 and 8-2)*

Controlled completion. [Selfstudy]
ANSWERS: **1.** _much_ furniture **2.** _many_ tables **3.** _many_ rings **4.** _much_ jewelry **5.** _much_ homework **6.** _many_ assignments **7.** _many_ jobs **8.** _much_ work **9.** _many_ questions **10.** _much_ information **11.** _many_ words **12.** _much_ new vocabulary

◇ WORKBOOK PRACTICE 7, p. 152. *A FEW and A LITTLE.* (Charts 8-1 and 8-2)

Controlled completion. [Selfstudy]

ANSWERS: **1.** _a little_ furniture   **2.** _a few_ tables   **3.** _a few_ rings
4. _a little_ jewelry   **5.** _a little_ homework   **6.** _a few_ assignments   **7.** _a few_ jobs
8. _a little_ work   **9.** _a few_ questions   **10.** _a little_ information   **11.** _a few_ new
words   **12.** _a little_ new vocabulary

◇ WORKBOOK PRACTICE 8, p. 152. *A vs. AN: singular count nouns.* (Charts 8-1 and 8-2)

Controlled completion. [Selfstudy]
A focused presentation in class of *a* vs. *an* would help the students. The main text presents
information in a footnote on page 210. More information is contained in the *Workbook* footnote
on page 152. The author will be sure this information is presented clearly in a chart in the next
revision of the text.

ANSWERS: **1.** _a_ game   **2.** _a_ rock   **3.** _a_ store   **4.** _an_ army   **5.** _an_ egg
6. _an_ island   **7.** _an_ ocean   **8.** _an_ umbrella   **9.** _a_ university   **10.** _a_ horse
11. _an_ hour   **12.** _a_ star   **13.** _an_ eye   **14.** _a_ new car   **15.** _an_ old car
16. _a_ used car   **17.** _an_ uncle   **18.** _a_ house   **19.** _an_ honest mistake
20. _a_ hospital   **21.** _a_ hand   **22.** _an_ aunt   **23.** _an_ ant   **24.** _a_ neighbor

◇ WORKBOOK PRACTICE 9, p. 153. *A/AN vs. SOME.* (Charts 8-1 → 8-2)

Controlled completion. [Selfstudy]

ANSWERS: **1.** _a_ letter   **2.** _some_ mail   **3.** _some_ equipment   **4.** _a_ tool
5. _some_ food   **6.** _an_ apple   **7.** _some_ clothing   **8.** _an_ old shirt
9. _some_ advice   **10.** _a_ suggestion   **11.** _an_ interesting story
12. _some_ interesting news   **13.** _a_ poem   **14.** _some_ poetry   **15.** _a_ song
16. _some_ Indian music   **17.** _a_ new idiom   **18.** _some_ new slang

---

CHART 8-3: MORE NONCOUNT NOUNS

• The intention of this chart is simply to provide information for the students to use if and as they can; it
will have varying degress of usefulness. The intention is not for the students to memorize these noncount
nouns. The information can be quite useful for learners who already know and use many of these words.
Students for whom much of the vocabulary is new may not benefit a great deal immediately in terms of
appropriate use of noncount nouns in their own speech and writing. For them this chart can serve
principally as a reference when they attempt the exercises and the *Workbook* practices.

☐ EXERCISE 4, p. 198. *Noncount vs. count nouns.* (Chart 8-3)

Controlled completion.
This exercise chooses some of the more common words in Chart 8-3 for student practice. The
only noncount nouns used in the exercises from here to the end of the noun unit are those listed
in Charts 8-2 and 8-3.

ANSWERS: **2.** is . . . weather **3.** Sunshine is **4.** knowledge **5.** fun **6.** luck
7. ideas **8.** intelligence **9.** gold is **10.** diamonds are **11.** movies
12. entertainment **13.** games **14.** generosity **15.** help **16.** patience **17.** patients
18. confidence **19.** progress **20.** courage **21.** pollution **22.** forests **23.** peace
24. hospitality **25.** beef . . . was **26.** is . . . fog

☐ EXERCISE 5, p. 199. *MANY vs. MUCH. (Chart 8-3)*

Controlled completion.

ANSWERS: **3.** much mail **4.** many letters **5.** much postage **6.** many stamps
7. much English **8.** much slang **9.** many words are **10.** much coffee **11.** many
sandwiches **12.** much sugar **13.** many courses **14.** much homework **15.** isn't
much news **16.** many articles are **17.** much fun **18.** many stars are **19.** isn't much
sunshine **20.** Is . . . much pollution **21.** much luck **22.** are many kinds **23.** is . . .
much violence **24.** much makeup **25.** many cars **26.** Is . . . much traffic

☐ EXERCISE 6, p. 201. *A FEW vs. A LITTLE. (Chart 8-3)*

Controlled completion.
NOTE: This text does not deal with the difference between *a few* vs. *few* or *a little* vs. *little*. See
Understanding and Using English Grammar, Chart 5-9.

ANSWERS: **4.** a few . . . desks **5.** a little help **6.** a few apples **7.** a little fruit
8. a little advice **9.** a little . . . money **10.** a few coins **11.** a little information **12.** a
few . . . hours **13.** a little toothpaste **14.** A little laughter **15.** a few laughs **16.** a
little . . . grammar **17.** a few flowers **18.** a little progress **19.** a little . . . chicken
[Point out the humor of having "a few more chickens."] **20.** a few chickens [Point out the possible
meaning of "a little chicken" = one small chicken.]

◇ WORKBOOK PRACTICE 10, p. 153. *Count and noncount nouns. (Charts 8-1→8-3)*

Controlled completion. [Selfstudy]
The troublesome final *-s/-es* is revisited. You might want use this practice in class discussion to
review pronunciation of final *-s/-es*. [See *Workbook* page 62 (Chapter 4, Practice 3) for
information about pronunciation.] Omission of final *-s/-es* in speech and writing, even when the
students understand the grammar thoroughly, may often be due to the fact that the learners
don't hear it clearly. Extra work on production of *-s/-es* surely never hurts and can only help
reinforce habits of correct usage.

ANSWERS: **1.** grammar_/_ **2.** noun_s_ **3.** language_s_ **4.** English_/_ **5.** makeup_/_
6. scenery_/_ **7.** mountain_s_ **8.** traffic_/_ **9.** automobile_s_ **10.** sand_/_
11. dust_/_ **12.** beach_es_ **13.** slang_/_ **14.** mistake_s_ **15.** information_/_
16. fact_s_ **17.** game_s_ **18.** weather_/_ **19.** thunder_/_ **20.** water_/_
21. parent_s_ . . . health_/_ **22.** circle_/_ . . . degree_s_ **23.** Professor_s_ . . . knowledge_/_
24. family_/_ . . . luck _/_ **25.** neighbor_s_ . . . help_/_ **26.** factor_ies_ . . . pollution_/_
27. pride_/_ . . . children_/_ **28.** people_/_ . . . intelligence_/_

◇ WORKBOOK PRACTICE 11, p. 154. *Count and noncount nouns. (Charts 4-1, 8-1 → 8-3)*

Controlled completion. [Guided Study]
As suggested for the preceding practice, review pronunciation of final *-s/-es*. This is not an easy
exercise for those students who are unfamiliar with some of the vocabulary. Ease of correct
usage usually depends on the learner's familiarity with the lexical items.

ANSWERS: **1.** Plants . . . things **2.** Scientists . . . things . . . groups . . . plants . . . animals . . . plants . . . animals **3.** Flowers . . . trees . . . Plants . . . deserts . . . oceans . . . mountaintops . . . regions **4.** Plants . . . houses . . . Plants . . . kinds . . . drugs . . . plants . . . plants . . . lives **5.** Crops . . . plants . . . crops . . . fields . . . disasters . . . floods . . . storms . . . farmers . . . problems **6.** things . . . animals . . . plants . . . plants . . . roots . . . leaves . . . insects . . . plants . . . birds . . . worms . . . insects . . . Reptiles . . . animals . . . eggs . . . insects

◊ WORKBOOK PRACTICE 12, p. 155. *Count and noncount nouns. (Charts 8-1 → 8-3)*

> *Written.* [Guided Study]
> The topics are designed to produce a variety of nouns. It is hoped that some of them will be noncount nouns.

◊ WORKBOOK PRACTICE 13, p. 155. *HOW MANY/HOW MUCH. (Charts 8-1 → 8-3; 4-1; 6-2)*

> *Controlled completion.* [Selfstudy]
> This practice reviews *many* vs. *much*, final *-s/-es*, and subject-verb agreement.
>
> ANSWERS: **1.** many letter_s_ *are* **2.** much mail_/_ **3.** many <u>men</u> *have* **4.** many famil_ies_ *are* **5.** many word_s_ *are* **6.** many sentence_s_ *are* **7.** much chalk_/_ *is* **8.** much English_/_ **9.** much English literature _/_ **10.** many English word_s_ **11.** much gasoline_/_ (much petrol_/_) **12.** much homework_/_ **13.** many grandchild_ren_ **14.** many page_s_ *are* **15.** many librar_ies_ ★ *are* **16.** many bone_s_ *are* **17.** many teeth_ /_ **18.** much water_/_ **19.** many cup_s_ **20.** much tea _/_ **21.** many glass_es_ **22.** much fun _/_ **23.** much education _/_ **24.** much soap _/_ **25.** many island_s_ *are* **26.** many people_/_ *were* **27.** many human being_s_ *are* **28.** many people _/_ **29.** many zero_es_ OR zero_s_ *are* **30.** many butterfl_ies_ ★ _/_

◊ WORKBOOK PRACTICE 14, p. 154. *A FEW vs. A LITTLE. (Charts 8-1 → 8-3)*

> *Controlled completion.* [Selfstudy]
> ANSWERS: **1.** a little music_/_ **2.** a few song_s_ **3.** a little help_/_ **4.** a little English_/_ **5.** a few more apple_s_ **6.** a little honey_/_ **7.** a little advice_/_ **8.** a few suggestion_s_ **9.** a few question_s_ **10.** a few people_/_ **11.** a few more minute_s_ **12.** a little light_/_ **13.** a little homework_/_

CHART 8-4: NOUNS THAT CAN BE COUNT OR NONCOUNT

• The nouns presented here are but a drop in the bucket of those that have dual count-noncount usages. The intention is simply to introduce the students to the idea that such a possibility exists in English. Point out that they may find count vs. noncount information in their dictionaries. Again, the purpose in this text is to get across the <u>concept</u> of a noncount noun, for it is this concept that will serve the students well as they gain experience with English and expand their usage ability. The ultimate goal is for learners to use nouns as count or noncount as unthinkingly as a native speaker does. In the meantime, it helps them to pay a little special attention to this phenomenon in English. In this chart, discuss how the noncount usages deal with "wholes" and the count usages with individual items.

★The -*y* is changed to -*i* and then -*es* is added. Example: *baby → babies.*

☐ EXERCISE 7, p. 203. *Count vs. noncount, same word.* *(Chart 8-4)*

Controlled completion.

ANSWERS: **1.** some lamb   **2.** Lambs are   **3.** time   **4.** times   **5.** papers
6. paper   **7.** a . . . paper   **8.** works   **9.** work   **10.** light . . . gets . . . it   **11.** are
. . . lights   **12.** hair . . . hair   **13.** hairs   **14.** coffees   **15.** coffee   **16.** glasses
17. glasses   **18.** glass   **19.** Iron is   **20.** Irons are

◇ WORKBOOK PRACTICE 15, p. 157. *HOW MANY/HOW MUCH.* *(Charts 8-1 → 8-4; 4-1; 6-2)*

Transformation. [Selfstudy]

ANSWERS: **1.** How many children do the Millers have?   **2.** How much money does Jake
make?   **3.** How many players are there on a soccer team?   **4.** How much homework do
you have tonight?   **5.** How many feet are there in a mile?   **6.** How many meters/metres
are there in a kilometer/kilometre?   **7.** How many suitcases did you take on the plane to
Florida?   **8.** How much suntan oil did you take with you?   **9.** How many pairs of sandals
did you take?   **10.** How much toothpaste/How many tubes of toothpaste did you take?
11. How many hours did the flight take?   **12.** How many times have you been in Florida?
13. How many apples are there in the two baskets?   **14.** How much fruit is there in the two
baskets?

**CHART 8-5: USING UNITS OF MEASURE
WITH NONCOUNT NOUNS**

• These units of measure are also called "partitives."

• Some other units of measure not introduced in the text are: *carton, dozen, head* (of lettuce or cabbage),
pack, package, roll (of film or paper towels), *tablespoon, teaspoon, tub* (of margarine). Additional
nonmetric terms not in the text are *ounce, pint, inch, foot, yard.*

• The United States is the only major country that does not use the metric system. Nonmetric terms
have little meaning to most students and little use unless the students are living in the United States and
have to do their own food or gas shopping.

• Nonmetric terms originated in English in the 1200s and are called "English" or "British units." The
metric system was created by French scientists in the late eighteenth century. At that time, each country
had its own system of measurements that had developed from local traditions. By the late nineteenth
century, most major countries had recognized the need for an international system of measurements and
had adopted the metric system. Great Britain, Canada, and Australia began converting to it in the 1960s.
The United States government is still wrestling with the problem of if and how to convert to metric.

• The spellings "metre" and "litre" are chiefly British. The spellings "meter" and "liter" are used in
American English.

□ EXERCISE 8, p. 204. *Units of measure (partitives) with nouncount nouns. (Chart 8-5)*

Semi-controlled completion.

There may easily be more than one possible completion. Often only one is idiomatic (i.e., the expression a native speaker would typically use) or culturally appropriate in most English-speaking countries. For example, in item 1 it would be possible to say "a glass of coffee," but "cup" is idiomatically and culturally appropriate.

ANSWERS: **3.** quart/gallon [bottle?] **4.** glass/cup [bottle? quart?] **5.** piece **6.** gallons [*Liter* would be possible here, but not *quart*.] **7.** bowl/cup **8.** piece **9.** bottle/glass [also common: can] **10.** pound **11.** sheets **12.** bowl/piece **13.** pieces **14.** loaf [pound?] **15.** spoonful **16.** tube **17.** bar **18.** piece **19.** piece **20.** pieces **21.** pieces

□ EXERCISE 9, p. 205. *HOW MANY and HOW MUCH. (Chart 8-5)*

Oral (books closed).

Before class, prepare one card or piece of paper for each item in the exercise. Write on it the quantity from the sentence. In class, seat students so that about half are facing the others and so that you can walk behind them. Tell them that you have secret information for each one to discover. Stand behind the first student who will answer. Hold up the card for item #1 so that everyone except that student can see the quantity on the card. Tell the student, "There are some good students in this class." Because this student can't see your card, s/he will have to choose between *how many* and *how much* to ask someone, "How many good students are there in this class?" The question should be addressed to any student on the opposite side of the room.

The other student answers with the quantity on your card. Always use the word "some" in your sentence, but change the words in parentheses to match your situation. Keep the pace lively by moving around the room behind the students.

EXPECTED ANSWERS: **1.** How many students **2.** How much mail **3.** How many states **4.** [See footnote on p. 205 of the main text.] **5.** How much butter/How many pounds of butter **6.** How many provinces **7.** How many pages **8.** How much (money) **9.** How much rice/How many cups of rice **10.** How many desks **11.** How much salt **12.** How many students **13.** How much (money) **14.** How many (different) kinds of fish **15.** How much English vocabulary **16.** How many people **17.** How much chalk/How many pieces of chalk **18.** How much gas(oline)/petrol OR How many gallons of gas(oline)/petrol.

◇ WORKBOOK PRACTICE 16, p. 158. *Units of measure with noncount nouns. (Chart 8-5)*

Controlled completion. [Selfstudy]

See the comments on Exercise 8 above. The same holds true in this practice and the following one.

EXPECTED ANSWERS: *(Others may be possible.)*
PART I: **1.** can/jar **2.** box **3.** bottle **4.** jar **5.** can **6.** box **7.** can **8.** bag/box **9.** bottle **10.** can/bag **11.** can/bag **12.** bag **13.** bottle/can **14.** can
PART II: **15.** cup/glass **16.** bowl **17.** slice/piece **18.** slice/piece **19.** slice/piece **20.** glass **21.** bowl/cup **22.** piece **23.** glass **24.** bowl/cup **25.** glass/cup **26.** bowl **27.** slice/piece **28.** bowl/cup **29.** bowl

◊ WORKBOOK PRACTICE 17, p. 158. *Units of measure with noncount nouns. (Chart 8-5)*

Controlled completion. [Guided Study]

ANSWERS: **1.** jar   **2.** bottle   **3.** box/bottle   **4.** jar/can (tin)   **5.** can (tin)
6. bag/box   **7.** jar   **8.** bottle   **9.** box/bag   **10.** can (tin)

◊ WORKBOOK PRACTICE 18, p. 159. *HOW MANY/HOW MUCH. (Charts 8-1 → 8-3; 4-1; 6-2)*

Oral; pair work. [Guided Study]
The intention here is to provide some directed conversation practice involving the target structures.

◊ WORKBOOK PRACTICE 19, p. 159. *Count and noncount nouns. (Charts 8-1 → 8-3)*

Written. [Guided Study]
The intention here is directed writing practice. Writing about food requires both count and noncount nouns.

◊ WORKBOOK PRACTICE 20, p. 160. *Noncount abstractions. (Chart 8-3)*

Combination. [Selfstudy]
This practice presents a few common sayings in English that the students might find interesting. These sayings illustrate the use of abstractions as noncount nouns. There is no reason to expect the students to know the proper completions. It depends on whether or not they have encountered these expressions before. Tell your students just to guess if they have never heard them. Use the practice as a springboard for a discussion of the students' interpretations of and reactions to these sayings. Do they have similar sayings in their languages?

ANSWERS: **1.** D   **2.** G   **3.** F   **4.** B   **5.** E   **6.** C   **7.** A

◊ WORKBOOK PRACTICE 21, p. 160. *Noncount abstractions. (Chart 8-3)*

Open completion. [Guided Study]
The purpose here is for the students to reach for nouns that are abstractions. Most of the noncount nouns given in the answers below can be found in the list in Chart 8-3. Students should work in groups. Suggest that they consult Chart 8-3.

POSSIBLE RESPONSES:

a.	**b.**	**c.**	**d.**
1. patience	1. greed	1. prosperity	1. homelessness
2. honesty	2. ignorance	2. peace	2. ignorance
3. courage	3. jealousy	3. freedom	3. hunger
4. reliability	4. dishonesty	4. progress	4. violence
5. compassion	5. laziness	5. justice	5. poverty
6. gentleness	6. cowardice	6. literacy	6. disease

CHART 8-6: GUIDELINES FOR ARTICLE USAGE

• This chart seeks to give an understanding of the basics of article use. It by no means covers the myriad uses of articles in English. Almost all students find article usage difficult to learn, and many teachers and textbook authors find articles difficult to teach. There are many idiomatic uses, complex patterns, intricate variations, and subtleties. Proficient use of articles can only come with experience over time. Tell your students not to get frustrated. Articles are just one small part of English.

• Most students need help with this chart; it contains too much information to be grasped independently. It is suggested that you combine an explanation of this chart with a discussion of the illustrations in Exercise 10. The dialogues in Exercise 10 mirror the organization of the examples in Chart 8-6. In other words, DIALOGUE 1 illustrates the grammar in examples (a), (b), and (c). DIALOGUE 4 illustrates the grammar in examples (d), (e), and (f). DIALOGUE 2 illustrates the grammar in examples (j), (k), and (l).

• Comparisons of meaning need to be made both vertically and horizontally in the chart and in Exercise 10. In other words, Example (a) *A dog makes a good pet* needs to be compared vertically with (d) *Dogs make good pets* and horizontally with (j) *I saw a dog in my yard* and (s) *Did you feed the dog.*

• In *Understanding and Using English Grammar,* see Charts D-1 and D-2 in the Appendix for more information about articles.

☐ EXERCISE 10, p. 208. *Articles: A, SOME, THE, Ø. (Chart 8-6)*

Oral.
The key point the students need to understand from this exercise is that article usage often depends upon what the speaker assumes the listener is familiar with and is thinking about. If they have shared knowledge and are thinking about the same object or person, the speaker uses *the.*

☐ EXERCISE 11, p. 210. *Articles: THE vs. A. (Chart 8-6)*

Controlled completion.
Again the key point is what the speaker assumes the listener is familiar with and thinking about.

ANSWERS: **3. the** party   **4. a** party   **5. a** table   **6. the** table . . . **the** front door   **7. a** graduate student . . . **a** professor   **8. the** professor   **9. the** zoo   **10. a** zoo   **11. a** quiet street   **12. the** restaurant [This item was intended to indicate that both speakers had the same restaurant in mind, but "a" is also possible.] . . . **the** street   **13. a** job . . . **a** restaurant   **14. the** cat   **15. a** cat . . . **a** dog   **16. the** kitchen   **17. a** big kitchen

☐ EXERCISE 12, p. 211. *THE vs. Ø. (Chart 8-6)*

Controlled completion.
Students can discuss this exercise in groups prior to class discussion.

ANSWERS: **2.** a. **Ø** Mountains   b. **The** mountains   **3.** a. **Ø** Water   b. **The** water   **4.** a. **The** information   b. **Ø** information   **5.** a. **Ø** Health   b. **the** health   **6.** a. **Ø** Men . . . **Ø** women   b. **the** men . . . **the** women   **7.** a. **Ø** problems   b. **the** problems   **8.** a. **the** happiness   b. **Ø** happiness   **9.** a. **Ø** Vegetables   b. **The** vegetables   **10.** a. **Ø** Gold   b. **The** gold [The spelling "karat" is AmE; the spelling "carat" is BrE and also AmE. A karat/carat is a unit for measuring the amount of gold in an object such as jewelry, with 24K being pure gold.]

☐ EXERCISE 13, p. 212. *THE vs. Ø. (Chart 8-6)*

Controlled completion.

ANSWERS: **3. the** milk . . . **the** refrigerator . . . **the** table   **4. Ø** milk [Perhaps mention that *milk* should be capitalized as the first word of the sentence, but keep the focus on article usage rather than capitalization.]   **5. Ø** wine   **6. the** wine   **7. Ø** English . . . **Ø** grammar   **8. The** grammar   **9. Ø** chemistry   **10. the** weather   **11. Ø** copper   **12. Ø** air   **13. The** air   **14. The** windows   **15. Ø** windows . . . **Ø** glass   **16. Ø** meat   **17. The** meat   **18. Ø** candles . . . **Ø** light . . . **Ø** electricity

☐ EXERCISE 14, p. 213. *THE for second mention. (Chart 8-6)*

Controlled completion.
Ask the students to find the first mention of each noun.
   Grammar note: Chart 8-6 teaches that *the* is used for second mention, and this exercise is tightly controlled to reflect that information. However, as a sort of caveat in case the question should arise in other contexts: *the* is not used for the second mention of a generic noun. For example:
   A: Do you have ***a pen*** *(generic noun)?*
   B: No. I have a pencil, but I don't have ***a pen*** *(generic noun).*
   COMPARE: I had ***a pen*** *(indefinite noun)* and a pencil.
      I gave Bob ***the pen*** and kept the pencil for myself.

ANSWERS: **1. The** cat was chasing **a** mouse. **The** mouse . . . **a** hole, but **the** hole . . . . **The** cat . . . **the** hole, . . . up **a** tree. **The** dog . . . **the** tree   **2.** bought **some** clothes. I bought **a** suit, **a** shirt, and **a** tie. **The** suit . . . . **The** shirt . . . and **the** tie   **3.** saw **a** man and **a** woman . . . . **an** argument. **The** man . . . **the** woman, and **the** woman . . . at **the** man . . . . what **the** argument   **4.** I had **some** soup and **a** sandwich for lunch. **The** soup was . . . but **the** sandwich   **5.** A: **an** accident   A: **A** man . . . **a** Volkswagen . . . **a** bus.   B: **the** accident   A: **The** man . . . **the** Volkswagen . . . **the** bus   **6.** B: on **a** picnic . . . **a** movie   B: **The** picnic . . . but **the** movie

☐ EXERCISE 15, p. 214. *A, AN, SOME, THE, Ø. (Chart 8-6)*

Controlled completion.

ANSWERS: **2. some** fruit . . . **an** apple   **3.** A: **The** fruit   B: **Ø** fruit   **4. Ø** gas   **5. The** gas . . . **The** gas   **6. some** gas [also possible: **Ø** gas]   **7. a** radio . . . **Ø** music   **8. the** radio . . . **The** music   **9. the** man . . . **the** president   **10. a** president   **11.** B: **a** blouse . . . **some** jewelry   A: **the** blouse   **12. the** floor . . . **the** corner . . . **the** sofa   **13. some** furniture . . . **a** sofa . . . **an** easy chair   **14. Ø** furniture   **15. a** vegetarian . . . **Ø** meat   **16. a** book . . . **the** life   **17. Ø** life   **18.** A: **the** lake   B: **a** good idea   **19. A** lake . . . **Ø** water . . . **a** sea . . . **a** pond . . . **An** ocean . . . **a** sea   **20. the** beach . . . **the** ocean   **21. Ø** fresh water . . . **Ø** seawater . . . **Ø** salt   **22. an** interesting experience . . . **A** man . . . **a** blue suit . . . **a** bouquet . . . **Ø** flowers . . . **the** man . . . **the** flowers . . . **the** door

◊ WORKBOOK PRACTICE 22, p. 161. *Using A or Ø for generalizations. (Chart 8-6)*

Controlled completion and transformation. [Selfstudy]

ANSWERS: **1. A** bird . . . Birds have feathers.   **2. Ø** Corn . . . *(none possible)*   **3. Ø** Milk . . . *(none possible)*   **4. A** flower . . . Flowers are beautiful.   **5. Ø** Water . . . *(none possible)*   **6. A** horse . . . Horses are strong.   **7. Ø** Jewelry . . . *(none possible)*   **8. Ø** Honey . . . *(none possible)*   **9. A** shirt . . . Shirts have sleeves.   **10. Ø** Soap . . . *(none possible)*

◇ WORKBOOK PRACTICE 23, p. 161. *Using A or SOME.* *(Chart 8-6)*

Controlled completion and transformation. [Selfstudy]

ANSWERS: **1. a** bird . . . I saw some birds. **2. some** corn . . . *(none possible)* **3. some** milk . . . *(none possible)* **4. a** flower . . . I picked **some** flowers. **5. some** water. . . *(none possible)* **6. a** horse . . . I fed grass to **some** horses. **7. some** jewelry . . . *(none possible)* **8. some** honey . . . *(none possible)* **9. a** new shirt . . . Tom bought **some** new shirts. **10. some** soap . . . *(none possible)*

◇ WORKBOOK PRACTICE 24, p. 161. *A/AN vs. THE: singular count nouns.* *(Chart 8-6)*

Controlled completion. [Selfstudy]

ANSWERS: **1. a** dog **2. the** dog **3. the** radio **4. a** radio . . . **a** tape player **5. a** desk, **a** bed, **a** chest of drawers **6. the** desk . . . **the** top drawer **7. the** basement **8. a** basement **9. a** subject and **a** verb **10. the** subject . . . **the** verb **11. a** meeting **12. the** meeting **13. a** long distance . . . **a** telephone **14. The** distance . . . **the** sun . . . **the** earth **15. the** telephone **16. a** question **17. the** problem **18. a** poem **19. the** lecture . . . **The** speaker . . . **an** interesting talk **20. a** cup . . . **the** cafe . . . **the** corner

◇ WORKBOOK PRACTICE 25, p. 163. *Ø vs. THE.* *(Chart 8-6)*

Controlled completion. [Selfstudy]

ANSWERS: **1. Ø** Dogs **2. the** dogs **3. Ø** Fruit **4. The** fruit **5. Ø** Children **6. the** children **7. Ø** Paper . . . **Ø** trees **8. The** paper **9. the** potatoes **10. Ø** Potatoes . . . **Ø** vegetables **11. Ø** Nurses **12. the** nurses **13. Ø** Frogs . . . **Ø** small animals . . . **Ø** tails . . . **Ø** turtles . . . **Ø** tails . . . **Ø** hard shells **14. The** frogs . . . **The** turtles **15. Ø** books . . . **Ø** textbooks . . . **Ø** workbooks . . . **Ø** dictionaries . . . **Ø** encyclopedias . . . **Ø** entertainment . . . **Ø** novels . . . **Ø** poetry **16. The** books **17. Ø** plants . . . **Ø** fruit . . . **Ø** vegetables . . . **Ø** plants . . . **Ø** meat . . . **Ø** plants **18. The** plants **19. An** engineer . . . **Ø** engineers . . . **Ø** bridges . . . **Ø** rivers . . . **Ø** valleys . . . **Ø** highways . . . **Ø** railroad tracks . . . **Ø** other places **20. the** bridges

◇ WORKBOOK PRACTICE 26, p. 164. *Using THE for second mention.* *(Chart 8-6)*

Controlled completion. [Selfstudy]

ANSWERS: **1. a** banana . . . **an** apple . . . **the** banana . . . **the** apple **2. some** bananas . . . **some** apples . . . **the** bananas . . . **the** apples **3. some** coffee . . . **some** milk . . . **The** coffee . . . **The** milk **4. a** desk . . . **a** bed . . . **The** desk . . . **The** bed **5. a** pen . . . **some** paper . . . **the** pen . . . **the** paper **6. a** bag . . . **some** sugar . . . **some** cookies . . . **The** sugar . . . **the** flour . . . **the** flour . . . **some** little bugs . . . **the** little bugs . . . **a** new bag . . . **The** new bag **7. some** birds . . . **a** tree . . . **a** cat . . . **the** tree . . . **The** birds . . . **the** cat . . . **the** cat . . . **the** birds **8.** Once upon a time, **a** princess fell in love with **a** prince. **The** princess wanted to marry **the** prince, who lived in a distant land. She summoned **a** messenger to take **some** things to **the** prince to show him her love. **The** messenger took **the** jewels and **a** robe made of yellow and red silk to **the** prince. **The** princess anxiously awaited **the** messenger's return. She hoped that **the** prince would send her **some** tokens of his love. But when **the** messenger returned, he brought back **the** jewels and **the** beautiful silk robe that **the** princess had sent. Why? Why? she wondered. Then **the** messenger told her: **the** prince already had **a** wife. [The first word following a colon can be either upper or lower case: either *The prince* or *the prince* is correct.]

◇ WORKBOOK PRACTICE 27, p. 166. *Using THE for second mention. (Chart 8-6)*

Controlled completion. [Guided Study]

ANSWERS: **(1) a** man   **(2) a** truck . . . **a** covered bridge . . . **The** bridge   **(3) a** small river . . . **the** man   **(5) the** man . . . **the** top   **(6) the** bridge   **(7) the** bridge   **(8) a** solution   **(10) the** solution [also possible: *a solution*]   **(11) the** man   **(12) the** truck   **(13) the** bridge . . . **the** river   **(14) a** great idea . . . **the** man   **(15) the** tires . . . **the** river [*tires* = AmE spelling; *tyres* = BrE spelling]

◇ WORKBOOK PRACTICE 28, p. 166. *Summary: A/AN vs. Ø vs. THE. (Chart 8-6)*

Controlled completion. [Selfstudy]

ANSWERS: **1. An** egg . . . **the** egg   **2. Ø** Eggs   **3. a** scientific fact . . . **Ø** steam . . . **Ø** water   **4. the** tape player . . . **the** shelves . . . **the** batteries   **5. Ø** Chalk . . . **a** necessity   **6. the** plumber . . . **The** sink . . . **the** water supply . . . **the** house . . . **the** leak   **7. Ø** Water . . . **the** water . . . **The** pollution   **8. a** taxi   **9. the** car . . . **a** minute . . . **the** kids . . . **the** car . . . **a** minute   **10. Ø** Newspapers . . . **an** important source . . . **Ø** information   **11. The** sun . . . **a** star . . . **the** sun . . . **Ø** heat . . . **Ø** light . . . **Ø** energy   **12. Ø** Ducks   **13. the** letter . . . **A** strong wind . . . **the** floor . . . **the** dog . . . **the** scraps . . . **the** wastebasket   **14. An** efficient transportation system . . . **an** essential part   **15. the** alarm . . . **the** door . . . **the** stove . . . **the** windows . . . **the** lights   **16. an** exceptionally talented person   **17. Ø** Money . . . **Ø** trees   **18. Ø** sick people . . . **A** farmer . . . **Ø** crops . . . **An** architect . . . **Ø** buildings . . . **An** artist . . . **Ø** new ways . . . **the** world . . . **Ø** life   **19. Ø** Earthquakes . . . **Ø** relatively rare events   **20. an** earthquake . . . **the** earthquake . . . **The** ground

◇ WORKBOOK PRACTICE 29, p. 168. *Summary: A/AN vs. Ø vs. THE. (Chart 8-6)*

Controlled completion. [Guided Study]

ANSWERS: **1. Ø** Good food . . . **Ø** pleasure   **2. Ø** Ice cream   **3. Ø** Pizza . . . **Ø** cheese . . . **Ø** tomatoes . . . **Ø** "Pizza" . . . **the** Italian word . . . **Ø** "pie"   **4. A: the** pizza   B: **the** big piece . . . **the** small one   **5. Ø** steamed rice . . . **Ø** fish . . . **Ø** vegetables . . . **The** rice . . . **The** fish . . . **The** vegetables   **6. The** food . . . **the** fish . . . **the** service . . . **the** waitress . . . **a** good tip   **7. the** continents . . . **the** world   **8. an** easy exam . . . **the** right answers . . . **the** questions . . . **the** exam   **9. a** job interview . . . **Ø** nice clothes   **10. a** long, thin, almost hairless tail . . . **Ø** Rats . . . **Ø** long, skinny tails   **11. Ø** wood . . . **Ø** coal . . . **Ø** heat . . . **Ø** gas . . . **Ø** oil . . . **Ø** electricity   **12. A** good book . . . **a** friend . . . **Ø** life   **13. Ø** Gold . . . **an** excellent conductor . . . **Ø** electricity . . . **a** spaceship   **14. the** kitchen . . . **a** sandwich   **15. Ø** coins . . . **Ø** shells . . . **Ø** beads . . . **Ø** salt . . . **Ø** paper   **16. the** salt . . . **the** pepper   **17. Ø** different countries . . . **Ø** different geography . . . **a** peninsula . . . **an** island nation   **18. Ø** fresh fish   **19. a** good program . . . **a** documentary . . . **an** old movie . . . **the** documentary   **20. Ø** Modern people . . . **the** universe . . . **the** moon . . . **Ø** life . . . **a** star . . . **the** universe . . . **the** sun

**CHART 8-7: USING EXPRESSIONS OF QUANTITY
AS PRONOUNS**

• The emphasis in this chart is on understanding the meaning of quantifiers used as pronouns. As with any other pronouns, meaning depends on antecedents.

• This chart is intended as an introduction to Chart 8-8. The important point for students to grasp from this chart is that expressions of quantity can be used as pronouns.

☐ EXERCISE 16, p. 216. *Expressions of quantity as pronouns. (Chart 8-7)*

Oral.

ANSWERS: **2.** *some* = some apples **3.** *some* = some bread **4.** *some* = some envelopes
. . . *any* = any envelopes **5.** *a little* = a little sugar **6.** *much* = much lined paper . . . *a lot* =
a lot of lined paper. . . *a little* = a little lined paper **7.** *a couple* = a couple of erasers
8. *any* = any blank floppy disks . . . *two* = two blank floppy disks . . . *many* = many blank floppy
disks . . . *four* = four blank floppy disks . . . *five* = five blank floppy disks . . . *a few* = a few blank
floppy disks . . . *some* = some blank cassette tapes . . . *many* = many blank cassette tapes . . . *a
couple* = a couple of blank cassette tapes

**CHART 8-8: NONSPECIFIC OBJECT PRONOUNS:
SOME, ANY, AND *ONE***

• The grammar in this chart can be confusing and difficult for students. You may want to do Exercise
17 prior to discussing the examples here and have the students inductively reach conclusions about
some/any vs. *them* and *one* vs. *it.*

• To demonstrate the use of *one:*

TEACHER: *Who has a grammar book (pen/notebook/etc.)?*
STUDENT A: *I have **one**.*
STUDENT B: *I have **one**.*
STUDENT C: *I have **one**.*
Etc.

Compared to the use of *it:*

TEACHER: *This is my grammar book (pen/notebook/etc.). I'm going to give it to Yoko.
Where's my grammar book?*
STUDENT A: *Yoko has **it**.*
TEACHER: *Give my grammar book to another person. Now where is my grammar book?*
STUDENT B: *Natasha has **it**.*
Etc.

☐ EXERCISE 17, p. 217. *Nonspecific vs. specific object pronouns. (Chart 8-8)*

Controlled completion.

ANSWERS: **2.** it . . . it . . . it **3.** one **4.** it **5.** some **6.** them **7.** it
8. one **9.** some **10.** it . . . some **11.** any . . . some . . . any **12.** them **13.** one
14. it

◇ WORKBOOK PRACTICE 30, p. 170. *Object pronouns: ONE vs. IT. (Charts 8-7 and 8-8)*

Controlled completion. [Selfstudy]

ANSWERS: **1.** one **2.** it **3.** one **4.** it . . . it **5.** it **6.** one **7.** one
8. it **9.** one **10.** it

◇ WORKBOOK PRACTICE 31, p. 170. *Object pronouns: ONE vs. IT. (Charts 8-7 and 8-8)*

Controlled completion. [Guided Study]

ANSWERS: **1.** it **2.** one **3.** one **4.** it **5.** one **6.** it **7.** it **8.** one
9. one **10.** it

◇ WORKBOOK PRACTICE 32, p. 171. *SOME/ANY vs. IT/THEM. (Charts 8-7 and 8-8)*

Controlled completion. [Selfstudy]

ANSWERS: **1.** it **2.** some **3.** some **4.** it **5.** them **6.** some **7.** any
8. it

◇ WORKBOOK PRACTICE 33, p. 172. *SOME/ANY vs. IT/THEM. (Charts 8-7 and 8-8)*

Controlled completion. [Selfstudy]

ANSWERS: **1.** them **2.** some **3.** some **4.** A: them B: them **5.** A: it B: it
. . . them A: it **6.** them **7.** any **8.** it **9.** them. . . it **10.** B: any A: some
B: it

☐ EXERCISE 18, p. 219. *Cumulative review. (Chapter 8)*

Error Analysis.

ANSWERS: **1.** There **is** a lot of **information** . . . . **2.** Ø Oil is . . . . **3.** Lions are wild
animals. OR **A lion is a** wild animal. **4.** . . . there **was** too **much traffic**. **5.** I drank
two **glasses of water**. **6.** . . . too **much homework**. **7.** . . . a lot of **vocabulary**. **8.** I
had **an** egg . . . . **9.** There **are** many **kinds** of . . . . **10.** I'm studying Ø English. **11.** I'm
living in **the** United **States**. **12.** Only twelve **students** . . . . **13.** . . . some **advice**.
14. . . . a few **problems** in Ø life.

☐ EXERCISE 19, p. 219. *Cumulative review. (Chapter 8)*

> *Written.*
> Topic 1 is intended to elicit nouns and quantifiers. Topic 2 is intended to elicit abstract nouns and generalizations.
>
> For Topic 2, suggest to your students that they give specific, concrete examples of the qualities they admire in the person they write about. For instance, if someone is admired for her/his generosity, can the writer tell a little story that illustrates this quality? Or at least give some examples of this person's generosity? If you want to instruct your students in the basic organization of English rhetoric, Topic 2 can be developed into a full-length (400 to 800 words) five-paragraph essay with introduction leading to a thesis sentence, topic sentences for the three body paragraphs, and a concluding paragraph. All generalizations should be supported by specifics.

☐ EXERCISE 20, p. 219. *Prepositions. (Chart 8-8)*

> *Controlled completion.*
>
> ANSWERS: **1.** on **2.** from . . . with **3.** from **4.** about **5.** for . . . about **6.** for **7.** about **8.** from **9.** to . . . about **10.** to **11.** into **12.** from **13.** by **14.** to

◊ WORKBOOK PRACTICE 34, p. 173. *Prepositions. (Chapter 8; Appendix 1)*

> *Controlled completion.* [Selfstudy]
>
> ANSWERS: **1.** from **2.** about . . . for **3.** to . . . about **4.** to . . . from . . . into . . . by **5.** for **6.** on **7.** about/of . . . with **8.** from . . . to **9.** about . . . from

◊ WORKBOOK PRACTICE 35, p. 174. *Prepositions. (Chapters 1 → 8; Chart 2-10; Appendix 1)*

> *Controlled completion.* [Selfstudy]
>
> ANSWERS: **1.** for **2.** in **3.** In . . . to **4.** for **5.** with **6.** at **7.** of **8.** to **9.** at **10.** in . . . on **11.** of **12.** to **13.** to **14.** from . . . of **15.** for **16.** about/of . . . at **17.** of . . . for . . . (up)on . . . for . . . In **18.** for . . . to **19.** A: about . . . about . . . with/at   B: from . . . in . . . to . . . for **20.** of . . . on